The Moral
Dimensions
of Teaching

John I. Goodlad
Roger Soder
Kenneth A. Sirotnik
Editors

The Moral
Dimensions
of Teaching

Jossey-Bass Publishers

San Francisco   •   Oxford   •   1990

THE MORAL DIMENSIONS OF TEACHING
by John I. Goodlad, Roger Soder, and Kenneth A. Sirotnik, Editors

Copyright © 1990 by: Jossey-Bass Inc., Publishers
350 Sansome Street
San Francisco, California 94104
&
Jossey-Bass Limited
Headington Hill Hall
Oxford OX3 0BW

Library of Congress Cataloging-in-Publication Data

The Moral dimensions of teaching
 John I. Goodlad, Roger Soder, Kenneth A. Sirotnik, editors.—1st ed.
  p.   cm.—(The Jossey-Bass education series) (The Jossey-
Bass higher education series)
  Includes bibliographical references.
  ISBN 1-55542-199-7 (alk. paper)
  1. Teachers—Professional ethics—United States. 2. Moral
education—United States. I. Goodlad, John I. II. Soder, Roger, date.
III. Sirotnik, Kenneth A. IV. Series. V. Series: The
Jossey-Bass higher education series.
LB1779.M67   1990
174'.9372—dc20   89-28755
                                                        CIP

Manufactured in the United States of America

The paper in this book meets the guidelines for
permanence and durability of the Committee on
Production Guidelines for Book Longevity of the
Council on Library Resources.

JACKET DESIGN BY WILLI BAUM

FIRST EDITION
     First printing: January 1990
     Second printing: November 1990

Code 9001

A joint publication in
The Jossey-Bass Education Series
and
The Jossey-Bass
Higher Education Series

Contents

Part Two: The Moral Mission of Education and Implications for the Teaching Profession

Preface

What are public schools for in a democratic society? What *should* they be for, and for whom? Whose interests are served and whose *should* be served in a system of compulsory education? What is the nature of the relationship between the interests of the individual, the family, the community, the state, and society? Are there reasoned answers to these and like questions, or is there just an assortment of value positions, each as "good" as the other? Or, to put it another way, are there not fundamental normative positions derived from moral and ethical argument that serve to ground appropriate answers to crucial educational questions such as these?

These questions and more are the subject of inquiry in *The Moral Dimensions of Teaching*. The chapter authors are all agreed that the answer to the last question is yes, and their arguments, taken as a whole, spin a web of normative intrigue from the reconceptualization and reconstruction of professionalism in teaching, to the proper role and function of American public education, to the inherent moral and ethical relationship between those who teach and those who are taught.

But why a book of this nature at this time? Questions about virtue and moral character—not only of individuals but of institutions—were perhaps more central to academic and public conversation several decades ago than they are now. When it comes to institutions of higher education, there appears to be an increasing tendency to label such matters "purely philosophical" and relegate them to esoteric niches in the graduate curriculum. Many educators and much of the community generally have come to eschew discussion of all matters moral and ethical concerning public schooling, preferring to focus instead on literacy and numeracy (as if such decisions did not rely on normative argument).

Teaching the young has moral dimensions, however, simply because education—a deliberate effort to develop values and sensibilities as well as skills—is a moral endeavor. The teacher's first responsibilities are to those being taught.

And teaching the young in schools adds dimensions to this moral responsibility, which teachers share with parents. All cultures seek to ensure that the young will learn whatever values, rituals, skills, and modes of behavior are deemed to be in the best interests of the group or the whole. Various formal, informal, and nonformal educative means are established to effect this enculturation. In the United States, this is done primarily through a system of compulsory schooling that most children enter at the age of five or six. Until the twentieth century, the goals set for this system had far more to do with educating the young for economic and civic responsibility than with educating them for personal development and freedom.

This charge to schools, in a system of compulsory attendance, enormously compounds the moral responsibilities of teachers, as the chapters of this book reveal. The lives of public school teachers, in particular, would be simplified if the fit between parents' expectations and state directives to schools were neat. Schools and the people in them are caught up in a host of contradictions and the inevitable conflicts between individual and group interests and well-being. One would hope that teachers and administrators are well prepared to deal with these contradictions and conflicts in steadfastly fulfilling their educational mission. Unfortunately, they are not.

Background

This book grew out of a comprehensive study of conditions and circumstances pertaining to the education of educators in the United States. In 1985, the book's editors created the Center for Educational Renewal in the College of Education at the University of Washington, with the aim of bringing about renewal in both schools and the programs that prepare teachers for them. Although extensive research into schools had already provided ample evidence of their problems and shortcomings, there was no comparable body of data about the education of teachers and school principals. We set out to ameliorate this situation through the Study of the Education of Educators.

Part of our work involved us in an examination of the education of workers in professions such as law, medicine, architecture, and public health. At the same time, there was increasing interest among major actors in the educational reform movement in ensuring professional status for teachers and teaching. We noted that this interest focused almost exclusively on the special knowledge and technical skills likely to characterize "professionals"—and the successful demonstration of these on tests. Largely missing from the dialogue and from major reports was any reference to the moral dimensions of teaching and a profession of teaching. Simultaneously, both scholarly books and articles and popular media were revealing growing, deep concern over widespread moral decay in every aspect and at every level of our society. A rhetoric of educational reform centering almost exclusively on the instrumental role of schools in creating jobs and on the technical competence of teachers appeared to us to be at best shortsighted and at worst off the mark.

Initially, we viewed the moral imperatives of education and schooling as one of four major themes on which to build a teaching profession and from which to derive the components of teacher education programs. Then we came to see that moral imperatives pervade the whole. Recognized and taken into account, they provide greater strength to the several themes. If these imperatives are neglected and ignored, the whole is weakened to such a degree that teaching becomes an occupation recognized at most for its technical expertise but not granted the public esteem that professional status requires.

In the questions to be addressed in our surveys and interviews, we included several designed to reveal the degree of awareness and commitment to these moral responsibilities in colleges and universities preparing teachers. Our fears were confirmed. First of all, teaching in our elementary and secondary schools is demeaned because it is held in low regard on university campuses and, indeed, in many schools and colleges of education. Relatively few teacher education programs offer courses addressing the role of the schools in a democratic society, the moral process of becoming humane, and some of the conflicts involved in squaring the educational needs of students with the special interests of the larger community. Few such programs are infused with a sense of moral mission. Further, only in a few of the settings we visited was there any structure designed to promote the inquiry that such a mission entails.

Given the general absence of the development of moral character as a goal of teacher education and the dominance of a behavioristic and technical approach to formal and informal socialization processes for those about to enter teaching, one would be surprised to find in schools ongoing dialogue and decision making in the moral domain.

Our discussions with students, faculty members, supervisors of student teachers, and others convinced us that our earlier decision to go ahead with this book was a good one. The findings, conclusions, and recommendations resulting from our study are soon to be reported in another volume, which will not include extensive explanation of what we mean by the moral dimensions of teaching. Yet these discussions revealed the necessity for elaboration. As Hugh Sockett points out in Chapter Seven, we lack the necessary vocabulary for moral discourse. *The Moral Dimensions of Teaching*, along with a few other recently published works, is designed to provide educators and future educators with part of that vocabulary and particularly with a feeling of need and a desire to participate with colleagues in the necessary dialogue.

While first drafts of chapters were being completed, two of the editors of this volume had a unique opportunity to engage in a year-long moral dialogue with a group of prospective school principals in the context of a seminar. In planning the program, the faculty agreed on the moral dimensions of the principalship as a theme not only to integrate the whole but also to be addressed specifically and directly. Subsequent discussion in the seminar focused on the different chapters of this book as each became available.

Sockett's observation regarding the lack of a vocabulary for moral discourse was confirmed early on with this group of carefully selected, experienced practitioners. At the outset, they found the issues to be intriguing and new—even somewhat foreign. Although they seemed to sense the significance and meaning of what they read, they had varying degrees of difficulty in expressing reactions to what the authors had written. Classes were organized according to the principle of distributed practice—that is, participants in the seminar had plenty of time to complete the readings over the two to three weeks between sessions. We were into the fourth session—that is, into the third month of the seminar—before a few members of the group began to contribute to the dialogue freely, comfortably, and with some passion. By the seventh month, almost all were connecting the readings and the discussions to situations that they were encountering in their apprenticeship roles in schools. While several still found the concepts to be awkward and not easy to convey in their own words, there was general agreement that the theme had been powerfully integrative.

The editors, all of whom took part in the visits and interviews at the teacher education settings, believe that what this group of experienced educators went through over a year should have begun in their initial teacher preparation programs. For them to have come so late to rigorous discourse about the moral dimensions of their work and profession is a serious indictment of the teacher education enterprise. In another volume, we will make recommendations designed to rectify this failing, discussing moral imperatives ranging from the responsibilities faced by a college or university in educating teachers to the responsibilities that must be assumed by the teacher education faculty. We hope that the ten chapters included in this book will prove useful, particularly to those educators who take our recommendations seriously.

Overview of the Contents

Chapters One through Four center on notions of profession and professionalization as applied to the occupation and act of teaching. John I. Goodlad opens the discussion in Chapter One with a consideration of the historical and political context in which we might view teaching as a moral matter, the multilayered nature of the teaching act, and the efforts to professionalize teaching. In

Chapter Two, Roger Soder decries the rhetorical grounding claimed by teachers in their professionalization attempts; he argues that claims based on the moral imperatives of teaching would be more accurate and more telling.

In Chapter Three, Barry L. Bull focuses on the relationships between teacher autonomy, licensing, freedom, and teaching as a public profession; he argues that freedom to teach the young is potentially self-defeating and risk-laden and that the office of the schoolteacher may thus legitimately be limited to those holding licenses, but he also argues that full professionalization of teaching is not justified. Gary D Fenstermacher, in Chapter Four, examines the basis for teacher professionalization claims and concludes that teaching is indeed a moral endeavor; he argues that teaching should avoid the hierarchical differentiation and distance from clients that characterize other professions.

The next five chapters shift the focus to the school and the classroom. In Chapter Five, Walter Feinberg addresses the moral responsibility of public schools from a historical and philosophical perspective and evaluates recent works that attempt to recapture a sense of the moral mission of American education. Kenneth A. Strike, in Chapter Six, directs our attention to the legal and moral responsibilities of teachers; in his discussion of the ethics of teaching, he addresses critically the central claims of the advocates of values clarification, as well as those of Lawrence Kohlberg and Nel Noddings. Hugh Sockett, in Chapter Seven, focuses on professional accountability, pointing up the tension between the need for public control and the need for professional autonomy; he suggests that such accountability be conceptualized as contingent on trust, public and professional partnership, and recognition of the moral agency of the teacher.

In Chapter Eight, Christopher M. Clark asks us to consider the relationship between the teacher and the taught in the classroom. He provides case descriptions to illuminate how decisions and actions with serious moral implications look and feel in context. Following along similar lines, Bruce R. Thomas, in Chapter Nine, discusses the moral universe of teaching through a presentation of three individual case studies and a consideration of the meaning of the Eight-Year Study; ultimately, Thomas tells us, schools depend on the moral agency of the individual teacher.

In the final chapter, Chapter Ten, Kenneth A. Sirotnik posits that teaching has five ethical roots: inquiry; knowledge; competence; caring; and freedom, well-being, and social justice. Drawing on the previous nine chapters, as well as on findings from the Study of the Education of Educators, he reflects on the meaning and implications of the moral dimensions for schooling, teaching, and preparing to teach.

Seattle, Washington   John I. Goodlad
December 1989   Roger Soder
                                              Kenneth A. Sirotnik

Acknowledgments

When it became apparent to us that the moral dimensions of teaching were to enter significantly into the design of a study of the education of educators, we sought the counsel of our colleague Donna H. Kerr. After deciding that the concepts warranted elaboration far beyond what would be possible in a report on the research, we drew up an outline of the major topics, themes, and perspectives to be included in this elaboration. Again we sought Kerr's advice—this time for the names of authors qualified to write chapters in a book on the subject. To her we extend our gratitude and appreciation. Our only regret is that her duties as vice-provost and director of planning for branch campuses (combined with other professorial responsibilities) at the University of Washington prevented her from preparing the chapter we wanted her to write.

All of the authors of the chapters in this volume were extraordinarily receptive to our suggestions regarding first drafts, some of which resulted in substantial rewriting. Best of all, they met the deadlines set for each stage of production. We express to them all our deep gratitude.

The contributing authors probably would have accepted our invitation with considerable enthusiasm even had there been no financial inducements. However, we did not have to put them to this test. We are grateful to the MacArthur Foundation for the grant that covered all costs and to Peter Gerber of the foundation for his recognition and support of this undertaking.

James I. Doi, now dean emeritus of the College of Education at the University of Washington, and Richard L. Andrews, then head of policy, governance, and administration of the college (now dean of the College of Education at the University of Wyoming),

vastly eased the process of creating the Center for Educational Renewal and steadfastly supported its work. To them and to our hard-
working, congenial colleagues in the center who have contributed
in various ways to this book, we express thanks and appreciation.
Special thanks go to Paula McMannon, who worked closely with
the authors in keeping the work on schedule, and to Jordis Young
for her superb editing of the final manuscript.

J.I.G.

R.S.

K.A.S.

The Editors

John I. Goodlad is professor of education and director of the Center for Educational Renewal, University of Washington. Born in Canada, he has taught at all levels, from kindergarten through graduate school. He served from 1967 to 1983 as dean of the Graduate School of Education, University of California, Los Angeles. He holds a B.A. degree (1945) in history and an M.A. degree (1946) in history and education, both from the University of British Columbia; a Ph.D. degree (1949) from the University of Chicago in education; and honorary degrees from nine universities in Canada and the United States.

Goodlad's research interests are in educational change and improvement and have been reported in more than twenty books and hundreds of other publications. An extensive study of schooling resulted in *A Place Called School* (1984). A subsequent comprehensive study of the education of educators is in press.

Roger Soder is senior researcher, Center for Educational Renewal, University of Washington. He attended the University of Chicago and did graduate work at the University of Washington. His sustained inquiry into an array of professions has brought to the center's work a useful perspective on the education of educators. Soder's research interests continue to focus on the ethics and politics of rhetoric.

Kenneth A. Sirotnik is professor and chair of the Area of Policy, Governance, and Administration, College of Education, University of Washington. Previously, he spent a number of years as senior research associate in the Graduate School of Education at the

University of California, Los Angeles (UCLA), teaching, writing, and participating in many educational research studies. Sirotnik's interests and publications range from topics in measurement, statistics, evaluation, and technology to issues of educational policy and local school improvement and change.

Sirotnik received his B.A. degree (1964) in mathematics, M.A. degrees (1966 and 1967) in measurement and statistics—the first in the field of education and the second in psychology—and his Ph.D. degree (1969) in education measurement, statistics, and evaluation, all from UCLA.

The Contributors

Barry L. Bull is associate professor of philosophy of education at the University of Minnesota. He received both his B.A. degree (1969) from Yale University and his M.A. degree (1970) from the University of Virginia in English, his M.A.T. degree (1972) from the University of Idaho in education, and his Ph.D. degree (1979) from Cornell University in philosophy of education. He has also worked in state government and as an education policy consultant. His articles have appeared in such journals as *Teachers College Record, Educational Evaluation and Policy Analysis,* and *Educational Theory.* His current research interests are in the ethics of teaching, teacher education, and multicultural education.

   Christopher M. Clark is professor of education in the department of Counseling, Educational Psychology, and Special Education at Michigan State University. His professional interests and publications include research on teacher thinking, teacher professional development, and the relationship between research and practice. He is the recipient of the Palmer O. Johnson Award for empirical research (1979) and the Interpretive Scholarship Award (1987), both from the American Educational Research Association, and of a Spencer Fellowship from the National Academy of Education (1979–1984). He received his B.S. degree (1963) from Villanova University in social studies and his M.A. (1972) and Ph.D. (1976) degrees from Stanford University in psychological studies in education.

   Walter Feinberg is professor of philosophy of education and educational policy studies at the University of Illinois, Urbana. He received his B.A. (1960), M.A. (1962), and Ph.D. (1966) degrees from Boston University in philosophy.

Feinberg's main interest is the relationship between school and society. His books include *Reason and Rhetoric: The Intellectual Foundations of Twentieth Century Educational Reform* (1974), *Knowledge and Values in Social and Educational Research* (1982, with Eric Bredo), *Understanding Education* (1983), and *Schools and Society* (1983, with Jonas Soltis).

Feinberg has served as the president of both the American Educational Studies Association (1978) and the Philosophy of Education Society (1988–89).

Gary D Fenstermacher is dean of the College of Education at the University of Arizona and professor of educational foundations. He received his B.A. degree (1961) in political science and his Ph.D. degree (1969) in philosophy and education, both from Cornell University. From 1968 to 1977, he served as head of the program in history and philosophy of education at the UCLA Graduate School of Education; from 1977 to 1985, he served as professor of educational foundations at the Virginia Polytechnic Institute and State University in Blacksburg, Virginia. His research interests include the philosophy of research on teaching, teacher education, and educational policy analysis.

Hugh Sockett is research professor and director of the Center for Applied Research and Development in Education at George Mason University. His main research activities are in the philosophical aspects of accountability and professionalism, in institutional development, and in moral education. He received his B.A. degree (1959) from University of Oxford in modern history and his M.A. (1967) and Ph.D. (1974) degrees from the University of London in philosophy of education.

Kenneth A. Strike is professor of philosophy of education at Cornell University. He holds a B.A. degree (1965) from Wheaton College in philosophy, an M.A. degree (1967) from Northwestern University in philosophy, and a Ph.D. degree (1968) from Northwestern University in philosophy of education.

Strike's research interests are in ethics, political philosophy, and professional ethics. His recent work has emphasized various issues in the ethics of teaching and the ethics of educational administration.

Bruce R. Thomas has for the last decade been a free-lance writer, teacher, and consultant based in Chicago, Illinois. He earlier served as founder/director of the center for Illinois Studies and as director of the Illinois Institute for Social Policy. He received a B.A. degree (1964) from Harvard University in American history and literature and studied for three years at Balliol College, Oxford University, on a Rhodes Scholarship.

The Moral
Dimensions
of Teaching

PART ONE

*On the Nature
and Commitments
of Teaching
as a Profession*

1

The Occupation
of Teaching
in Schools

John I. Goodlad

A Special Case of Teaching

Most people teach during their lives. Some teach a great deal—parents, in particular, and people paid to teach in schools, colleges, and various other institutions and enterprises. Indeed, teaching is so pervasive that perhaps all of us should be taught something about it.

There is a good deal to learn. Some of it is common to all teaching: how to motivate, how to maintain attention, how to distribute learning time effectively, and more. There are those who claim the ability to teach the basic principles of teaching in a few days or even less. But there are relatively few situations in which these general principles suffice.

Principles common to all teaching do not carry the teacher of diesel engine maintenance very far. And what this teacher knows about both principles of teaching and diesel engines will not suffice for teaching in a barber's college. Each teaching situation has its own set of subject matter specifics, be it teaching the basics of diesel engine care, hair design, cooking, or mathematics. The good teacher is deeply versed in these specifics as well as in well-founded techniques for helping others understand them.

This description falls far short, however, of conveying the full complexity of most teaching situations. The parent who feels rather good about his or her teaching of an infant may be in for

3

surprises and will need new learning when the infant becomes ambulatory. Teaching one child at home turns out to be quite inadequate preparation for teaching twenty-five children in a first-grade class. The successful first-grade teacher is in for a lot of fresh learning when, for the first time, several children in the new class speak only Spanish but the teacher does not. Principles common to all teaching, however acquired, do not carry the classroom teacher of children or youths very far.

Contextual factors in school classrooms profoundly influence teachers' instructional behavior. These include the size of the class group, the size of the room, supplies and equipment, the health of the students, the number of absentees, whether the day is Monday or Friday, whether it is raining or snowing and for how many days, the socioeconomic and racial makeup of the class, whether the class is multigraded, how often the principal comes into the classroom and what she or he does there, the frequency and nature of interruptions from outside, the current smog level, and on and on. And there is nothing in the above list about the personal worries of individual students and the teacher, all of which add to the context. What now about those common principles and techniques? "No method or impersonal theory relieves the trainer (teacher) of the burden of judgment."[1]

The burden of judgment is compounded by increased contextual complexity. The context of teaching in schools is richly layered. In addition to the obvious classroom elements described above, there are arrangements in schools that strongly influence and set boundaries on teachers' domains of judgment. These are subject to change by orders of the principal or people beyond the principal. They include promoting and reporting policies, the assignment of pupils to classes and grades, recess and lunch schedules, policies and practices in selecting and distributing instructional materials, playground rules, the use of public address systems, grouping and tracking policies and practices, and more.

Beyond the school are additional influences that impinge on the classroom either directly or through the principal, parents, and others. These include district policies, which sometimes are so specific that they dictate such instructional matters as how reading is to be taught. Supervisors come into classrooms, sometimes to check up on compliance with district regulations, sometimes to inject their own ideas, sometimes to pass judgment on teachers' performance, sometimes just to be helpful.

Schooling is a very open system. Parents do not wait for a quarterly report to the stockholders or confine their complaints to board meetings. They go directly to their children's teachers. Pressure groups have books and other materials banned from classrooms or exert pressure to get rid of "open" classrooms or "open" inquiry into sensitive social issues. Legislatures pass bills that affect what is to be taught and how it is to be taught.[2]

Are teachers to be heard and to bear some burden of judgment in the decisions made at each layer of remoteness from the classroom? The arguments for teacher participation in shaping school conditions and circumstances—the culture of the school—to enhance the relationship between teacher and child and the quality of teaching decisions are powerful ones.[3] Further, since legislatures make decisions that to a degree define and restrict teachers' authority to decide, should not teachers' voices be heard in making these decisions as well? Or should teachers' decisions be confined strictly to the didactics of instruction?[4]

Clearly, the answers to these questions have powerful implications for teacher education and teaching as a profession. Indeed, if the last of these questions is to be answered in the affirmative, then the claim that teaching in school classrooms is a profession becomes difficult to defend. The professional lore required then appears to the general public to be thin—little different from or more than what anyone seeking to teach something to others requires and insufficient to warrant professional status. Soder, in Chapter Two, makes much of this public warranty with respect to professions.

If there is little of a special nature about instruction that schoolteachers must know, and if they are to play no role in decisions at other layers of the system of schooling, then professional status must rest on subject matter knowledge. Now the claim grows weak, indeed. There are tens of thousands of people with college degrees in academic subjects who make no claims of professional standing for their accomplishment. Lawyers and teachers of the law stake their claims on special knowledge not generally shared. If teachers are to claim professional status tied to subject matter, such must rise out of the special knowledge required for their role in inculcating it.[5]

Arguments for a profession of teaching in schools must arise out of the special layered context of the work, the complexity of this context, and the special knowledge, skills, and personal characteristics required for the burden of judgment entailed. Perhaps everyone should learn something about teaching. But learning something about teaching does not, in itself, equip or entitle one to teach children or youths in schools if it is generally recognized that such teaching is a special case warranting professional status.

The Unraveling of Coalitions

Questions about the extent and nature of teachers' decision-making role in the total context of their teaching will not be answered easily or soon. Tensions between public and teacher prerogatives have been with us throughout the evolution of our educational system.[6] The rhetoric frequently juxtaposes public control and the interests of the "teaching profession." Yet public recognition of teaching in schools as a profession must still be in doubt or there would be no need for continued protestation by groups such as the National Education Association (NEA) and the American Federation of Teachers (AFT) that say that this special case of teaching is, indeed, a profession.

To the tension between public control and "professional" prerogatives has been added a tension between segments of what Conant observed to have been a coalition of school-related groups. He noted the emergence of

> certification regulations [that] were in a sense imposed on universities and colleges as a result of pressure from a coalition of state Department officials and public school people. . . . The professors of education, for their part, found that their own convictions coincided with those of state Department and public school personnel, and realized, too, that their source of greatest support was outside the university faculty; as a result, they were more careful to cultivate the outside group.[7]

This coalition, however, fell apart over the next quarter of a century. Once organized in departments of the National Education Association, various groups broke off into their own independent organizations: American Educational Research Association, Association for Supervision and Curriculum Development, National Association of Elementary School Principals, National Association of Secondary School Principals, and others. Creation of the first two of these moved large numbers of education professors out of and away from NEA and its teachers. Creation of the second two effectively reduced the number of joint meetings of principals and teachers at local, state, and national conferences. School superintendents, once in the Department of Superintendence of the NEA, found their professional niche in the American Association of School Administrators, fast growing in size and status during the post-World War II years.[8] Although there had been considerable separation of departments from one another, there had been, too, a certain organizational unity among the segments so that "the education profession" appeared at times to speak with a single voice and to be, in fact, a coalition of like interests.

This professional coalition at one time was joined with lay citizens and groups in a larger political coalition that fought successfully for financial and moral support of public education. Of the delegates to the 1955 White House Conference on Education, only one-third were educators; two-thirds were lay citizens. Bailey cites some of the factors in the unraveling of coalitions from 1965 to 1980: demographic changes, tax revolts, the Vietnam legacy, civil rights movements, the urban fiscal crisis, teachers' unions, evaluative research, and the growing role of the media in creating simplistic public perceptions of education.[9]

The unraveling of the public coalition was predictable, for it had excluded from the beginning a growing segment of the population. There was no place in it for blacks and Native Americans. And there was little or no place for them in the school perceived by these minorities to be in the service of the dominating white coalition. These conditions and perceptions prevail, to considerable degree, today. There will not again be the professional and lay coalition that supported public education until it includes the interests of all

children. Without a broad inclusion of self-interests, the public interest will suffer.

In the unraveling of the coalition, the interests in education
of each group narrowed and hardened. Parents, now a minority
group, found themselves almost alone with school employees in
mustering tax support for schools and then, with children no longer
in schools, often joined the majority in voting against tax levies.
Most school district bond initiatives failed during the 1970s and
early 1980s. Various groups sought policies that would establish
their special interests in schools: multicultural and bilingual instruction, classes for the gifted, provisions for the handicapped,
global education or no global education, time for prayer, drug and
alcohol education, after-school programs, and so on. The voucher
plan was presented as a way to secure for everyone at public expense
what many people seek in private schools. Community withered as
both a place and a concept. With this withering, the idea of a common school well and equitably serving the commonweal withered,
too.[10]

The spinning off from the NEA of groups representing educators not teaching in elementary and secondary school classrooms
was not generally seen at the time as a splintering of the professional component of the education coalition. For example, in discussions during the 1967–68 academic year regarding possible
separation from the NEA of the American Educational Research
Association (AERA), the executive director of the NEA referred
mostly to the additional financial burden that such a step would
entail for the AERA. There was little talk of the implications of
separating researchers and classroom teachers into separate organizations. A polling of the AERA membership revealed no sign of
regret.[11]

The disintegration of the coalition was more than the division of schoolteachers, administrators, and professors and the
hardening of the lines between them. Today, high school teachers
have their closest affiliations with subject matter organizations such
as the National Council for the Social Studies and, through conferences and publications, interact with university professors. Elementary teachers are more likely to identify with a field such as special
education, music education, or early childhood education than with

teachers as a whole. They perceive their vocation more in this special context than in the generic one. The curricula of teacher education line up accordingly—just a little introduction to the historical, philosophical, and social context of schooling and then on to the subject and its teaching or to the methods of teaching each of a half dozen subjects. There are literally dozens of teaching specialties scattered across several schools and colleges in the medium-sized to large American university. A common center is barely discernible.

In the 1960s, the NEA set out deliberately to build its strength through a nationwide drive for improved conditions for teachers and the right to bargain for them, often coming head to head with the American Federation of Teachers in the process. Internal budgets were aligned accordingly, to the comparative neglect of what previously had been seen as the professional services role. The collective bargaining process brought confrontation with administrators down to the level of the building principals. The gap between teachers and administrators widened at a very personal, not just organizational, level.

This gap already had widened with the rapid expansion and bureaucratization of schooling during the school population explosion of the 1950s and 1960s. Skills in management became more important for superintendents and principals than educational knowledge and expertise. Their certification requirements and graduate degree programs reflected this perspective.

Large numbers of teachers coming into schools during these years did so with emergency teaching certificates, ultimately picking up in odd sequences the courses necessary to satisfy state requirements. They were not carefully socialized into a teaching profession, knowledgeable about and respectful of the accompanying rights, responsibilities, and privileges. Much of what was subsequently required of them to earn in-service credits built into salary scales was satisfied through district workshops and institutes. The declining role of schools of education in providing post-baccalaureate in-service education for teachers, coupled with the end of the teacher shortage by the 1970s, precipitated a severe decline in teacher education enrollments and a crisis for many such schools. The close relationship they had cultivated with "the outside group," to use Conant's words, was drawing to a close.

New signals from inside most universities turned the attention of professors of education inward. Within two decades following the end of World War II, the priorities in the rhetoric of university expectations and faculty recognition shifted. Whereas teaching had come first, service was expected, and scholarly work was hoped for in most colleges and universities, research became a must at institutions called universities. The appointment of the historian C. Vann Woodward to a professorship at Yale in the mid-1950s not only broke the magic $20,000 salary ceiling but sent out a significant signal to the academic world: no teaching required for the first year. This would give Woodward more time for what had attracted Yale to him in the first place—his scholarly work.

This is not the place to discuss in detail the strains in higher education settings caused by the shift in the balance of priorities. Many of the places named universities in the 1950s and 1960s, once normal schools and then teachers' colleges, only recently had become regional state universities. Large numbers of faculty members, including those in colleges of education, viewed themselves as hired to teach. Many were not prepared for careers in research, by either mind-set or training. Often, there were no reductions in teaching load or allocations of resources to facilitate research activity. Teacher education is labor intensive. Professors involved in it, whether from education or from other departments, perceived themselves as both put upon and, to a degree, deceived by the demanding, changed expectations.

A handful of schools of education in well-established major research universities viewed the growing research orientation as an opportunity rather than a debilitating condition. Favored by the low teaching loads first gained by colleagues in academic departments and substantial federal funding, they aggressively hired each other's most able young scholars and created what are now closer to educational research institutes than teacher-preparing colleges. Some of these new appointees secured joint appointments with arts and sciences departments and did scholarly work similar to that of professors in these departments. Many knew little about schools or teacher education, and, if appointed initially to teach courses such as educational psychology to prospective teachers, they quickly got out of teaching them when they secured research grants and tenure.

Clifford and Guthrie document the evolution of ten such research-driven schools of education.[12] By the 1980s, professors of education in these schools, if involved with future teachers at all, were more likely to be studying them than preparing them to teach.[13] Yet even these schools experienced, in varying degrees, the tension between "the external demand for practical professional programs and the campus norms," as Clifford and Guthrie describe the contradictions faced by the school at the University of California, Berkeley.[14]

It was into this divided, fragmented, and to a degree feuding and discredited educational community that the politically initiated call for reform was injected by the report *A Nation at Risk*.[15] Frazier has described well the divisive context and defined the collaborative effort necessary to broad-scale improvement.[16]

In response to *A Nation at Risk* and what Darling-Hammond described as "a batch of excellence" reports,[17] states added still another to the substantial bundle of mandates to control the schools already in place by 1983. By the time several major additional reports of national significance appeared in 1986, adding teacher education to the agenda,[18] they were viewed as part of the call for a second wave of school reform, the first increasingly being perceived as having not washed very far. Two years later, the reform effort, even in the highly visible arena of "children and youth at risk," was perceived by some to be, at best, scattered and inadequate.[19]

Clearly, the call, pitched frequently at the level of national crisis and alarm, failed to rally sufficiently the many fragmented groups. Had a coalition of educators and concerned lay citizens—comparable to the one now gone—been in place, the results might have been quite different.

Why this rather long discourse on the unraveling of coalitions for our schools, particularly the "professional" component, in the first chapter of a book addressing the moral dimensions of teaching and the teaching profession? There are two fundamental reasons. First, the now-separate groups of educators must get their several mansions back in the same house, even if they continue to view their respective mansions as home.[20] They must once again become a coalition. But coalitions have something other than organizations to hold them together and direct their activities. They have a common sense of mission. In education and schooling, that mission rests heavily on moral grounds. The definition of these moral grounds has the potential for also defining a mission for teachers, administrators, and teacher educators that is seen to be in the common interest. Such a common mission, in turn, holds promise for defining a profession of teaching in ways that the public might recognize and respect—a necessary condition for the establishment of a profession. Here we have the second reason for describing in a book on the moral dimensions of teaching a disintegration that, if sustained, will effectively inhibit and perhaps even prohibit the emergence of the teaching profession now widely deemed essential to an excellent system of education.

Toward a Common Professional Core

There has been much talk recently of the need to create a "true" profession of teaching, talk that seemingly is based on the premise that creating such a profession will lead to better schools. Seldom have the words *profession, professional, professionalism,* and *professionalization* been bandied about so extensively in so many different quarters. Strangely, this rhetoric has been accompanied by an alarming lack of discourse on the nature of a profession. Consequently, definitions and assumptions vary widely— from holding a teaching certificate to holding a certificate and a master's degree to membership in a "professional" organization.

It is not surprising, then, that widely varying reform initiatives cloak themselves in the language of advancing a true profession while pursuing often contradictory ends. For example, the Carnegie Forum report *A Nation Prepared: Teachers for the 21st Century* pictured professional teachers with master's degrees taking substantial control not only over national board certification and, of course, their own teaching decisions but also over schoolwide decisions. The implication that head or lead teachers, presiding over teams of colleagues, might run the school brought protests from principals' organizations and words of appeasement from Carnegie Forum representatives. Although most lay citizens probably would want to stay out of quarrels between principals and teachers over the division of decision-making authority, the idea of moving the power from district offices to local sites appeals to many. With this view goes the expectation that those closest to parents—principals and teachers—would work together toward school improvement.

Simultaneously, however, there has emerged a movement to "professionalize" principals through master's degree preparation programs focused on management, not necessarily built on preparation to teach and experience as teachers. Indeed, the program in New Jersey was intended to break the "monopoly" of teachers over the principalship. Initial descriptions of the role of principals were not specific regarding the controversial issue of their authority over the instructional activities and evaluation of teachers.[21] The principal trained in management was to take one course in curriculum and instruction, have training in supervision, and observe instruction so as to be a little bit knowledgeable, but program descriptions do not address questions of authority and responsibility in these areas. Nonetheless, it is widely assumed that principals do have authority, especially in regard to the evaluation of teachers.

A quite different point of view guides some other principal-preparation programs, several of them in settings partially funded by the Danforth Foundation.[22] Prospective principals are selected from the teaching ranks and brought into master's degree programs in which universities and school districts collaborate closely.[23] Those chosen are, first, good teachers who are perceived to have leadership potential.

Carried to their logical conclusions, programs designed to go outside of the teaching ranks to select individuals for training in management roles lead to a sharp separation between a profession of teaching and a profession of school management, somewhat parallel to the separation of physicians (of all specialties) from hospital managers or superintendents. Just as hospital managers have no supervisory or evaluative authority over physicians, it is reasonable to make parallel assumptions regarding the supervisory authority of school managers (principals) over teachers. It is easy to see why the leadership of both the NEA and the AFT would welcome such a development. It is equally easy to see why the leadership of the elementary and secondary principals' organizations would oppose it. It also is easy to see why the role of the principal as instructional leader was welcomed by many principals but looked on with suspicion by many teachers. It is apparent that teachers will be particularly hostile to the instructional leader concept of the principalship if individuals assuming the implied role are recruited out of non-teaching ranks and trained exclusively or primarily in management.

It is interesting that, even though the concepts of principal as manager and principal as educational leader are fundamentally opposed, both lead one to the conclusion that teaching is central to the schooling enterprise and is the place to begin in talking about a profession, whether it is a profession of teaching or a profession of education to which people besides practicing teachers belong. The primary responsibility of a teacher, technically and morally, is to the students being taught. Teacher education, first and foremost, must prepare teachers to assume this responsibility. It must not be delegated to or assumed by others, such as principals, any more than a physician's responsibility to patients may be delegated to or assumed by hospital managers. Although this is more obvious to most people in regard to the doctor-patient relationship, it certainly is not obscure in regard to the teacher-student relationship.

The role of the principal now becomes seen as supporting this teacher-student relationship, of helping to make it maximally productive and satisfying. This is the role of the principal, whether prepared as manager, educational leader, or both. But it also becomes apparent that the teacher-become-principal who also is knowledgeable about the role of schools in our society and skilled in the teaching of adults is likely to enhance the context of teaching and be valued by teachers and parents alike. The public might begin to perceive as professionals the diverse groups of teachers and administrators who refer to themselves as such when they come together around a common mission of educating children and youths in schools.

Dare we be optimistic about defining and building a profession that the public might recognize and respect? The cards appear stacked against it. In spite of the vital connection between schools and our individual and collective welfare—argued so passionately and convincingly in educational reform reports—it is difficult to arouse much passion in the cause of school improvement. It is not surprising that it is equally difficult to create the belief that teaching is a high and noble calling to which our most able young citizens must be attracted and for which they must be rigorously prepared and well paid. We are, as a people, scarcely beyond the conventional wisdom of believing that teaching is a calling for women who will teach school for a few years prior to rearing their own children. We are only beginning to become aware that the once-ensured supply of women is no longer there. Changing circumstances force us to look more realistically and intelligently at the demands that are being placed on our schools, the expectations these create for teachers, and the requirements to be met in recruiting, educating, and rewarding teachers. These requirements are those that one associates with a profession.

We have been inclined, many of us, to think of a profession as a calling, conjuring up images of idealistic young men and women preparing themselves to serve God or humankind or both. At times, teaching is so envisioned and depicted, as in the movie *Stand and Deliver* or Sylvia Ashton Warner's book *Teacher*.[24] Our admiration usually is for a specific, humane, selfless teacher, not schoolteachers as a group or teaching as an occupation. And so, parents and professors advise their children and brightest students not to become teachers.[25] At dances and social gatherings, young teachers often lie about their occupations. And reform reports on schooling argue tellingly for higher salaries for teachers, usually omitting completely such idealistic notions as teaching being a noble calling. Salaries often are compared with those in occupations paying more but clearly not in the category of "callings."

In hours of interviewing students in teacher education programs and administrators and faculty members in colleges and universities, it became clear to my colleagues and me that ignoring the appeal of teaching as a calling is a serious error. When I asked students in groups about how others responded to their goals of becoming teachers, they looked at one another and broke into giggles and laughter. "My friends think I'm crazy," was a frequent response. "My parents are disappointed," some said. "Teachers have tried to talk me out of it," was a disturbingly frequent response. But then, some admitted to the rather grudging admiration of friends. "Teaching kids is very important," said these friends; "somebody has to do it." Almost doggedly, these young people had

stuck to their determination to teach while admitting to little recognition and financial reward for teachers—frequently citing salary
expectations well below those that actually would prevail for most
at the time of beginning their teaching careers.

Interviews with older men and women returning to postgrad-
uate teacher-preparing programs after years at other work were
equally revealing and rewarding. This is a large and growing group
on campuses all across the United States. They, too, referred to the
antiteaching persuasion of friends, coupled with admission of admiration, and the low salaries and lack of appreciation by our society in general. But teaching was what many of them had long
wanted to do and at last were about to do. Almost all were making
substantial economic sacrifices to be enrolled in the program. Most
were forced to abandon part-time jobs in order to meet the requirements of student teaching. Many viewed schoolteaching as exceedingly important and potentially satisfying—as a calling.

The dismaying part of our learning during our visits to college and university campuses was the general failure of the institutions to capture and build on the concept of teaching as a calling.
Except in a few noteworthy instances, there was little or nothing in
recruitment literature and program descriptions to suggest the
moral responsibility of the institution taking on teacher education,
the need to recruit people committed to dedicating their lives to
teaching, an ongoing counseling effort to weed out the diffident,
and a process during which those chosen were to be carefully socialized into their responsibilities as stewards of schools and mentors of
the young. It proved difficult to engage students, particularly the
college-age, undergraduate group, in issues surrounding the role of
schools in a democratic society and the implications of this for
teachers. It was not always easy to engage faculty members in the
implied dialogue. Many said that these young future teachers were
too young and immature to get seriously into such issues. No
wonder that Bloom's *Closing of the American Mind* touched such a
sensitive nerve.[26]

A large part of the argument for recognizing teaching as a
profession addresses the emergence of a solid body of knowledge to
guide and direct teachers' instruction. Berliner, for example, argues
that educational research is fully prepared to bring to the education

profession the kind of power that research brought to medicine.[27] I am convinced that even though there is fragility in the extant body of knowledge,[28] much progress in this area will continue to be made. The need is particularly great in the area of marrying the knowledge of the practitioner with that of the researcher. There already is enough pertaining to classroom behavior and interactions of students and teachers that, if mastered, would separate school-teachers sharply from the average citizen and from teachers of barbering and diesel engine repair.

In recent years, various groups—testing organizations and state regulatory bodies—have pushed toward encapsulating in tests items designed to elicit some of the more specific pieces of this knowledge. Increasingly, passing such tests not only has become a requirement for securing or renewing a teaching certificate but also is perceived to convey professional status. Sockett has persuasively sounded an alarm, arguing that a teaching profession must be guided by a set of moral and ethical norms internalized by teachers and articulated in a code of ethics.[29] There is substantial agreement among the authors of these chapters, all of whom address some aspect of this moral dimension.

The Layered Context of Teaching

Earlier in this chapter, I referred to the comprehensive study of the education of educators that colleagues and I conducted over a five-year period, 1985–1990. The first two years of this effort were spent in conceptualizing the study and translating our decisions into a design for gathering data in a purposefully representative sample of colleges and universities.[30] Early on, we confronted the need to clear our heads regarding the meaning of *profession* and its derivatives and, particularly, to clarify our thinking regarding the nature of "a profession of teaching," if indeed such should be claimed. An analysis of other occupations calling themselves *professions* helped.[31]

A major purpose in all of this was to arrive at a set of norms against which the conduct of teacher education in our sample of institutions might be judged.[32] We were especially interested in determining whether there existed in each college or university a shared institutional or programmatic vision of teaching in the nation's schools toward which educational efforts were being directed. It seemed reasonable to assume that such a vision would acquire its substance and clarity from a conception of what schoolteachers should reasonably be expected to do.

We then set out to develop our own vision. The early phase of our inquiry was depressing. By the mid-1980s, many states were well advanced in the folly of defining the education to be gained by children and youths in schools in the form of behavioral proficiencies easily tested. Teachers, in turn, were to secure the competencies believed required to inculcate these proficiencies in their teacher education and staff development activities. Earlier, California had sought to mesh the requirements of two legislative bills into a fully interlocking, rationalized system combining these processes of reductionism. Folly was added to folly in the passage of a bill designed to require principals to evaluate teachers on the basis of their demonstrated ability to teach to specific instructional objectives.

Little harm and perhaps some good might be accomplished through teachers learning to do this. But, commonly, this is where the vision of what education, teaching and instructional leadership are all about stops. Indeed, many teachers and principals coming through crash in-service workshops in this behavioristic mode bristle at the suggestion that this approach is at best insufficient and at worst wrongheaded. It has, of course, a certain appeal to efficiency-minded administrators and lay citizens.

The concept of teaching as a profession takes on a hollowness when teaching is defined in this limited way. It is akin to viewing surgery as merely a series of mechanistic movements and the education of a surgeon as training in them. Of course, the movements must become automatic, but, even mastered, they do not a surgeon make.

We were further depressed by the repetition (in the so-called second wave of educational reform following the 1983 publication of *A Nation at Risk*) of all the old bromides regarding the improvement of teacher education that have appeared in reform reports for a century.[33] It seemed to us, considering reports on the condition of college education in the United States,[34] that one could not casually assume that the standard undergraduate fare provides adequate general or, for that matter, subject matter major preparation for today's teachers. Depending heavily on an extensive mentoring component for future teachers not well prepared to make critical judgments did not make sense to us, in view of the widespread dissatisfaction with the existing quality of teaching in schools.

The reports of the Carnegie Forum and the Holmes Group, both appearing in 1986, put teacher education squarely on the reform agenda but, by omission, alerted us to shortcomings in their otherwise useful contributions. For example, after carefully studying the report of the latter, *Tomorrow's Teachers*, my colleague Roger Soder bluntly concluded: "The question of context, of ends, is one that the Holmes Group report ignores."[35]

In short, as a result of our study, we arrived at the conclusion that teaching, a profession of teaching, and teacher education must derive their mission and their substance from the richly layered context within which teaching decisions are made. Not only are there layers of context, but each layer is complex and not predictable or understandable from the perspective of scientific principles alone. Even if a well-developed science of teaching were available, its mastery by teachers would not provide sufficient guidance for the burden of judgment they carry, its full definition would not adequately frame a profession of teaching, and teacher education programs based on only this science would be seriously deficient. Virtually all of teaching in schools involves values and is guided by normative principles. This is true at every level of the context.

When we first began to grapple with these normative considerations, we attempted to group them into the moral leg of a four-legged stool on which teaching as a profession rests. Increasingly, we came to see that normative considerations are a part of each leg and do not constitute a discrete entity. They pervade the whole, becoming moral imperatives for teaching, a profession of teaching, and teacher education. These moral imperatives arise out of the school's responsibility for enculturating the young, the necessity for and challenge of providing access to knowledge for all students, the unique relationship between the teacher and the taught in the context of compulsory schooling, and the role of teachers in renewing school settings.

The Moral Dimensions

Enculturation. From their earliest beginnings, our tax-supported schools were viewed as necessary for the induction of the young into the culture. This expectation intensified with the founding of the Republic. The language of school purpose emphasized educating for responsibility—as citizen, parent, and worker. Education for self-realization is a twentieth-century concept in the United States. But, as Kerr points out, "Inasmuch as valuing one's self and one's plans and abilities is a cultural achievement, self-respect presupposes education as initiation into some culture."[36] Not only are our schools charged with this responsibility; they are unique among institutions in this respect.

The most obvious moral deficiency in this area has been our treatment of Native Americans and blacks; our schools for a long time were for neither. Even today, we are driven to include them in the educational system more for instrumental than for moral reasons. Remedying the long period of neglect will be difficult, even for teachers driven by moral imperatives, especially if their own experience and education have failed to equip them with some understanding of why those minorities often see little reason to succeed in an institution of schooling that they perceive to be serving the aspirations of whites.[37]

It becomes apparent that the general education of all schoolteachers must provide them with critical perspectives (historical, philosophical, and sociological) on the nature of democratic societies, with particular reference to their own political democracy. This is not now ensured by passage through an undergraduate curriculum. Since we cannot afford the risks of omission, the implied intellectual encounters must be specified in a preteaching curriculum. It is difficult to imagine that colleges and universities presuming to educate teachers are not able to ensure such a curriculum in the educational experience of all students planning to become teachers. Nonetheless, few ensure it now. It is difficult to imagine a true profession of teaching standing idly by in the face of evidence that a given teacher-preparing institution is unable to provide such ensurance. Still, the teaching profession has been virtually mute on this issue and has been content, it appears, with the vague rhetoric of more general education for teachers.

Teachers need more than the general education described. They also need to acquire both an understanding of the critical role of schools in enculturating the young and a sense of moral justice regarding the right of all to the necessary education. For the most diffident, seemingly uninterested students to drop out of school early removes the problems of teaching them. But it shifts elsewhere responsibility for the enculturating process—and, of course, there is no such elsewhere. Protestations to the effect that stumbling students are better off out of school and in jobs are a cruel sham. Yet such an argument appears to make logical sense if one ignores the moral responsibility for keeping all students meaningfully engaged in school and the equity issues involved in sending young people ill prepared into the job market. We dare not ignore this responsibility, however. Our society simply cannot afford teachers who fail to understand and assume the moral burden that goes with developing humane individuals within the context of a political democracy. Teacher-preparing institutions share the moral burden.

Access to Knowledge. The most frequently and clearly articulated goals for schools define a central role of promoting intellectual processes through encounters with knowledge. Unfortunately, knowledge too often is translated into inert bits and pieces—in a sense, the garbage left behind in the human dialogue rather than the stuff of dialogue itself. Large numbers of teachers and, of course, their students fail to realize that embedded in the subject fields of the school curriculum are the ordered ways created by humankind for structuring experience. These are the tools for understanding the physical universe, comparing cultures, appreciating the arts, communicating in a wide range of circumstances, feeling at home in one's environment, and so on.

The richer one's repertoire for interpreting human experience, the greater the prospect for living a rich life. Teachers who do not know well the subjects they teach fail to develop in their students the "canons of assessment" embedded in the subject fields of the school curriculum.[38] They fail to do the very thing that the school alone as a social institution purports to do. Again, it becomes apparent that college curricula left to emerge more or less by chance around faculty interests or the happenstance of class schedules are likely to deny future teachers the kind of general and specialized knowledge they must have. An entire society suffers the consequences.

Teachers must be actively aware, too, of how casual, misguided decisions with regard to grouping and tracking students, apportioning the domains of knowledge and knowing in the curriculum, allocating daily and weekly instructional time, scheduling, and other practices often distribute access to knowledge unfairly and inequitably. There is, of course, a knowledge base to be drawn on in making these decisions wisely; it is part of the knowledge that is the foundation for a profession of teaching.

But there are moral issues here, too. Opportunities to gain access to the most generally useful knowledge are maldistributed in most schools, with poor and minority children and youths on the short end of the distribution.[39] This is morally wrong, whatever the arguments regarding teachable classes, teachers' comfort, parents' preferences, and even achievement. It is possible—indeed, likely—that college students will go through their general education requirements and academic majors, perhaps to the level of a master's degree, without even thinking about these inequities in schooling. But it is intolerable for future teachers to remain ignorant and unconcerned. And so their professional education must ensure the necessary loss of innocence.

The Teacher and the Taught. There is not in our society the kind of consensus regarding the need for teachers to know *how* to teach that there is regarding their need to know *what* they teach. Yet most reform reports admit to there being something worth learning in the former category. Virtually every state specifies that instruction in methods of teaching be included in the curriculum of future elementary school teachers; less such instruction is required for secondary school teachers and none at all for college and university teachers. Apparently, the closer the students are to adulthood, the less the need for the teacher to be well versed in teaching methods.

I already have argued in this chapter the case for a substantial and growing body of knowledge about teaching sufficient to meet the "special knowledge" criterion of a professional and a profession. Some of it is generic to all teaching; most is specific to the special case of teaching in schools for children and youths. But there is something more about this special case that calls for moral, not scientific, judgment. It is the compulsory nature of schooling.

Large numbers of teachers teach voluntary students who will simply leave if their dissatisfaction grows too great. Many students are in voluntary learning settings because they are motivated by a desire to paint or to ski or to qualify for jobs that will pay them more or be more satisfying than their present jobs. Usually, there is a close connection between taking a course or class and something of valued utility in their lives.

Almost all of these powerfully motivating factors are missing for young people under the age of sixteen who are in schools. They did not choose to be there; they see little there as utilitarian in their lives; the connections between classes or courses and personal betterment of some kind are remote. Intrinsic motivation, so lauded in psychological literature, is largely missing. The likelihood of intrinsic motivation being present for athletics, vocational subjects, and the arts is greater than for history, algebra, and mathematics. The first three rank high in liking and interest among many secondary school students,[40] but it is English, mathematics, science, and social studies that are most valued in schools and required for admission to college. Students' motivation for these subjects is closely tied to their motivation for more school. This kind of motivation, in turn, is tied to family background and economic status and is unevenly distributed in the culture.

Do schools have a responsibility to be aware of these nonschool factors in student motivation? Apparently, they assume so, for if they did not, the many provisions for special needs would not characterize schools as they do today. But how far should they go with special programs and arrangements? To what lengths should teachers go to reach the diversity of students in their charge?

The fact that our society requires that children attend school (or the equivalent) places a unique burden on the teacher-student relationship and makes of teaching in public schools a very special case of teaching, separating it from teaching in private schools. The private school is not, after all, the setting of last resort. Dismissed from private school for whatever reason, one still may claim the right to attend a public school.

The practical, moral implications of compulsory schooling for exercising judgment as a teacher are many. Does the child who was absent for illness have a greater right to make up time with a teacher than does the child whose parents simply kept him or her out? Time to learn is an exceedingly important factor in students' accomplishments, but how much additional time for Marie is warranted? Is it all right to deny Tom his interest in drawing when he does not finish his arithmetic? If I give Michael a *D* in biology, he will not have the grades he needs for a driver's license—and his family badly needs the part-time job that a car will enable him to take. The moral crunch for many decisions made by people outside of schools finally comes down to teachers in schools. We want our teachers to be sensitive and caring, but the more they are, the greater the decision-making dilemmas in which they find themselves. The more limited our vision of what teaching in schools is and what it requires of teachers, their preparation, and their support, the more we shortchange them and ourselves.

Renewing School Settings. In 1988, Boyer wrote:

> During the last five years, this nation has been en-
> gaged in the most sustained drive for school renewal
> in its history. Governors have placed education at the
> top of their agendas. Corporate leaders have, for the
> first time, argued vigorously on behalf of public
> schools. And federal debate has become increasingly
> intense.[41]

The report introduced by Boyer summarizes teachers' responses to a series of questions on implementation of specific reform proposals and their reactions to the reform movement in general. The responses reveal a substantial perception by teachers that conditions that the movement supposedly had addressed and that were of considerable concern to them had not got better or had got worse. Nearly 70 percent said that the push for reform deserved a *C* grade or less; one teacher in five gave it a *D* or *F*.

There is an ironic contradiction in these orgies of school reform that sweep the country from time to time. They lament the condition of our schools; frequently and in strident language, they invoke the importance of teachers, lay more demands for accountability on them—and then leave them out of the process. We never seem to learn that the schooling enterprise simply does not improve significantly when approached in this way. The substantial body of literature offering critiques of the federally driven reform efforts of the 1960s was scarcely referred to during the state-driven reform efforts of the 1980s—a costly omission.

If schools are to become the responsive, renewing institutions that they must, the teachers in them must be purposefully engaged in the renewal process. It does not matter whether a good deal of the impetus and many of the ideas for reform come from outside, so long as what comes into the school is seen as reasonable and useful by those engaged on the inside. This is a lesson we should not need to discover every twenty-five years. But, apparently, we do.

Even when we do learn it, which usually comes late in a reform cycle, we learn it in only an academic way. We do not translate the learning into concrete action. Teachers are employed and paid for 180 days a year, give or take a few. These days are spent in teaching. Some districts throw in a few staff development days, usually requiring attendance at a district setting outside the school.[42] The focus is rarely on the context of their teaching—the conditions and circumstances of their own schools that deeply affect their daily efforts. Addressing school-based issues must be reserved for the few hours a month, almost always at the end of a weary day, when staff meetings are held. But these are too few, too short, and too scattered in intent and substance to get at anything in the school that is of underlying importance. "School renewal" becomes a nonevent, one more in the cycle of nonevents that characterize the school improvement enterprise.

Renewal—whether of ponds, gardens, people, or institutions—is an internal process, whatever the external concerns and stimulants. It requires motivation, dedication, systematic and systemic evolution, and *time*. A second or a third reform wave calling on teachers as the prime actors will be no more successful than a first wave pushed by policymakers if the conditions necessary to renewal are not developed. Teachers employed for 180 days and required to teach 180 days simply will not renew their schools. It is ludicrous and self-deceiving to believe that they will. Further, such an expectation borders on the immoral.

The answer is not 160 days of teaching with 20 additional days of employment for planning. It is 180 days for teaching and 20 or more additional days for institutional renewal. We can begin to look seriously at teaching as a profession when it no longer is a part-time job. Teaching will become a full-time occupation when the public sees the need for it. Ironically, the part-time status sustained to date maintains a public impression that teachers have something less than the commitment expected of professionals. Many work at plebeian jobs during the summer.

The fact that administrators, including principals, are employed by the district during the summer further restricts the participation of teachers in decisions affecting the context of their teaching. Administrators use this time to make decisions about many things—often including the staff development activities and schedules for teachers during the coming year. Some of these decisions intrude into the classroom, which in higher education is the exclusive domain of the professor. Teaching in elementary and secondary schools enjoys only a truncated version of this prerogative, thus remaining a truncated profession. Yet teachers are held accountable for the learning of their students, often directly to the very administrators responsible for narrowing their domain of decision making. To the degree that administrators are management-trained and management-oriented rather than education-oriented, the tension over turf is exacerbated and too often resolved in the collective bargaining process rather than through dialogue.

Although I argue for teacher prerogatives in all of the contextual layers and domains of decision making that influence their teaching, I am not sanguine about the *immediate* benefits of removing the restraints. I already have identified the cruel irony in giving teachers authority to accompany their responsibility in the full range of the school's role and function without simultaneously creating the circumstances necessary for their effective performance. The question is not whether they should have this authority but how the rightful authority of both teachers and administrators is to serve in the best interests of students in schools.

There is irresponsibility in significantly expanding teachers' authority without educating them to use it well. Using it well requires both knowledge and moral sensitivity. These are acquired, in large part, through critical, disciplined socialization into the full array of expectations and responsibilities a democratic society requires of its teachers. This is unlikely to occur if teaching in schools is seen to require only the generic skills common to all teaching. Nor is it likely to occur if passage through a general undergraduate curriculum and mentoring with an experienced teacher are to be the route to teaching, as is so frequently recommended. Nor is this disciplined socialization commonly occurring in teacher education programs as now conducted.

Summary

I have argued for a teaching profession grounded in the judgments that teachers in schools must make to maximize the education of all children and youths. These judgments must extend far beyond the students and classroom for which each teacher is responsible. Judgments beyond the immediate classroom are shared with others—administrators, parents, and citizens who have a stake in our democracy and the school's role in making it work. Unless teachers participate in these judgments, their classrooms are likely to be polluted by decisions that make their classroom tasks more difficult. Virtually all of these judgments require special knowledge and, in the end at least, are normative. They involve values and valuing in addition to relevant knowledge.

There is, as yet, no clear taxonomy of the necessary decisions at each contextual level, from the classroom to state policy. Consequently, the nature of the knowledge needed for the various educational decisions to be made and the normative issues likely to be encountered in each are not at all clear. Inquiry necessary to the development of such a taxonomy remains vague and unfocused but has begun.[43]

The core to which each category of the taxonomy of educational decisions must connect is normative, with the focal question being "What are schools for?" All else stems from the answer. If schools are to serve the sole purpose of teaching children to read, write, and spell, we obviously do not need them. The job can be done inexpensively and efficiently through computer-based skill centers in the local shopping mall. "Park your kid in the spelling lab and shop," blinks the new sign, twenty-four hours a day. A teaching profession built on generic principles of teaching is an expensive hoax.

But if the answer to the question of what schools are for is more complex—is seen to encompass such things as responsibility for critical enculturation into a political democracy, the cultivation (with the family) of character and decency, and preparation for full participation in the human conversation—then teachers (carefully selected teachers, themselves well educated, who understand the layers of contextual complexity and who have engaged in reflection and dialogue on the moral issues involved) become necessary.[44] Such teachers and their calling warrant the designation "professional." They must be both liberally and professionally educated.

Further, they must be educated commonly (that is, together) in programs with a common professional core. To this core are added specialties such as physical, multicultural, science, English, or primary education or teaching. But all teachers should be educators first and specialists second.

I have argued also, more implicitly than explicitly, that administration, including the principalship, is one of these added specialties. All who work in schools and carry the title "teacher" or "principal" or "supervisor" are educators, whether teaching in a classroom or seeing to it that the conditions there are maximally educational for all. Those who administer and supervise must understand what is maximally educational so that they are able to help teachers achieve the necessary circumstances.

If the principalship comes to be defined as a management role, as it may, its future status is, at best, cloudy. Most certainly, the public will support the steady movement of teachers toward increased autonomy in a wide range of decisions, not just inside the classroom but beyond. Parents will see as most central and important those people with whom they interact regarding the care and welfare of their children in school. Teachers will become the indispensable professionals. Managers of schools—versed in generic management—will be viewed as interchangeable with managers of retail stores, markets, and insurance agencies and decreasingly viewed as educators. Teachers, not administrators, will become the recipients of plane tickets to attend educational meetings.

The alternate course is for the administration of schools to move more in the direction of academic administration in major universities, one of the few areas for which higher education may be a desirable model for elementary and secondary schools. To considerable degree, deans are like principals, responsible for a unit of a larger organization. But nearly all academic deans are professors first, a designation and status they retain with doggedness and determination. Like principals, they deal with personnel, budgetary matters, and a variety of publics. But, unlike principals, their security and professional status rest on the professorship to which they commonly return after a term or two as dean. They are teacher-scholars first and administrators second.

A vocation is not a profession because those in it choose to call it one. It must be recognized as such. Teachers may refer to themselves as professionals because they have passed examinations on a core of generic understandings and principles regarding teaching. But they are unlikely to be publicly regarded as professionals merely for doing so, because people in many other occupations earn licenses in this way and are regarded neither by themselves nor by the public as professionals.

In summary, the conditions necessary to legitimate self-proclamation of professional status include a thorough understanding of the role of education and schooling in a democratic society, an understanding of knowledge and ways of knowing that serve to interpret human experience, high-level competence in the special knowledge and skills required to educate the young in these ways of knowing, and substantial awareness of the standards of excellence and equity that must characterize schools and classrooms.

Public recognition of teaching in schools as a profession will come in part as the now separated specialties come together in pursuit of a common vision defined as the attainment of these conditions by all who educate. This recognition is likely to come more quickly if those who supervise, administer, and teach teachers are seen as joined in this mission. But full recognition of teaching in schools as a profession depends on teachers, individually and collectively, demonstrating their awareness of and commitment to the burdens of judgment that go with a moral enterprise. Teacher-preparing institutions and teacher educators carry a heavy responsibility for the education and professional socialization of teachers who will come to possess the necessary awareness and commitment.

Notes

1. V. Hearne, "Horses," *New Yorker,* Aug. 18, 1986, p. 44.
2. H. W. Hill, "Societal Decisions in Curriculum," in J. I. Goodlad and Associates (eds.), *Curriculum Inquiry* (New York: McGraw-Hill, 1979), pp. 101–127.
3. See, for example, M. Cooper, "Whose Culture Is It, Anyway?" in A. Lieberman (ed.), *Building a Professional Culture in Schools* (New York: Teachers College Press, 1988), pp. 45–54; D. H. Kerr, "Authority and Responsibility in Public Schooling," in J. I. Goodlad (ed.), *The Ecology of School Renewal,* Eighty-Sixth Yearbook (Part I) of the National Society for the Study of Education (Chicago: University of Chicago Press, 1987), pp. 20–40.
4. For a perspective on the degree to which teachers' roles are so restricted, see A. E. Wise, *Legislated Learning* (Berkeley: University of California Press, 1979). For descriptions and analyses of the ways such restrictions impinge on teachers' behavior, see L. M. McNeil, *Contradictions of Control: School Structure and School Knowledge* (New York: Routledge, 1988).
5. B. R. Wilson, "The Teacher's Rôle—A Sociological Analysis," *British Journal of Sociology,* 1962, *13* (1), 23.
6. L. A. Cremin, *The Genius of American Education* (New York: Vintage Books, 1965).
7. J. B. Conant, *The Education of American Teachers* (New York: McGraw-Hill, 1963), p. 11.
8. For a perspective on the once all-encompassing National Education Association, see E. B. Wesley, *NEA: The First Hundred Years* (New York: Harper & Row, 1957).

9. S. K. Bailey, "Political Coalitions for Public Education," *Daedalus,* Summer 1981, *110,* 35–38.

10. For discussions of the common school and of the mutual roles of such a school and the home, see J. I. Goodlad, "Common Schools for the Common Weal," in J. I. Goodlad and P. Keating (eds.), *Access to Knowledge: An Agenda for Our Nation's Schools* (New York: College Entrance Examination Board, 1989); J. J. Schwab, "Education and the State: Learning Community," in *The Great Ideas Today* (Chicago: Encyclopaedia Britannica, 1976), pp. 234–272.

11. The writer participated in these discussions as president of the AERA.

12. G. J. Clifford and J. W. Guthrie, *Ed School* (Chicago: University of Chicago Press, 1988).

13. H. Judge, *American Graduate Schools of Education* (New York: Ford Foundation, 1982).

14. Clifford and Guthrie, *Ed School,* p. 290.

15. National Commission on Excellence in Education, *A Nation at Risk* (Washington, D.C.: U.S. Government Printing Office, 1983).

16. C. M. Frazier, "The 1980s: States Assume Educational Leadership," in J. I. Goodlad (ed.), *The Ecology of School Renewal,* Eighty-Sixth Yearbook (Part I) of the National Society for the Study of Education (Chicago: University of Chicago Press, 1987), pp. 99–117.

17. L. Darling-Hammond, "Policy and Professionalism," in A. Lieberman (ed.), *Building a Professional Culture in Schools* (New York: Teachers College Press, 1988), p. 56.

18. The reports of the National Governors' Association, *Time for Results* (Washington, D.C.: National Governors' Association, 1986); and of the Carnegie Forum on Education and the Economy, *A Nation Prepared: Teachers for the 21st Century* (Washington, D.C.: Carnegie Forum on Education and the Economy, 1986) addressed the reform of both schools and teacher education. The report of the Holmes Group, *Tomorrow's Teachers* (East Lansing, Mich.: Holmes Group, 1986), addressed teacher education almost exclusively.

19. L. Olson, "Despite Years of Rhetoric, Most Still See Little

Understanding, Inadequate Efforts," *Education Week,* 1988, *8* 1, 16.

20. At the time of this writing, the NEA is discussing a proposal to bring into membership currently unorganized support personnel and higher education faculty members.

21. S. Cooperman and L. Klagholz, *A Principal Residency Program* (Trenton: New Jersey Department of Education, 1987).

22. Danforth Foundation, *Annual Report, 1987-1988* (St. Louis, Mo.: Danforth Foundation, 1988), p. 10.

23. See, for example, that of the BYU–school district partnership as described by D. D. Williams, "The Brigham Young University–Public School Partnership," in K. A. Sirotnik and J. I. Goodlad (eds.), *School-University Partnerships in Action* (New York: Teachers College Press, 1988), pp. 129–130.

24. S. A. Warner, *Teacher* (New York: Simon & Schuster, 1963).

25. It is encouraging to note that recent polls show increases in the percentage of parents who would be pleased to see their children become teachers.

26. A. Bloom, *The Closing of the American Mind* (New York: Simon & Schuster, 1987).

27. D. C. Berliner, "Knowledge Is Power," in D. C. Berliner and B. V. Rosenshine (eds.), *Talks to Teachers* (New York: Random House, 1987), p. 31.

28. Berliner used the word *fragile* to describe the knowledge base of teaching in a letter to the author dated Aug. 29, 1988.

29. An exchange of views between Shulman and Sockett usefully frames a large part of the debate (now and probably for some time into the future) regarding the professional bases of teaching. See L. S. Shulman, "Knowledge and Teaching: Foundations of the New Reform," Harvard Educational Review, Feb. 1987, *57,* 1–22; H. T. Sockett, "Has Shulman Got the Strategy Right?" *Harvard Educational Review,* May 1987, *57,* 208–219; L. S. Shulman, "Sounding an Alarm: A Reply to Sockett," *Harvard Educational Review,* Nov. 1987, *57,* 473–482.

30. For an account of this early work, see J. I. Goodlad, "A Study of the Education of Educators: Values-Driven Inquiry," *Phi Delta Kappan,* Oct. 1988, *70,* 105–111; K. A. Sirotnik, "A Study

of the Education of Educators: Methodology," *Phi Delta Kappan,* Dec. 1988, *70,* 229–305.

31. R. Soder, *Professionalizing the Profession: Notes on the Future of Teaching,* Occasional Paper no. 4, (Seattle: Center for Educational Renewal, College of Education, University of Washington, 1986).

32. Under the rubric of "teacher education," we subsumed the education of three groups of educators: teachers, "special" educators, and principals.

33. Z. Su, *Teacher Education Reform in the United States (1890–1986),* Occasional Paper no. 3 (Seattle: Center for Educational Renewal, College of Education, University of Washington, 1986).

34. See, for example, Bloom, *The Closing of the American Mind;* F. I.. Boyer, *College: The Undergraduate Experience in America* (New York: Harper & Row, 1987).

35. R. Soder, "Tomorrow's Teachers for Whom and for What? Missing Prepositions in the Holmes Group Report," *Journal of Teacher Education,* Nov.-Dec. 1986, *37,* 2.

36. Kerr, "Authority and Responsibility," p. 23.

37. J. Ogbu, "Overcoming Racial Barriers to Equal Access," in J. I. Goodlad and P. Keating (eds.), *Access to Knowledge: An Agenda for Our Nation's Schools* (New York: College Entrance Examination Board, 1989).

38. Kerr, "Authority and Responsibility," p. 23.

39. For a comprehensive review with supporting data, see J. Oakes, *Keeping Track: How Schools Structure Inequality* (New Haven: Yale University Press, 1985); Goodlad and Keating (eds.), *Access to Knowledge.*

40. J. I. Goodlad, *A Place Called School* (New York: McGraw-Hill, 1984), pp. 198–224.

41. E. L. Boyer, "Report Card on School Reform," in Carnegie Foundation for the Advancement of Teaching, *Report Card on School Reform: The Teachers Speak* (Princeton, N.J.: Carnegie Foundation for the Advancement of Teaching, 1988), p. 1.

42. K. A. Tye, *The Junior High School* (Lanham, Md.: University Press of America, 1985), pp. 284–289.

43.   Knowledge thought relevant to curriculum and instruction is
      now rather well defined; see, for example, M. Wittrock (ed.),
      Handbook on Research on Teaching, 3rd ed. (New York: Mac-
      millan, 1986); P. W. Jackson (ed.), *Handbook on Research on
      Curriculum* (in press); American Association of Colleges for
      Teacher Education, *Knowledge Base for the Beginning
      Teacher,* M. C. Reynolds (ed.), (Oxford, England: Pergamon
      Press, 1989). Other categories are now being identified but,
      taken together, fall far short of a taxonomy.
44.   See J. I. Goodlad, *Some Propositions in Search of Schools*
      (Washington, D.C.: Department of Elementary School Princi-
      pals, National Education Association, 1962); J. I. Goodlad,
      What Schools Are For (Bloomington, Ind.: Phi Delta Kappa
      Education Foundation, 1979).

2

The Rhetoric
of Teacher
Professionalization

Roger Soder

For many academics, it may seem that returns from the study of professions and professionalization have become marginal, with less and less to be mined and more and more to quibble about. Perhaps Laurence Veysey summed up these feelings with the title of his review of yet another work on the history of professions: "Who's a Professional? Who Cares?"[1]

But what has become a minor quibble for some academics remains of central and practical concern for dozens of occupational groups who are preoccupied with joining the ranks of the already established professions. For these groups, profession is the ultimate in status, the elite position in the world of work. Their responses to Veysey's questions are, respectively, "We are!" and "We do, passionately!" These responses would be the same—particularly in the case of the one occupational group we will consider in detail—in either the last decades of the previous century or all of this one.

There are three noteworthy aspects of this general desire to be a professional, a member of a profession. First, although professional status is seen as elite, virtually all occupational groups can try out: entry to the scramble for elite status is democratic. Second, groups can keep trying. If you do not feel that you have been accorded professional status, rest a few years and go at it again. There are no penalties for failure. Third, it matters little for most occupational groups whether other groups win professional status. There is room for everyone in this race, and each striving occupational group has been willing to let others win—as long as it wins, too. In all of this, one senses resemblances to the dodo's decision in the Looking Glass caucus race: All have won and all shall have prizes.

Among the most venerable of these several groups looking to win and looking for prizes in the race for professional status are teachers and their organizations. As a group, teachers have been striving in this race longer than most, and they have been among the least successful in legitimating their claims to professional status. The historical literature is replete with reflections of this striving. Early-twentieth-century adjurations to teachers (and to those involved in the training of teachers) reveal two recurring themes: (1) a sense of already being a bit off the mark in the status drive and (2) a desire to consider teachers as at least potential candidates for membership in the inner circles of the "real" professions.

One notes, for example, these themes in comments of John Dewey in 1904:

> I doubt whether we, as educators, keep in mind with sufficient constancy the fact that the problem of training teachers is one species of a more generic affair— that of training for professions. Our problem is akin to that of training architects, engineers, doctors, lawyers, etc. Moreover, since (shameful and incredible as it seems) the vocation of teaching is practically the last to recognize the need of specific professional preparation, there is all the more reason for teachers to try to find what they may learn from the more extensive and matured experience of other callings.[2]

Some fifty years later, the themes emerge in refined and familiar form. We listen first to Francis Chase, speaking at a 1953 NEA conference:

> The needed improvements in education cannot be achieved unless we cloak teachers with professional freedom and responsibility. This professional responsibility must be accompanied by professional competence. When the American public recognizes that the

teacher with a group of children has essentially the
same kind of professional responsibility that the surgeon has in the operating room, there will be a public
demand for professional salaries and professional
preparation. Then we shall not need to concern ourselves so much about the status of the teacher.[3]

A similar instance was provided by Ralph McDonald at the same
meeting of minds:

In this country at the present time we are in the throes
of the movement to convert elementary school teaching into a profession. The movement has progressed
to the point that I now feel safe in saying that it will
definitely succeed. In fact, I will go so far as to predict
that by 1975, despite all obstacles, elementary school
teaching will be a full-fledged profession in the United States.[4]

In our own time, an examination of the current rhetoric suggests
that the themes of "why ours is a profession" and "how do we get
others to treat us as professionals" are of continuing concern.

In May 1985, the Carnegie Forum on Education and the
Economy announced the appointment of a panel to develop plans
to make teaching a "true profession." The panel's report, *A Nation
Prepared: Teachers for the 21st Century*, puts heavy emphasis on
professionalization.[5] Later in the same year, the heads of the National Education Association and the American Federation of
Teachers announced major plans to "professionalize" the occupation.[6] *Tomorrow's Teachers*, a report of the Holmes Group on the
reform of teacher education, appeared a year later. It, too, placed
considerable emphasis on making teaching a profession.[7]

Four questions are raised by these announced strategies to
professionalize what is already claimed to be a profession: (1) Can
an occupational group, through purposive efforts, raise its professional status? (2) What might those efforts look like? (3) What conditions must obtain in order that those efforts might best succeed?
and (4) Do such strategies serve good purposes, or might they?

Professions, Professionalism, Professionalization

It is clear that teachers have long considered themselves members of a profession, with their self-proclamations of membership in this particular class of occupations indicated early on. The primary purpose of the National Teachers' Association—later to become the National Education Association—was, according to its venerable preamble, "to elevate the character and advance the interests of the profession."[8] William Russell's paper presented at the founding meeting of the NTA in 1857 noted that teachers needed a professional organization "to reap whatever benefits our medical brethren derive from their national association" and to ensure for teaching the "proper distinction between a profession and any ordinary vocation."[9] The preoccupation with elevating teaching from vocation to profession has continued, uninterrupted, to our own time.

Although it is clear that teachers consistently have claimed membership in the class of "profession" (as opposed to the apparently less exalted class of "trade," "vocation," or "occupation"), less clear is what membership might imply. But lack of clarity in professionalization rhetoric is not limited to the occupational group of teachers; just precisely what constitutes the class of "profession" has been the subject of considerable speculation and disagreement for the greater part of this century.

The academic literature on professions and professionalization is vast. For our purposes here, we can only view salient aspects of this sometimes exalted and cynical terrain, noting that Eliot Freidson's *Professional Powers* is a useful and concise guidebook for those who wish to explore it in detail.[10]

From the 1930s to the 1970s, the study of the professions did tend to be exalted, with students of the genre piously celebrating professions as a positive force for the stabilization of society. This was an uncritical time for most American social science, with a Panglossian   everything-is-for-the-best-in-the-best-of-all-possible-worlds view prevailing in many academic quarters. The literature in the sociology of professions reflected this prepotent view. By and large, it was assumed that those in professions were benign and altruistic beings serving society by combining the virtues of ra-

tionality, technique, control, and codes of ethics and only inciden-
tally (albeit deservedly) reaping pecuniary and other rewards.[11] As
for the prestige, autonomy, and well-being that came with being a
professional, I would suggest that these attributes were seen by sociologists as reflecting a secularization of an earlier Puritanism: With
their money and high place in society, professionals were the new
visible saints, with outward manifestations of inner grace.

The major questions treated in the literature focused on discovery of traits purportedly common to all professions or on speculations as to ways in which professions best served society and
functioned as stabilizing forces. Both "traits" advocates and the
functionalists tended to speculate on these matters from a relatively
limited view of the world. Was one interested in the ways the profession of medicine served society? Then one discoursed with other sociologists specializing in medical sociology or, better yet, with doctors. It apparently did not occur to researchers to consider the perceptions of patients or other just plain folk.

This essentially benign view of professions tended to overlook the less edifying aspects of the struggle for occupational upward mobility and control. Medicine, for a time the *ne plus ultra* of
professions, was rife with factional disputes, and the bloody and
Byzantine battle for control, including the arm-twisting of legislators in state after state and an unrelenting public relations campaign extending over decades, suggests that this occupation did not
get its power by some sort of a priori good or natural process.[12] Most
other occupations have been involved in similar struggles, albeit
with more modest resources. Thus, teamsters have fought with iron-
workers over who should have control over the unloading of reinforcement bars at a job site; chiropractors have lobbied legislators to
deny massage therapists the right to manipulate the spinal column;
embalmers have seen to it that American citizenship is a prerequisite for licensing; and plumbers have contended that cities rather
than states should impose and control residence requirements.[13]
These struggles were largely overlooked by those seeking to discover
inherent generic traits of professions, as they were overlooked, too,
by functionalists whose guiding ethos was the maintenance of the
status quo.

With the shift in the 1970s to criticism of the foundations of virtually all American institutions, the focus of the literature on the sociology of professions changed sharply. Whereas in earlier times it was argued that professions serve all of society and only secondarily professional group members, revisionists now argued that the primary function of professions is to serve the elite, to maintain inequitable and hegemonic class relations, and to further the self-interests of group members.[14] In one way or another, these views are variants of George Bernard Shaw's dictum that all professions are conspiracies against the laity.

Others see the emergence of professionalization primarily as a struggle to gain hegemony over amateurs, rather than over a lower class. For example, Theodore Hamerow notes that the transformation of the study of history from an avocation to a profession exacerbated tensions between the gentleman-scholars and the newly prepared professional technicians armed with doctorates and backed by professional organizations and journals. "The professionals accused the amateurs of sacrificing scholarship for melodrama, the amateurs charged the professionals with a deadly pedestrianism which destroyed the human dimension of history."[15] Although the professionals in higher education have clearly won what seemed to be a Manichaean battle, professionalism is not always seen as a good thing. Hamerow suggests that professionalizing history might well have helped raise the level of technical competence, but "the advance has come at the expense of spontaneity and breadth of view; it has encouraged routinization and conformity."[16] Looking more broadly at higher education as a profession, one observer argued that humanists and natural scientists tend to view professionals with disdain: "The term *professional*, rather than blanketing the entire university, as is often more crudely thought, adheres with special explicit force only to those elements within it which reflect a utilitarian world-view."[17]

Others, guided less by ideology, were simply inclined to view the matter with what one senses to be a dash of world-weary cynicism. Thus, Veysey could claim that when considering the notion of profession, "Some degree of enhanced social status is the only true common denominator of the varied occupations that are given this label" and that the "usual definitions of professionalism prove to be the partisan creation of utilitarian-minded social scientists."[18]

Lay views of professions and professionalism are less informed by functionalist piousness or sociological jargon (although, it should be noted, such lacks do not necessarily make these views less useful or insightful than their academic counterparts). One must derive lay "meaning" of *profession* from the sources in the popular culture: As I have noted, there has been little sustained research to determine these meanings as held by the general public. What one does find is that many of the lay senses or "meanings" have counterparts among the academic views.

One recurring notion is the distinction between those who do something for pay and those who do the same thing for free. You do it for money? You're a professional. One hears this distinction during discussions, say, of whether participation in the Olympic Games should be limited to "amateurs" or whether "professionals" should be allowed in. This is probably the most commonly heard view of *profession*.

Another popular notion (again with a counterpart in the academic literature) centers on the notion of professional disinterest and detachment. Thus, after knocking out his opponent in the first round, heavyweight boxer Mike Tyson could respond to queries about the impact of his personal problems with "No matter what happens in my life, I'm a professional. The job has to be done."[19] This cool detachment of the professional is found in much of the crime and suspense literature: It is common to find a cold-blooded murderer described not as a psychopath but as a professional killer. Frederick Lewis Allen talks of "professional gangster-racketeers."[20] From the professional's point of view, such detachment is indeed necessary to get the job done. From the client's point of view, however, detachment is frustrating and alienating, as experienced by Tolstoy's Ivan Ilych:

> To Ivan Ilych only one question was important: was his case serious or not? But the doctor ignored that inappropriate question. From his point of view it was not the one under consideration, the real question was to decide between a floating kidney, chronic catarrh, or appendicitis. It was not a question of Ivan Ilych's life or death, but one between a floating kidney and

appendicitis . . . for the doctor, and perhaps for every-
body else, it was a matter of indifference, though for
him it was bad. And this conclusion struck him painfully, arousing in him a great feeling of pity for himself and of bitterness towards the doctor's indifference
to a matter of such importance.[21]

Doctors are not the only ones who get involved in difficulties
of professional detachment. A journalist could try to justify the
publication of an exposé of a judge after which the judge committed
suicide in terms of professional detachment:

The rush for a scoop seems a crass and cynical motive
for an undertaking that prompts a man to take his life.
But journalists, like lawyers and judges, are only professionals. We believe in the common good and hope
the truth shall set us free, but when we get down in the
trenches, we're driven, like all professionals, by the
thirst for and the joy of accomplishment. And that
means scoops.[22]

In addition to matters of money and detachment, we find a
third common theme: technical prowess or excellence. Thus the
expression "What a pro," suggesting respect accorded someone who
has pulled off a brilliant maneuver under pressure. There is a sense
of standards being met by a professional, a sense of considerable
competence. In *Blithe Spirit,* Noel Coward captures this sense
nicely:

Ruth: Do you realize what your insane meddling has done?

Madame Acarti: I have been a professional since I was a child,
Mrs. Condomine—"Amateur" is a word I cannot tolerate.

Ruth: It seems to me to be the height of amateurishness to evoke
evil spirits and not be able to get rid of them again.[23]

But being considered a professional can also be seen as a put-
down—as being viewed, for example, as a professional partygoer,

one who does something for form or because it is a job, rather than really having one's heart in it.

The dictionary—another arbiter of popular culture—is as inconclusive as other sources. The *American Heritage Dictionary* tells us that a profession is "an occupation or vocation requiring training in the liberal arts or the sciences and advanced study in a specialized field." So far, it would seem that here we are on familiar ground, with nice, neat images of medical schools and law schools and the like. But just below, under *professional*, things get untidy: As an adjective, the word can mean "engaged in a specific activity as a source of livelihood: a professional actor" or "performed by persons receiving pay: professional football." And as a noun, *professional* can mean "(1) A person following a profession, (2) One who earns his livelihood as an athlete, (3) One who has an assured competence in a particular field or occupation." So much for clean definitions. How quickly we can move from physicians to car thieves to carnival barkers (and all sorts of other folks, as long as competence is assured) all within the scope of a few lines! The term, then, is loosely defined in the popular culture, leading to some rich ambiguities. Thus, an assistant general counsel of the CIA could claim that "Espionage is the world's second oldest profession, and just as honorable as the first."[24]

Despite difficulties of definition, there are suggestions in the popular culture that being a professional is, at the very minimum, considered desirable and acceptable. One clear suggestion is the attention paid to the much-maligned and apparently envied Young Urban Professionals, or yuppies. There are, heaven knows, considerably more young urban workers around than there are yuppies, but *worker*, at least in America, just does not have the same resonance as *professional*. Likewise, among those seeking companionship through personal want ads, typically in *New York* and other city magazines, the blessed word *professional* comes into play as both a descriptor and a desideratum, along with the de rigueur white wine by the fire and walks on the beach.

The literature, both academic and lay, is indeed vast, disturbing, and hardly conclusive. It is not my purpose here to try to develop final definitions of *profession* and related terms satisfactory to all for all times or to argue for a grand synthesis of controverted conceptual frameworks. Personal limitations aside, the job cannot be done. In a very basic sense, the job cannot be done because these notions of profession, professionalism, and professionalization are social constructs and can "mean" only what a group of people in a given culture at a given time might want them to mean. These notions cannot—should not, at any rate—be reified: A profession does not exist in the same way a stone exists, and to define and look for a profession in the same way one would define and look for a stone will only lead to confusion and frustration.

But *profession* does exist as a social construct, and we can at least speculate as to its social "meaning." My own speculations as to the broad social meaning of profession for most people, including most teachers, would probably follow Becker: "Among the more desired and admired statuses is to be a member of a profession."[25] Thus, I believe most people's meaning will incorporate a sense of prestige, a sense of higher status, a sense of greater rewards (both pecuniary and otherwise). To want to be a professional, at the very least, is to want to be something that most people find desirable and acceptable.

If *profession* and related terms are social constructs, then we must be concerned with perceptions of those who claim to be professionals and those who must legitimate and accept those claims. Thus, what is of concern here is that *teachers* consider their occupation to be a profession, and, as discussed below, they consider it to be so in the sense that they consider medicine a profession. What is of concern here is that others in society have looked askance at the teachers' claims. It is to these concerns that we now turn.

Teacher Status and Professionalization

Although it is comforting to think of Mark Hopkins, the log, and the student, the dominant personification of the teacher in early America is, rather, Ichabod Crane:

> This "odd mixture of small shrewdness and simple credulity" was no hero to the men, and when Brom Bones in his ghastly masquerade frightened Ichabod out of town and smashed a pumpkin on his credulous

head, he was passing the symbolic judgment of the American male community on the old-time school-master.[26]

Robert Wiebe also alludes to the image of Ichabod Crane:

If the greatest public need for professionalism was in medicine, the greatest occupational need was in teaching. Ridiculed over the nineteenth century as Ichabod Cranes and fussy schoolmarms, teachers embodied the apparent paradox of exceptionally low prestige in a land that acclaimed universal education. Actually, there was no paradox. To most Americans of the nineteenth century, universal education referred only to the bare rudiments, a basic version of the three R's, which countless people were qualified to teach. Few could live on the teacher's starvation salary, few saw opportunities for advancement, and therefore very few—often the Ichabod Cranes and the futile old maids—devoted a life to it. Far more often teaching was a way-station, for a James A. Garfield and a Henry M. Teller in search of careers and for young ladies in search of husbands.[27]

Many teachers were indentured servants. As Jonathan Boucher, writing in Maryland in 1773, noted,

Not a ship arrives either with redemptioners or convicts, in which school masters are not as regularly advertised for sale, as weavers, tailors, or any other trade; with little other difference, that I can hear of, excepting perhaps that the former do not usually fetch so good a price as the latter.[28]

Consider, too, R. Carlyle Buley's unflattering assessment:

Many teachers were ignorant, others merely queer. Good teachers were hard to get, nor were the low pay

and lack of training facilities entirely accountable; it
would seem that teaching has always attracted (or else
protected and retained) more than its share of the constitutionally inept and impractical.[29]

Main also presents a telling description of the status of
teachers in revolutionary America:

> Social classes existed in early America, but their pre-
> cise definition is as unclear as the prestige order was
> flexible. Everyone pretended to exalt the farmers, giv-
> ing to professional men and still more to merchants
> an inferior status, and to artisans no status at all. In
> practice, however, Americans looked for leadership to
> their professional men as well as to the well-to-do
> landowners, while in the North merchants were
> granted high rank. The truth is that the social climber
> did not have to change his occupation except of course
> that he could not simply remain a laborer—or a
> teacher.[30]

One can argue that doctors and lawyers, too, were subjected
to criticism and often held in low esteem in early America.[31] The
point is that doctors and lawyers, beginning in the early twentieth
century, managed to overcome these earlier negative stereotypes,
while teachers did not. Most teachers, too, are no doubt aware of the
long-standing views of their occupation held by others. The sentiments underlying the old saw "Those who can, do; those who can't,
teach; those who can't teach, teach teachers" are commonly reflected
in the literature.

In an early sociology of education classic, Willard Waller
notes that:

> Concerning the low social standing of teachers much
> has been written. The teacher in our culture has al-
> ways been among the persons of little importance, and
> his place has not changed for the better in the last few
> decades.[32]

The low status of teachers, according to Waller, is due, among other things, to the belief that

> teaching is quite generally regarded as a failure belt. There is some justice in this belief. A popular epigram of a few years ago had it that teaching was the refuge of unsaleable men and unmarriageable women. The epigram is unjust to many individuals, [like] any generalization so sweeping, but it mirrors accurately a general belief.[33]

Other sociologists have similarly noted the low status of teachers. The Lynds, writing three years before Waller, observed that "few things about education in Middletown are more noteworthy than the fact that the entire community treats its teachers casually." Teachers, according to the Lynds, "are for the most part nonentities," with Middletown paying them "about what it pays a retail clerk." The underlying reason for the low status of teachers was cultural: "The often bitter comments of the teachers themselves upon their lack of status and recognition in the ordinary give and take of local life are not needed to make an observer realize that in this commercial culture the 'teacher' and 'professor' do not occupy the position they did even a generation ago."[34]

Such sociological analyses have been echoed in more recent times with little change. Teachers (along with librarians, social workers, and nurses) have the dubious distinction of being considered as belonging to a "semiprofession" or an "emerging" profession,[35] with all of the implications of second-class status implied by such labeling. In a widely quoted analysis, Glazer asserts that the "major professions are medicine and law; the minor professions [including education] are all the rest."[36] C. Wright Mills considered teachers as the "economic proletarians of the professions."[37]

It is not only by sociologists' pronouncements that ye shall know them. The occupational status of teachers is reflected, too, in the popular culture: In addition to the credulous Ichabod, teachers (and the rest of us) know of Tom Sawyer's schoolmaster, Our Miss Brooks, Miss Grundy, and Mr. Flutesnoot.

Teachers, too, know that a central recurring theme of the

criticisms of the education of teachers is the relatively low academic ability of those who would enter the field.[38] It is difficult to
avoid a sense of lowly status when one is told repeatedly that most
of the people entering your chosen field of endeavor are academi-
cally deficient when compared with those intent on other lines of
work and that the few bright teachers, such as they are, tend to bail
out of teaching at the first opportunity.

The general sentiment has long appeared to be that not only
are the worst and the dumbest stumbling into teaching but, with
few exceptions, the lesser lights are staying on. As one observer put
it, "We can expect only the dumb and the dull to linger in teaching
careers . . . our teaching corps is unacceptably incompetent."[39]

Teachers know, too, of the generally unflattering assessments
of the quality of their training programs. The indictments are common and have a common theme, as reflected in this comment by a
historian writing some twenty years ago:

> Nor was quality guaranteed when educationists began
> turning out hordes of teachers crammed with method-
> ology and jargon to match, but commonly not
> matched by a command of the subject they were pre-
> paring to teach.[40]

More recently, John Goodlad tells us that "Teachers education programs are disturbingly alike and almost uniformly inadequate." Unless major gambles are undertaken to achieve radical
breakthroughs, "Future attempts to improve teacher education—
and subsequently, our schools—are doomed to repeat the puny,
inadequate efforts of the past."[41]

Training programs are suspect, which reflects poorly on
those who are trained in those programs. The trainers, too, have
been portrayed in less than glowing terms:

> Study, reflection, debate, careful reading, even, yes,
> serious thinking is often conspicuous by its absence.
> What is passed off as "research" is either really train-
> ing program evaluation or trivial nosecounting. . . .
> The unreflective, unquestioning (if frighteningly

well-meaning) professor is still, alas, the rule. May his
tribe decrease.[42]

Considering the welter of opinion from all sides, teachers are
well aware of their relatively low standing in the status market.
They tend to accept the low estimates of others (although, as I shall
argue, they think that those estimates are undeserved). Unlike those
in other professions, they tend to indulge in harsh self-criticism:

> The tempered restraint that characterizes the criti-
> cisms of medicine by doctors and of law by lawyers is
> unknown in the teaching profession. Perhaps it is that
> educators, having been convinced of their lowly status
> by centuries of condescension, neglect, and contempt,
> are likewise unrestrained when they view their own
> profession.[43]

Accordingly, while teachers through their organizations proclaim theirs to be a profession in every way like the "other" professions, the rhetoric has a certain hollowness. The rhetoric also
appears, at times, to take on a peculiarly oxymoronic quality. For
example, one writer cites with approval this strategy proposed by
the NEA's National Commission on Teacher Education and Professional Standards (NCTEPS) in 1952: "The profession of teaching
should be made a socially acceptable one, its members functioning
as effective members of the community."[44]

And while teachers like to listen to the rhetoric, they listen
with some uneasiness and some ambivalence. Teachers sense (or
think they sense) the possibly amused reaction of the "real" professionals, the academicians, and the sociologists to their claims, and
they wonder, perhaps, whether their claims are not overwrought.
The reaction of these other observers to the claims, teachers might
well imagine, is rather like the indulgent response of airplane passengers to the youngster who announces he is a "pilot" because he is
wearing a pilot pin.

Such reactions are not always made explicit. A doctor or a
lawyer might not display such a reaction or publicly voice such
disdain of the teacher's claims to professionalism or of the teacher's

claims to be one with the medical or legal professions. But teachers can get a sense of such reactions from some professional groups, if only by default. (Teachers know that while they advert to the "real" professions, the adversion is not symmetrical. There are no instances in the literature, for example, in which those involved in medicine have claimed that their professional standing could be improved by their emulating teachers.)

Academicians, on the other hand, tend to be less reticent in their responses to the claims of teachers. If, for example, a treasured—if possibly dubious—attribute of a "real" profession is a base of theoretical knowledge, transmitted in an academic setting, consider how teachers might react to the sardonic comments of Jencks and Riesman:

> In teaching, on the other hand, it would be hard to demonstrate that even today there is any body of knowledge about pedagogy that can be transmitted from old-timers to apprentices. Yet enormous efforts have been made to professionalize teaching and to ensure that all recruits will go through the same motions of acquiring whatever expertise there is.[45]

It was one thing for a professor of education to say, in 1906, that

> The more I see of teachers and teaching, the less confidence I have in anyone's power to say with precision or in great detail what abilities and qualities are essential to success in the classroom.[46]

But teachers in the last few decades would prefer to believe that their profession had at long last begun to arm itself with some sort of knowledge base. To read that all that had happened was, in effect, an effort that was to be dismissed with a patronizing "Go through the motions of acquiring whatever expertise there is" is a bit disconcerting.

Consider, too, the comments of Jencks and Riesman regarding the status of normal schools that have become colleges and universities:

> Then the legislature typically responded by reorganiz-
> ing *all* the teacher training institutions, including
> some that were not really "ready." Or at least the legis-
> lature conducted such reorganizations on paper. In
> practice the change often takes a full generation to
> accomplish. Thus many of the places now called state
> colleges or universities still have more Ed.D.s than
> Ph.D.s on the faculty, more girls than boys in the
> student body, and more docility and low-level voca-
> tionalism everywhere than one would find in better-
> established institutions.[47]

It is not necessary to be a Yale critic to argue that the slights contained in this paragraph are many and painful; even a superficial exegesis reveals a high level of disdain for teacher education (as well as disdain for those with Ed.D.s and for women).

Both the theoretical basis of teaching and the appropriateness of training teachers in a university setting have been questioned by at least two certified academic Olympians. Abraham Flexner, writing in 1930, argued that "Of the professional faculties, a clear case can, I think, be made out for law and medicine; not for denominational religion, which involves a bias, hardly perhaps for education, certainly not at all for business, journalism, domestic 'science,' or library 'science.' "[48]

Six years later, Robert M. Hutchins propounded the notion that teacher training belonged in a technical institute apart from the university.[49] (Hutchins also suggested that training programs for medicine, law, and other "professions" be housed elsewhere in "institutes." Again, however, it should be noted that medicine and law managed to gain considerably in status—as did their training programs—while teaching did not.)

The preoccupation with occupational prestige is, as has been suggested, hardly the peculiar province of teachers. But what gives the preoccupation particular importance to us—and a certain poignancy—is the high level of status discrepancy in the teaching occupation.

Status discrepancy, as considered here, is a measure of the relationship between perceived self-value (and the implications of that self-value) and perceived valuing by others. Considered as such, status discrepancy is not related to overall status per se. For example, doctors think that their work is important and that they should thus be accorded high status; in terms of perceived value by others, doctors are indeed accorded high status. Shiners of shoes do not think that their work is important and do not think that they should be accorded high status (and they are not).[50] Both doctors and shoe shiners are illustrative of occupational groups with low status discrepancy.

Teachers, on the other hand, most likely provide an example of high status discrepancy. Given the historical themes of the teacher professionalization rhetoric, it is reasonable to suggest that teachers believe that their work is important but that they also believe that they are not accorded the high status they deserve.

As a hypothesis to test in further research, we suggest that much of the rancor that apparently permeates the occupation of teaching stems from the high level of status discrepancy between perceived self-value and valuing by others. That rancor, often reminiscent of the resentment of Dostoevsky's splenetic underground clerk, will not, we might argue, be assuaged by taking a standardized test to prove that one knows basic skills or by putting one's framed diploma on the classroom wall.

The similarity between this particular notion of status discrepancy and means-ends analysis of Robert Merton and others should be noted. Merton speaks of the "dissociation between culturally prescribed aspirations and socially structured avenues for realizing these aspirations."[51] Along similar lines, Burton Clark discusses the "responses of organized groups to means-ends disparities, in particular focusing attention on ameliorative processes that lessen the strains of dissociation."[52]

But what we are suggesting here moves us in a somewhat different direction. Means-ends analysis implies cultural prescriptions for aspirations that are applied generally and accepted generally. In the case of teachers, the prescriptions for aspirations come from the teachers *themselves,* rather than from the larger society.

The problem experienced by teachers is that others in the society do not accept the prescriptions.

It is, in part, from this high level of status discrepancy that the arguments for emulation arise. Make teaching a "real" profession (like medicine), and all will be well, the argument runs. That is to say, status discrepancy will be reduced, with teachers getting that which they believe they deserve. The argument stems from other motives as well. When teachers argue for emulation, are the arguments in some way specious? Do teachers desire the *prestige* associated with the "real" professions, or do they desire the *money* normally associated with those professions, or *both*? Or on the other hand, are teachers sincere in arguing that elevated professional status will lead to better schools, better students, and a better society?

I would argue that the question of motives, while interesting, need not be addressed here. The point is that teachers—for *whatever* reasons—strongly believe that it is important to emulate the "real" professions; and they believe that their professional status, through purposive efforts, can be elevated to that of the real professions.

The teacher professionalization literature suggests that when teachers advert to the "real" professions worthy of emulation, they advert almost exclusively to medicine or law.[53] One does not find in the teachers' rhetoric much mention of the desirability of emulating nursing, social work, or librarianship. (These are, after all, considered—by both teachers and others—as "semiprofessions," and why model your professional desires after groups having the same second-class status as your own?)

But one also does not find many references to other occupational groups generally accorded higher professional status in our society (for example, engineering, dentistry, architecture). The reluctance of teachers to advert to these professions as models is probably due to a sense that these professions, while worthy (and of greater status than teaching), do not have quite the prestige and power of medicine and law.

And, as we might expect, there are no instances we know of in the teacher professionalization rhetoric in which other occupational groups, albeit exhibiting many of the "attributes" of professions, are cited as exemplary models. Other traditionally "nonprofessional" occupations are mentioned, but only as negative referent points ("Garbage collectors make more money than we do"), not as exemplars.

The silence in the rhetoric regarding plain old occupations, crafts, and trades suggests once again that the gravitation toward selected professions is based less on a dispassionate analysis of attributes, efficacy, and value to society and more on manifest power and prestige.

Many occupational groups can claim with considerable justification (or at least as much justification as teachers) esoteric knowledge, socialization, extended formal training, testing, and state licensing. But it is difficult to imagine beleaguered teachers bemoaning their status, dreaming of the day when they will have good training programs and high status and power "just like the beauticians." Training in cosmetology might well require literally thousands of hours in a clinical program before the initiate can enter the ranks of practitioners, but that requirement is of little significance to teachers looking for a lock on the occupational status and prestige market.

Of all the hundreds of occupations, only a few will serve as useful models in the eyes of teachers, and, of those, medicine is the premier model. It is premier because of its legitimated power, prestige, and status. But just as important, medicine is the premier model for teachers because of its mutability, its wondrous ascension in the twentieth century.

Had medicine maintained the same status throughout history, it could not serve as a model, because its status would be seen as immutable, inherent in the nature of things. As has already been suggested (see note 31), medicine was once—and not very long ago at that—a weak, splintered occupation with little prestige and power. But just as one can speak of individual status mobility, so can one speak of the mobility of the occupations themselves. If physicians could change their status, could not teachers?

For these two reasons, then—current high status and historically low status—teachers expect medicine to provide the answers to their dilemma of status discrepancy. Accordingly, we must look carefully at the medical profession and its history to divine the reasons for the change in status from low to high. But first, some summary remarks on teacher status are in order.

First, the status of teaching in America has been relatively low. But just as the status of other professions is mutable, so has been the status of teaching. The conditions that prevailed during the eighteenth and nineteenth centuries and the early years of the twentieth century have changed. The emergence of teacher unionization and teacher militancy in the 1950s resulted in relatively higher pay, better working conditions, and the removal of some social restrictions. Changes in some aspects of status, however, do not lessen the arguments we have made for status discrepancy and the desire for enhanced status; rather, the small changes that have been made can be seen as reinforcing the desire for additional change.

Second, the preoccupation with status change is not limited solely to individual teachers; nor do all individual teachers, we would hypothesize, exhibit the same levels of dissatisfaction with status discrepancy and the same levels of desire for increased status. It may well be that there are major differences between the views of individual teachers and the views expressed by leaders of teachers' unions, trainers of teachers, and those in related organizations. It remains to be seen whether teachers qua teachers view the pronouncements of others as acceptable analyses of the situation or as irrelevant to their needs.

Third, as suggested early on in this chapter, many data regarding perceptions of teachers and others need to be obtained and analyzed in order to support or reject the basic arguments propounded here. Again, however, one purpose of this chapter is to suggest the need for data and to suggest the framework in which those data might be obtained and considered. The historical data and at least a portion of the current literature suggest, at any rate, perceived status discrepancy and a desire to reduce that discrepancy, and the data suggest a strong tendency on the part of teachers and their organizations to look to the medical profession as the exemplar.

Accordingly, it is to the history of the exemplar that we must now turn. Following our examination of the transformation of medicine, we must determine what purposive efforts, if any, under what necessary conditions, if any, have a reasonable probability of leading to a similar change in the status of teaching. We must also determine whether such efforts, even if feasible, are otherwise desirable.

The Changing Status of Medicine

The status of the doctor in America remained relatively low during the eighteenth and nineteenth centuries. Doctors were portrayed as "auxiliaries to the King of terrors" in the late 1700s; the great majority of doctors were viewed as incompetents.[54] The relatively low status of medicine was reinforced by the antiprofession sentiments of the Jacksonian era: Between 1826 and 1852, ten states rescinded laws governing the licensing of doctors.[55] Licensing of doctors was seen as favoritism toward a particular class, and there was a general sense that, in effect, one could be one's own doctor.

Throughout most of the nineteenth century, doctors continued to be subjected to attacks. Newspaper articles in the mid-1850s, for example, referred to "poisoning and surgical butchery" and declared that the profession was a "stupendous humbug." The profession's sense that all was not well is reflected in medical publication editorials: "On the Declining Relations of the Medical Profession to the Public" was one; another was "To What Cause Are We to Attribute the Diminished Respectability of the Medical Profession in the Estimation of the American Public."[56]

Concerns about low status led to the formation of the American Medical Association in 1847; at the organizational meeting of the AMA, those concerns were noted by its president: "The profession to which we belong . . . has become corrupt, and degenerate, to the forfeiture of its social position, and with it, of the homage it formerly received spontaneously and universally."[57] Commenting two years later, a special committee of the AMA declared that "It was not difficult to trace this abasement of the profession to its true cause. It had ceased to be a highly educated class."[58] (One must note, in passing, the recurring tendency to invoke notions of halcyon days: "the homage it formerly received"; "it had ceased to be a highly educated class." The teaching profession is not the only group to indulge in sentiments about how great things were in the good old days.)

By the second decade of the twentieth century, however, the

status of doctors had increased considerably, and by the 1930s, doctors reached the pinnacle, with their status exceeded only by that of justices of the Supreme Court.[59] Their power had become considerable, their prestige legitimated. Doctors had become the epitome of social mobility, the Horatio Alger strive-and-succeed prescription writ large.

As one would expect, the social mobility of the medical profession has been the subject of considerable interest. Rather than attempt to treat the vast body of literature on the topic, this section will examine selected references in an attempt to discern the critical circumstances and factors leading to the abrupt and dramatic rise in the status of doctors.

Shryock provides a representative example of the literature in suggesting five factors that accounted for the relatively low prestige of medicine:

1. Low standards for recruitment of entrants
2. Poor medical schools
3. General laxity of licensing laws
4. Lack of scientific basis for practice
5. Competition between practitioners and public condemnation of one practitioner by another[60]

With the advent of medical education reform, the passage of strict licensing laws, the emergence of "scientific" medicine, and the restriction of competition, medicine was able, according to this argument, to gain considerable power and prestige.

Along similar lines, Kunitz argues that medicine came to power in large part because of the demands of the Progressive Era for recognition and control of social problems:

> The result of recognizing problems in need of control resulted in the emergence of new occupations which asserted special competence in particular problem areas and ultimately claimed a license from society for autonomous professional status. However, not all occupations were equally successful in attaining this status. Medicine succeeded brilliantly; and I have sug-

gested that this was the result of having a theory
which was of great explanatory value in dealing with
a series of explanatory problems, infectious diseases.[61]

Other factors have been identified, factors operating in concert and supporting the Progressive Era demands for control. Jarcho
has noted that economic conditions were becoming more favorable:

During the three decades from 1860 to 1890 a logarith-
mic growth had doubled the nation's population, its
population density, and its per capita wealth. An important by-product was the creation of a small number
of multimillionaires, some of whom developed into
practical philanthropists. At about the same time the
application of newer scientific methods of medicine
began to yield the definite promise of effective prophy-
laxis for disease.[62]

For other analysts, the well-known reforms in medical education are the critical factors, although there is disagreement as to the
motives for reform. The appearance and broad acceptance of the
Flexner Report[63] have often been cited as signaling the great sea
change; with the subsequent demise (or continuing demise, as some
have suggested) of the proprietary medical school, the rise in admis-
sions standards, the emergence of medical school teaching and research as a career, and the acceptance of the certainty and universality of medical knowledge,[64] medicine was to consolidate its political
base and legitimate its professional claims.[65]

Markowitz and Rosner suggest that the AMA united in advocating medical education reform and also cite larger political factors
involved in the reform:

They did so because they believed that the economic
and social situation of individual doctors and the profession as a whole at the turn of the century was bad.
In part this arose from the general feeling of crisis that
permeated the society during the depression of the
1890s. In addition, physicians and other professional

groups saw their status and power being eroded and engulfed by the tremendous growth of the industrial giants. The large corporation, having achieved its power through consolidation and control, increasingly dominated the land. Doctors likewise organized and sought to reform medical education in order to solve a number of professional problems. Many believed that medicine had to become more scientific. A goodly number of physicians were outraged at the inadequate facilities for instruction at many medical colleges. But, in addition, many doctors and medical spokesmen forthrightly argued that organization and reform were necessary to assure the physicians' own financial security and greater status and power in the community at large. These goals were not seen as contradictory. In fact medical spokesmen argued that only as the profession achieved high social standing, became more restrictive and provided its members with a good livelihood could it provide scientific, efficient medical care to the nation. Through reform the profession also solved a number of other internal problems: they commenced the consolidation of the components of a newly emerging university medical school complex; restricted intraprofessional competition; organized medicine's long-term opposition to group practice and government financed hospital and clinic care; and also institutionalized a two-class medical care system.[66]

Others have argued from a Marxist (or quasi-Marxist) point of view, suggesting that the rise of the medical profession was linked to the rise of industrial capitalism. By this line of reasoning, the alliance between the AMA and the capitalist class was reinforced to legitimate the class structure and lessen class conflict.[67]

Still others have focused on dimensions of market control. Larson, for example, identifies seven market control factors that were favorable to the medical profession:

1. A salient, universal, and relatively invisible
    service
2. Independence from the capital and goods market
3. An unorganized and fragmented clientele
4. A standardized and clearly defined cognitive basis
5. Standardization and institutionalization of the
    production of producers
6. An independent relation to other markets, thus
    requiring the state to protect against incompe-
    tents through licensing
7. Affinity with dominant ideological structures[68]

A useful analysis and summary of the factors leading to the
ascension of medicine is found in Paul Starr's *The Social Transformation of American Medicine.* Starr suggests eight critical factors
bearing on the transformation:

1. *Growth in specialization and hospitals,* leading to a shift from
    dependence on patients to dependence on colleagues
2. *Control of labor markets,* cutting off the supply of cheap pro-
    fessional labor and resulting in doctors' mediating relation-
    ships between technical personnel and the labor market
3. *Socialization of capital investment,* with doctors able to use
    hospitals and technical innovations at virtually no charge;
    health departments and schools performing diagnostic work
    and making referrals, thus increasing demand for doctors'
    services
4. *Absence of countervailing power,* with no organized groups of
    buyers to counter the market power of doctors
5. *Lack of integrated organization,* with split lines of authority
    between professionals and administrators, contributing to the
    preservation of the sovereign power of doctors
6. *Revolution in local transportation,* which reduced the isolation
    of medical practice, improved efficacy of intervention, and
    brought greater dependence by patients on doctors
7. *Emergence of medical technology and scientific breakthroughs,*
    which increased manifest effectiveness of doctors, increased the
    asymmetry of the doctor-patient relationship, and increased the

collegial exercise of authority and collegial claims to objective judgment

8. *Market power,* through which doctors were able to gain and solidify their position by meeting the felt needs of the larger society experiencing complex changes[69]

No one factor, or even two or three factors, will adequately explain the rise of the medical profession. For example, the emergence of scientific medicine might appear to be critical. It is tempting to adopt the reasoning that advances in scientific medicine, reinforced by the Flexner Report, led to major reform and thus to power. But, as Starr cautions, "Science may improve the efficacy and productivity of a profession without making it rich or revered; knowledge must be transformed into authority, and authority into market power, before gains from scientific advances can be privately appropriated by a profession."[70]

It is with this insight that we begin to move to solid ground. Acknowledged skills must be coupled with cultural authority—authority gained through external legitimacy. Legitimacy in turn involves "respect and deference, especially from the more powerful classes, [to] open the way to resources and legally sanctioned privileges."[71]

The authority of medicine, then, rests in large part on the combination of *knowledge* complexity—scientific knowledge and technical innovations—and *cultural demand,* resulting, as Starr suggests, in *legitimate complexity.*

Starr's views are in accord with the penetrating analysis of Terence Johnson, who, in speaking of the professions in general, suggests:

> The assertion made that an occupation group rarely enjoys the resources of power which would enable it to impose its own definitions of the producer-consumer relationship suggests that *professionalism* as defined in the literature is a peculiar phenomenon. It is only where an occupational group shares, by virtue of its membership of a dominant class or caste, wider resources of power that such an imposition is likely to

be successfully achieved, and then only where the actual consumers or clients provide a relatively large,
heterogeneous, fragmented source of demand.[72]

When the many interrelated factors are reviewed, the notion
of legitimate complexity appears to provide the critical key to understanding the successful rise of the medical profession. It was not
simply a matter of doctors desiring power and monopoly and an
asymmetrical relationship between doctor and client. Many occupational groups have sought such monopolistic power and control
without success. Doctors managed to gain privileges, power, higher
incomes, and social status not solely through their own internal
efforts but because their own efforts at consolidation and control
were congruent—fortuitously, from the doctors' point of view—
with external societal interests and values.

This necessarily brief excursion into the history of the rise of
medicine in the early twentieth century suggests that professions (or
at least the medical profession) do not follow the pattern of development suggested by the "traits" proponents. The attribution of
traits—either by members of a profession or by sociologists—is, in
effect, after the fact and has little explanatory power.[73]

As Johnson persuasively argues, professions are not occupations per se; professions are the means of controlling an occupation.
Likewise,

Professionalization is a historically specific process,
which some occupations have undergone at a particular time, rather than a process which certain occupations may always be expected to undergo because of
their "essential" qualities.[74]

It is thus that one can argue that doctors did not attain their
preeminent position merely because they claimed to be altruistic or
because they claimed to possess a scientific body of knowledge or
because they claimed to "police their own" or because it became
more difficult to get into medical schools or because medical school
training became more extensive. Rather, doctors achieved their
preeminence and gained mastery of the profession (or, more ap-

propriately, the occupation) because of a combination of economic and social factors. These factors can be summarized as follows:

1. The increase in the manifest efficacy of medicine occasioned by scientific discoveries and technology
2. The linking of scientific medicine and medical training
3. The belief, beginning in the Progressive Era and supported by a wide variety of political groups, that medicine could no longer be a matter of self-administered first aid
4. The increasing—and fragmented—demand for medical services
5. The willingness of powerful interest groups to support the medical profession through funding of hospitals, research centers, and medical schools

These factors were, as we have noted, external to the profession, capitalized on by doctors but not created by doctors; these factors were interrelated. Manifest efficacy of treatment stimulated demand and stimulated disbelief in personal powers to deal with one's medical problems. Fragmented demand and a lack of countervailing power stimulated the trend toward monopoly control, and resources (stimulated by both public health demands and scientific discoveries) were thus directed to one occupational group.

It is these interrelated factors that led the medical profession to assume, in Starr's words, *legitimate complexity*—the real source of a profession's authority, power, and prestige. With these several factors in mind, we now return to our central question. What purposive efforts, if any, under what conditions will be necessary for the teaching profession successfully to assume the status of doctors?

Doctor Status/Teacher Status

The preceding discussion of the transformation of the medical profession makes it clear that a similar transformation of the teaching profession would necessarily involve much more than self-proclamations of professionalism and the hanging of framed diplomas on the classroom wall. Major changes would have to take place within both the teaching profession and the larger societal context.

We have identified the several factors leading to the transformation of the medical profession. Using these factors as our guiding criteria, the following six changes would be necessary.

1. New Technology. A new technology of schooling and learning would have to emerge, similar to the development of science and technology in medicine. The new technology would necessarily have the following characteristics:

First, the new technology would have to be demonstrably superior to current methods of schooling in the production of manifestly different outcomes, in much the same way that diptheria antitoxin was demonstrably superior to bloodletting. The results would have to be obvious and consistent and obviously related to the technology. The technology would have to be universally applicable.

Second, the new technology would have to produce results highly valued by society, and valued particularly by powerful groups controlling access to resources within the society. Without high valuing, there would be little demand. For example, a technology that could produce students all of whom could score at least 780 on either portion of the Scholastic Aptitude Test would have little impact if there were no societal demand for test-bright students. It should be stressed that such a demand could be argued for by the new educational technologists, but the demand could not come from them: Demand is an external function.

Third, the new technology would necessarily require professional judgment in its application. There would have to be some element of selection of facts and procedures from among several alternatives and some (albeit small) element of risk. If the new technology merely involved, let us say, attaching students to a machine in order to turn them into brilliant test takers, anybody could perform this routine task with a minimum of training. The new technology, in other words, would have to be characterized by complexity for claims to professional exclusiveness to be taken seriously.

Finally, there would have to be general external appearances of agreement among the new educational professionals as to the nature, scope, and efficacy of the new technology. In much the same way as the medical profession emphasized the universality of scientific knowledge and presented a more or less united front to the public, disagreements about the new technology would have to be kept "within the church."[75]

2. Training Linked to the New Technology. Training in the new technology would, as would the technology itself, have to be manifestly efficacious. With very few exceptions, the only way one could learn how to make professional judgments in using the new technology would be by completing a prescribed course of study in a teacher training program. The course of study would necessarily be standardized, with little variation from institution to institution. Claims for universal efficacy of treatment would not be accepted as long as there was too much variation in training. In addition, the new teacher training programs would, without exception, have to be accredited. Legitimation of professional training could not occur as long as some programs were accredited and others were not.

3. Public Support for Restricted Practice. In line with the notion of a delimited and standardized course of study, the public would have to come to believe that only those people so trained in the new technology should be allowed to practice as teachers. Strict licensing laws, derived from this belief, would have to be enacted in each state; such licensing would have to replace current practices of certification.

4. Public Valuing of Schooling. Schooling would have to become an actual—as opposed to a merely rhetorical—priority of the society. The priority would have to be deeply felt, and felt across social classes. In particular, schooling would have to be seen as a priority among those groups controlling allocation of resources. Reflecting this actual priority, considerable resources would have to be allocated from both the government and the private sector for educational research and development. Such allocations would be necessary both to increase knowledge production and to reinforce, through symbolism, the priorities of the society. (Medicine, of course, provides examples of both functions. We might also cite as an example the U.S. space exploration program, which, until perhaps recently, was accorded real as opposed to rhetorical priority.) The specific output of the new technology would have to be ac-

cepted and supported, as we have said. Beyond that, the general idea
of schooling as having high value would have to be incorporated as
part of the general culture and operating ideology.

5. Fragmented Demand for Services. Demand for schooling
would have to be fragmented, with no competing interest groups
capable of meeting the demand through alternative delivery of services. Necessarily, only those licensed to practice as teachers could be
allocated resources and given the power to make critical decisions.
Whatever the virtues of competition might be, those virtues do not
include legitimation of professional claims.

6. Bifurcation of Authority. The lines of authority in the
schooling bureaucracy would have to be bifurcated, with teachers
given the authority to make decisions as to the application of the
new technology and school administrators effectively denied that
authority. Along the same lines, teachers would have to be given the
authority to determine the proper activities of support staff in much
the same way that doctors determine activities of nurses, interns,
technicians, and other medical personnel.

We have outlined six interrelated requirements that, we
argue, must be satisfied if teaching is to be accorded the same professional status that medicine has enjoyed for the last sixty years. Having done so, we can now turn to an assessment of the probabilities
of meeting these requirements.

Meeting the Requirements: Can Teaching Do It?

In assessing the probabilities of teaching becoming as medicine, let us make three assumptions as to the best possible political
and social context: (1) that there is consensus among teachers regarding the advisability of mounting a serious full-scale professionalization effort, (2) that there is a similar consensus among teacher-
related groups, and (3) that the effort is accorded high priority, with
considerable resources somehow made available. Assuming a best-
case context, let us then consider our six requirements to determine
the probable success of the effort.

1. New Technology. The probability of teachers (or anybody else, for that matter) developing a new technology is very low. There is nothing in the current research literature that suggests even a remote possibility of an emerging technology that will produce manifestly efficacious and universal outcomes, let alone outcomes that will be highly valued by society.[76] Predictions of this sort have the notorious reputation of being proved wrongheaded; virtually every major scientific breakthrough has been preceded by an "expert" telling us why nothing of the sort will happen for eons. Perhaps, by analogy, something similar will occur in the field of learning and behavioral psychology. Perhaps, but it seems highly unlikely.

The optimist might argue that such an assessment is far too gloomy and negative: There are, after all, more things in heaven and earth and laboratories than are dreamt of in our philosophy. But optimism, while comforting, is too thin a reed to carry the burden of a major effort to professionalize teaching.

2. Training. It would be difficult to construct a new training program for teachers that was based on a nonexistent technology. One could, of course, construct new training programs with all sorts of expectations in mind, but it would be unreasonable to expect that a training program minus the required technology would have much bearing on the professionalization effort.

3. Public Support for Restricted Practice. If the criterion is public support for restrictions based on a new technology linked to new training programs, then the probability of meeting the criterion is close to zero. Given the history of licensing in America, one might argue that strict licensing for teachers might come about: Many occupations have received licensing protection. But, as we have seen, licensing per se does not give an occupation the sought-after prestige of the medical profession.

4. Public Valuing of Schooling. Here, the requirement focuses on both valuing of the necessary new technology and valuing of schooling more generally. It has already been suggested that it is unlikely that a new technology will emerge; therefore, the probability of meeting the requirements is quite low. Is it not possible, however, that the society might reorder its values, giving schooling a much higher ranking in reality than it does now, despite the lack of a manifestly efficacious technology? Again, the optimist might like to entertain such a hope, but it is difficult to imagine large-scale reordering of values without the motivating factor of an efficacious technology. For what other reasons would a society that for so long has placed a low actual value on schooling feel compelled to change?

5. Fragmented Demand for Services. The requirement here suggests that demand be fragmented, with no competition among various interest groups for meeting the demand. If, as we have assumed, there is no emergent new technology, then no interest group, including teachers, would be in a position to compete; hence, the requirement could not be met.

6. Bifurcation of Authority. Simply demanding changes in power relationships would most likely not have much effect. Absent the technology, the related training, the demand, and public support, there would be little to legitimate the demands. Again, one can, as has been the case, put forth demands for greater authority for all sorts of reasons. It is, however, unlikely that such demands would form even part of the basis for professionalization efforts. Rather, such demands would be viewed as merely self-serving or as an internal struggle for power among teachers, administrators, and paraprofessionals.

Professionalization Rhetoric

It is evident from the foregoing assessment that teaching cannot achieve the high status of medicine by following the medical model of professionalization. In this analysis, teaching fails to meet any of the six major criteria, and there is nothing either in the context of the theory and practice of teaching or in the larger society to suggest even a slight probability that the criteria will be met at some future time.

What is necessary to successfully follow the path of medicine cannot be achieved; a fortiori, the current attempts to follow that path will continue to be ineffectual. One of those attempts, as we have noted, involves passing some sort of examination as a prerequisite for certification. Quite clearly, the examinations currently required by some states will not contribute to professionalization à la medicine and may in fact have a negative result. To claim that testing for attainment of basic skills is somehow the equivalent of medicine's National Boards is merely to underscore the real and considerable differences between medicine and education—and hardly in favor of education.

Perhaps new, more comprehensive and difficult examinations can be constructed. But even assuming that the political obstacles are overcome (obstacles that have existed, apparently, since William Russell's day), it is difficult to imagine any examination having much significance as long as a new technology is lacking. It is indeed possible to construct a rigorous test, but if the test has no clear bearing on the necessary legitimate complexity of professional work, the test will be viewed as yet one more example of obscurantist hairsplitting by the educationists. Alternatively, lacking legitimate complexity as its basis, a rigorous test will be viewed no differently from tests required for licensing in many other occupations and thus will have little impact on professionalization efforts. (Tests for licensing of beauticians might well be rigorous, but that fact has little bearing on the status of beauticians.)

Symbolic attempts at professionalization á la medicine—the hanging of one's diplomas on the wall for example—clearly will have no positive impact. There is little magic in the world, and superficial imitations of outward manifestations of power are at best a placebo. Indeed, such symbolic attempts might well have a negative impact in that they may be viewed as naive.

Other symbolic attempts, such as becoming a member of symphony or museum boards of directors because that is what doctors do,[77] may be personally stimulating (and difficult to manage, what with the myriad assignments to correct and lessons to plan) but will do little to effect the desired professionalization. Sitting next to a doctor at a board meeting will not make one a doctor or give one a doctor's status.

The fundamental difficulty with all of these attempts to superficially emulate the historical conditions and apparent outcomes of medicine is rooted in the underlying source of rhetorical argument that teachers are using. The teachers' rhetoric of professionalization is flawed because of the line of argument on which they have chosen to rely. In terms of traditional rhetoric, one can choose from three lines or sources of argument: definition, similitude, and circumstance. Richard Weaver has examined these three sources and their implications in considerable depth; here we can note them briefly.[78]

The argument from genus, or definition, presumes the existence of classes with fixed characteristics. One argues, in effect, from the nature of the class. Thus, in arguing against slavery, Abraham Lincoln took the position that there is one genus of human beings; human beings are equal and deserving of justice and sympathy and dignity; blacks are of that genus and are not mere property; slavery is therefore wrong.

The argument from circumstance seeks to assess the current situation and allows the facts of the situation to determine policy or conclusions. Because facts of the situation (as opposed to inherent characteristics of genera in the argument from definition) can change, this source of argument borders on the expedient. To say that we should surrender because we are surrounded is to argue from circumstance. This was the argument used by the Athenians against the Melians in the Peloponnesian War. Why should the Melians surrender? Because the Athenians were stronger. If any states do maintain their independence, "it is because they are strong, and . . . if we do not molest them, it is because we are afraid."

The third source of argument is similitude. In arguing from similitude, one claims that there are essential correspondences between classes. In effect, this is an argument based on analogy, on "just as x, so is y." A similitude argument, to be effective, must show that the correspondence is apt, proven, and accepted.

Of the three main sources of argument, teachers' rhetoric of professionalization relies most heavily on the argument from similitude. The teachers' argument is, in essence, "We should be accorded the same prestige as doctors because we are doing what doctors did to get where they are." There is nothing particularly incorrect about the form of this similitude argument. But the line of argument

cannot help but force those who are listening to shift from considerations of inherent merit to considerations of correspondence.
"We're like doctors," teachers say. "Prove it," replies the audience.
As we have seen, proof is not forthcoming. It cannot be forthcoming
because the major criteria cannot be met. By the very structure of the
teachers' rhetoric, the efforts to achieve professionalization á la medicine are self-defeating.

Such efforts are demoralizing, not only because they are self-
defeating but also because they are inauthentic. As Etzioni notes,
inauthenticity results when there is a superficial appearance of responsiveness while the underlying conditions remain alienating.[79]
By engaging in arguments from similitude—or by accepting their
leaders' arguments—teachers, I would suggest, cannot help but experience a sense of frustration and helplessness and consequent
anger directed at themselves, their leaders, or the society. The arguments shift the focus to the nonessential, with consequent waste of
political capital, while the underlying alienating conditions remain
ignored.

All told, it would seem, the fundamental problem of teacher
status discrepancy, viewed in terms of the historical conditions of
the medical model, is a double bind. The major efforts needed to
meet the six major criteria are impossible to make. The minor efforts that *are* possible to make are inconsequential and debilitating.

Must we accept the doleful conclusion that there is nothing
to be done? Is there no way out of the double bind? We believe that
there is a strategy, albeit difficult and demanding, that has a possibility of success, and it is to a discussion of that strategy that I now
turn.

Teacher Professionalization: Beyond the Double Bind

Gregory Bateson tells of the Zen master who holds a stick
over the pupil's head, saying "If you say this stick is real, I will
strike you with it. If you say the stick is not real, I will strike you
with it. If you don't say anything, I will strike you with it." One
way out of this double bind is to take the stick away from the
master.[80]

As we have demonstrated, teachers are in their own double

bind, the double bind of preoccupation with emulating the medical model of professionalization: That which is necessary is impossible; that which is possible is irrelevant and self-defeating. Teachers must do as the Zen student; they can move beyond their double-bind situation by taking away the stick.

It is possible for teachers to move beyond the double bind because the preoccupation with medicine is self-imposed and can be stopped. The dreams of becoming as doctors are no more than dreams, and the pursuit of those dreams is, as Laing suggested in another context, rather like "hunting a hare whose tracks are in the mind of the hunters."[81]

Once teachers (and their leaders) cease attempts to define themselves as "professionals" in terms of the ideal of the medical model, they will begin to free themselves from the tyranny of their own dreams. It will not be easy to move beyond the double bind, to say, with John Lennon, "The dream is over." The preoccupation with medicine has a long history; the ideology is pervasive. Letting go of the dream will be difficult without some underlying rationale.

Perhaps what will make the necessary effort seem worthwhile despite the difficulties is an awareness of new possibilities. Once freed from the self-imposed tyranny of their dreams, teachers will be able to begin the restructuring of their professionalization rhetoric and will be able to begin the redefinition of their situation in ways more likely to be viewed as legitimate by the larger society.

In the discussion of teachers' professionalization rhetoric, it was suggested that the use of arguments from similitude was unproductive. By letting go of the medical model, teachers will be able to shift their rhetoric from similitude arguments to bedrock arguments from definition. Rather than encouraging self-defeating comparisons with doctors, teachers will be able to argue from their own definition of themselves and their work context.

The bedrock argument from definition that teachers can use has a moral basis. As Becker suggests, public willingness to accord honors to an occupation derives from a collective sense of the moral praiseworthiness of that occupation.[82] Teachers can legitimately argue for such worthiness because of the moral imperative that results from the nature of children and the nature of the relationship of the teacher, the parent, and the child. What teachers need to do is to examine the essential nature of children and the teacher-child-parent relationship and to develop this theme in their rhetoric of professionalization. The nature of the relationship is the reason that teaching is morally praiseworthy.

As an illustration of one way to proceed to develop an argument from definition, we could look at the teacher-child-parent relationship with particular reference to the historical fact of compulsory schooling. Parents are required by law to send their children to school. Those parents with necessary resources can send their children to private schools; those with resources and time can opt for home schooling. For the great majority of parents, however, public schools represent the only means to comply with the law.[83] In general, then, there is equality of surrender.

Equality of surrender, I would argue, should imply equality of treatment. That is to say, children should not be subjected to differential responses because of differences in social class, ethnicity, gender, or other factors over which children have no control. It has long been recognized that there is, in fact, inequality of treatment (and inequality of outcomes, for that matter). But the existence of inequality does not justify inequality. Equality of surrender must imply equality of treatment. Therefore, those responsible for the treatment of children in schools have a moral obligation to ensure equality of treatment.

Children by nature are defenseless. Children by tradition are taught to distrust strangers. But parents, in complying with compulsory schooling laws, turn their defenseless children over to virtual strangers. (Consider the amount of information most parents seek in selecting a baby-sitter versus the amount of information those same parents have about public school educators.) The surrendering of children to the state's schools thus represents a considerable act of trust. The state claims that surrender is for the general good; the parent accepts the claim but demands in return a guarantee that the child will be kept free from physical and mental harm. Those responsible for the physical and mental health of children in schools have a moral obligation to ensure that children are kept from harm.

Compulsory schooling, then, carries with it immense moral obligations and provides the legitimate basis for restructuring teacher professionalization rhetoric. It is curious that such should be the case. After all, by traditional reckoning, teaching has been considered a lesser profession in large part because of the nature of the clientele served by teachers. The compulsory nature of schooling (as opposed to the voluntary setting in medicine) and the low social status of children have been cited as functional reasons for the low status of teaching. As I have demonstrated, however, it is precisely *because* children are compelled and children are defenseless and have low status that teaching has moral obligations and thus moral praiseworthiness. That which has been posited as the obstacle turns out to be the enabler—and therein lies a certain irony.

Teachers' arguments from definition do not necessarily have to be derived from the current compulsory nature of schooling in America. Teachers could argue that all children have the right to learn, irrespective of whatever schooling laws happen to prevail. The argument here could be illustrated as follows: We believe that children have a right to grow physically; we are sickened whenever we read of a disturbed parent who has physically confined a child for weeks and even years. Such physical deprivation revolts us to the core because it denies the child the chance to manifest his or her human qualities. To be deprived of the opportunity to learn is just as revolting, because it, too, denies the child the essential humanity of the child. We have no right to deprive; we have every obligation to enhance the physical and mental growth of the child. Teachers, by definition of their relationship to children, are critical agents in ensuring children's humanity. (It will be noted that this argument has little to do directly with keeping up with the Japanese or making Detroit stronger or strengthening the dollar.)

Either illustration shows how the rhetorical base can be shifted, with positive results. As part of this shift to a new base, teachers could begin the redefinition of their work context (and, consequently, their training programs). That the conditions and circumstances of teaching are in need of redefinition has been amply documented.[84] The new rhetorical base will lend much greater credibility to efforts to redefine the work context because the arguments for change can be based legitimately on moral grounds, rather than (as is often perceived) on motives of pecuniary gain or bureaucratic maneuvering.

The shift in rhetorical grounding illustrated here will be demanding. It will involve much more than one-time pronouncements from teachers' leaders, much more than a press conference or an editorial or two in a house organ. We are dealing here with fundamental shifts in the rhetoric of teachers, with the letting go of a long-held dream. Such shifts will require much persistence over time to move beyond the superficial to the essential.

Beyond the fundamentally important shift in rhetoric, the strategy must necessarily entail changes in related areas. If, for example, the primary defining factor of teaching is the compulsion of the defenseless, then there will need to be careful examination of such matters as (1) the process by which people are selected into training programs, (2) the nature and ends of preservice training, (3) the selection and evaluation of teachers, and (4) the continuing education of teachers. All of these elements must be articulated in ways that will reinforce the underlying rhetoric, and the reinforcement must be made manifest to the public.

There is no guarantee that the strategy will be successful. Necessarily, any professionalization strategy involves a public response, and we cannot predict with certainty that the response to our suggested strategy will be positive. We can predict, however, that the current strategies to professionalize teaching will continue to be ineffectual because they are based on the wrong rhetoric and inevitably doomed to failure. We can argue that a restructured rhetoric, coupled with a redefinition of the work context and training programs, provides a much more legitimate basis for acceptance of teachers' claims. It seems more reasonable to attempt a strategy that might work than to follow one that surely cannot work.

But whether a new rhetorical strategy "works" should not be the determining factor in deciding to stay with the strategy. When Abraham Lincoln argued from definition about the nature of humanity and the moral wrongness of slavery, he did not cast about for new sources of argument when he was not immediately successful in persuasion. In like manner, teachers should not cast aside their argument from definition about the nature of humanity and the moral praiseworthiness of teaching just because the polls and levy elections do not reflect immediate positive results. If teachers wish to have their claims to higher status and respect realized, they must stick with the bedrock argument from definition. No other source of argument will do. As I have shown, if teachers try to argue from similitude, they will continue to be frustrated, because the comparisons are inappropriate and self-defeating. If they wish to argue from circumstance, they will never allow themselves to seek a better vision, because the circumstances will always seem bleak and overwhelming. What Richard Weaver tells us is true: Nothing catches up with you faster than the topics or sources of argument you choose to use to win the support of others.

Notes

1. L. Veysey, "Who's a Professional? Who Cares?" *Reviews in American History,* 1975, *3,* 419–423. In a similar vein, see L. Veysey, "Plural Organized Worlds of the Humanities," in A. Oleson and J. Voss (eds.), *The Organization of Knowledge in Modern America, 1860–1920* (Baltimore: Johns Hopkins University Press, 1979), pp. 51–106.

2. J. Dewey, "The Relation of Theory to Practice in Education," in C. A. McMurry (ed.), *Third Yearbook of the National Society for the Scientific Study of Education* (Chicago: University of Chicago Press, 1904), p. 10.

3. F. Chase, "The Improvement of Teacher Certification—Next Steps," in *Annual Report of the National Education Association National Commission on Teacher Education and Professional Standards* (Washington, D.C.: National Education Association, 1953), p. 88.

4. R. McDonald, "The Certification of Teachers: Challenge and Opportunity," in *Annual Report of the National Education Association National Commission on Teacher Education and Professional Standards* (Washington, D.C.: National Education Association, 1953), pp. 33–34.

5. See "New Panel's Goal: To Make Teaching 'True Profession'" *Education Week,* May 29, 1985, *4,* 1, 12; see also Carnegie Forum on Education and the Economy, *A Nation Prepared: Teachers for the 21st Century* (New York: Carnegie Forum on Education and the Economy, 1985).

6. *Education Week,* Sept. 4, 1985, contains three articles dealing

with NEA and AFT plans. For interviews with Mary Hatwood Futrell and Albert Shanker, see pp. 6–7; see also "Unions: A Campaign to 'Professionalize' Teachers," pp. 1, 32; "Hiring of Untrained in Shortage 'Crisis' Makes Sham of Reform, Futrell Warns," pp. 1, 34.

7. Holmes Group, *Tomorrow's Teachers* (East Lansing, Mich.: Holmes Group, 1986).

8. National Teachers' Association, *Proceedings, 1857* (Syracuse, N.Y.: Bardeen, 1909), p. 311.

9. National Teachers' Association, *Proceedings, 1857,* pp. 16, 21. An early advocate of the need for a "certificate of competency to teach, warranted by a teachers' association" (p. 23), Russell argued for an examination

> at the hands of the actual members of the profession, as is virtually the case at the present day when a lawyer is admitted to the bar, a physician to the membership of a State or national medical association, or a licentiate is ordained for the ministry [pp. 21–22].

Although Russell extolled the virtues of licensure controlled by the teachers' association, he recognized the difficulties of reaching agreement on the matter:

> Whatever disposal is made of the subject of professional rank and recognition for teachers, the great considerations of personal duty in regard to associated and united effort for the advancement of education, are the subjects that lie immediately before us. It was not to be the only time that teachers' associations recognized, but declined to face squarely, the complications of licensure, examinations, and competency, while electing, rather to deal with the perceived exigencies of organizational politics [p. 24].

10. E. Freidson, *Professional Powers* (Chicago: University of Chicago Press, 1986).

11. For representative views, see H. M. Vollmer and D. L. Mills

(eds.), *Professionalization* (Englewood Cliffs, N.J.: Prentice-Hall, 1966).

12. Two useful works on the rise of medicine are P. Starr, *The Social Transformation of American Medicine* (New York: Basic Books, 1982), and E. Shorter, *Bedside Manners* (New York: Simon & Schuster, 1985).

13. Issues of occupational licensing tend to be overlooked in the professionalization literature, with licensing taken as a matter of course. But licensing is a reflection of political struggles and power relationships; it is not automatically provided to an occupation by the state. For useful discussions of occupational licensing, see J. A. Cathcart and G. Graff, "Occupational Licensing: Factoring It Out," *Pacific Law Journal,* 1978, *9,* 147–163; S. L. Carroll and R. J. Gaston, "Occupational Licensing and the Quality of Service: An Overview," *Law and Human Behavior,* 1983, *7,* 139–146; H. S. Cohen, "Professional Licensure, Organizational Behavior, and the Public Interest," *Milbank Memorial Fund Quarterly,* Winter 1973, *51,* 73–88; W. Gellhorn, *Individual Freedom and Governmental Restraint* (Baton Rouge: Louisiana State University Press, 1956); W. Gellhorn, "Occupational Licensing—Nationwide Dilemma," *Journal of Accountancy,* Jan. 1960, *101,* 39–45; W. Gellhorn, "The Abuse of Occupational Licensing," *University of Chicago Law Review,* 1976, *44,* 6–27; W. B. Graves, "Professional and Occupational Restrictions," *Temple Law Quarterly,* 1939, *13,* 334–363; T. G. Moore, "The Purpose of Licensing," *Journal of Law and Economics,* 1961, *4,* 93–117; D. B. Hogan, "The Effectiveness of Licensing: History, Evidence, and Recommendations," *Law and Human Behavior,* 1983, *7,* 117–138. A good collection of articles on the subject is found in S. Rottenberg (ed.), *Occupational Licensure and Regulation* (Washington, D.C.: American Enterprise Institute for Public Policy Research, 1980); of particular interest is Rottenberg's "Introduction" (pp. 1–10) and "Professionals and the Production Function: Can Competition Policy Improve Efficiency in the Licensed Professions?" (pp. 225–264). An excellent historical summary is provided by L. M. Friedman, "Freedom of Contract and Occupational Licens-

ing, 1890-1910: A Sociological Study," *California Law Review*, May 1965, *53*, 487-534.

14. See M. S. Larson, *The Rise of Professionalism* (Berkeley: University of California Press, 1977); T. J. Johnson, *Professions and Power* (London: Macmillan, 1972); I. Illich, "The Professions as a Form of Imperialism," *New Society*, Sept. 1973, *13*, 663-666, along with an earlier work, C. Gilb, *Hidden Hierarchies* (New York: Harper & Row, 1966).

15. T. S. Hamerow, *Reflections on History and Historians* (Madison: University of Wisconsin Press, 1987), p. 54.

16. Hamerow, *Reflections on History and Historians*, pp. 52, 54.

17. L. Veysey, "Higher Education as a Profession: Changes and Continuities," in N. O. Hatch (ed.), *The Professions in American History* (Notre Dame, Ind.: University of Notre Dame Press, 1988), p. 19.

18. Veysey, "Who's a Professional?" p. 420.

19. As reported in the *Seattle Post-Intelligencer*, June 27, 1980, p. D1.

20. F. L. Allen, *Since Yesterday* (New York: Bantam Books, 1965), p. 147.

21. L. Tolstoy, *The Death of Ivan Ilych* (A. Maude, trans.) (New York: New American Library, 1960), pp. 121-122.

22. *Seattle Weekly*, Aug. 24, 1988, p. 24.

23. N. Coward, "Blithe Spirit," in N. Coward, *Three Plays* (New York: Grove Press, 1979), p. 64.

24. P. Knightley, *The Second Oldest Profession* (New York: Norton, 1987), frontispiece quotation.

25. H. S. Becker and others, *Boys in White: Student Culture in Medical School* (Chicago: University of Chicago Press, 1961), p. 4.

26. R. Hofstadter, *Anti-Intellectualism in American Life* (New York: Knopf, 1964), pp. 315-316.

27. R. Wiebe, *The Search for Order, 1877-1920* (New York: Hill and Wang, 1967), pp. 117-118.

28. As quoted in H. K. Beale, *A History of Freedom of Teaching in American Schools* (New York: Scribner's, 1941), p. 11. The use of indentured servants as teachers was also noted in 1727 by a Baltimore cleric: "There are some private schools within

my reputed district which are put very often into the hands of those who are brought into the country & sold for Servants. . . . When a Ship arrives in the River, it is a common expression with those who stand in need of an instructor for their children,—Let us go & buy a School Master." [As quoted in W. S. Perry (ed.), *Historical Collections Relating to the American Colonial Church,* Vol. 5 (Davenport, Iowa: 1878), p. 47.]

29. R. C. Buley, *The Old Northwest Pioneer Period, 1815–1840,* Vol. 1 (Indianapolis: Indiana Historical Society, 1950), p. 372.

30. J. T. Main, *The Social Structure of Revolutionary America* (Princeton, N.J.: Princeton University Press, 1965), p. 219.

31. Main, *The Social Structure of Revolutionary America,* discusses the status of doctors (pp. 144, 201–202) and lawyers (pp. 205–206). See also Starr, *The Social Transformation of American Medicine,* introduction and chaps. 1–3; K. M. Ludmerer, *Learning to Heal* (New York: Basic Books, 1985), chap. 1.

32. W. Waller, *Sociology of Teaching* (New York: Wiley, 1965), p. 58. (Originally published 1932.)

33. Waller, *Sociology of Teaching,* p. 61.

34. R. S. Lynd and H. M. Lynd, *Middletown* (San Diego, Calif.: Harcourt Brace Jovanovich, 1929), p. 209.

35. For a typical discussion, see A. Etzioni, *The Semi-Professions and Their Organization* (New York: Free Press, 1969).

36. N. Glazer, "The Schools of the Minor Professions," *Minerva,* July 1974, *12,* 346–364. Glazer also claims that medicine and law "are what is in mind when one defines the professions or when one estimates the degree of 'professionalism' of various occupations" (p. 347).

37. C. W. Mills, *White Collar* (New York: Oxford University Press, 1951), p. 129.

38. See, among many examples, J. Koerner, *The Mis-Education of American Teachers* (Boston: Houghton Mifflin, 1963); W. T. Weaver, *America's Teacher Quality Problem: Alternatives for Reform* (New York: Praeger, 1983); see also P. C. Schlechty and V. S. Vance, "Recruitment, Selection and Retention: The Shape of the Teaching Force," *Elementary School Journal,* 1983, *83,* 469–487; V. S. Vance and P. C. Schlechty, "The Dis-

tribution of Academic Ability in the Teaching Force: Policy Implications," *Phi Delta Kappan*, Sept. 1982, *64*, 22–27.

39. D. H. Kerr, "Teaching Competence and Teacher Education in the United States," *Teachers College Record*, Spring 1983, *84*, 531. For earlier examples of similar sentiments, see A. Bestor, *Educational Wastelands: The Retreat from Learning in Our Public Schools* (Urbana: University of Illinois Press, 1953); M. Smith, *And Madly Teach: A Layman Looks at Public School Education* (Chicago: Regnery, 1949); M. Smith, *The Diminished Mind: A Study of Planned Mediocrity in Our Public Schools* (Chicago: Regnery, 1954).

40. H. J. Muller, *Freedom in the Modern World* (New York: Harper & Row, 1966), p. 306.

41. J. I. Goodlad, *A Place Called School* (New York: McGraw-Hill, 1984), pp. 315, 318. See also "Tomorrow's Teachers: A Report of the Holmes Group," *Chronicle of Higher Education*, Apr. 9, 1986, pp. 27–37.

42. T. R. Sizer and A. G. Powell, "Changing Conceptions of the Professor of Education," in J. S. Counelis (ed.), *To Be a Phoenix: The Education Professoriate* (Bloomington, Ind.: Phi Delta Kappa, 1969), p. 73.

43. E. B. Wesley, *NEA: The First Hundred Years* (New York: Harper & Row, 1957), p. 136.

44. T. R. Miller, *Annual Report of the NEA/National Commission on Teacher Education and Professional Standards* (Washington, D.C.: NEA, 1953), p. 74.

45. C. Jencks and D. Riesman, *The Academic Revolution* (New York: Doubleday, 1968), p. 203.

46. M. V. O'Shea, "Relative Advantages and Limitations of Universities and Normal Schools in Preparing Secondary Teachers," in M. Holmes (ed.), *The Education and Training of Secondary Teachers*, Fourth Yearbook of the National Society for the Scientific Study of Education (Chicago: University of Chicago Press, 1905), p. 94.

47. Jencks and Riesman, *Academic Revolution*, p. 234.

48. A. Flexner, *Universities: American, German, English* (New York: Oxford University Press, 1930), p. 29.

49. R. M. Hutchins, *The Higher Learning in America* (New Haven, Conn.: Yale University Press, 1936), pp. 114–115.

50. See, for example, G. W. Hartmann, "The Prestige of Occupations: A Comparison of Educational Occupations and Others," *Personnel Journal*, Oct. 1934, *13*, 144–152.

51. R. K. Merton, "Social Structure and Anomie," in R. K. Merton, *Social Theory and Social Structure*, rev. ed. (New York: Free Press, 1957), p. 134.

52. B. R. Clark, "The 'Cooling-Out' Function in Higher Education," *American Journal of Sociology*, May 1960, p. 569.

53. Of the many paeans to the wonders and joys of medicine and law, Robert Schaefer's comparison of the working conditions of teachers and those in the more exalted professions is of particular interest:

> Other professions which involve person-to-person relations provide some respite—refreshing moments when the concentration required in projecting an idea, an ideal, or a product can be eased. The doctor, for example, spends only a part of each day conferring with patients. He has almost never to deal with his clients in a group, and most of those he sees are too weak and too low-spirited to resist him. Only a few attorneys serve as trial lawyers, and those few, unlike teachers, are required to face their judges and juries a mere fraction of the working day. [R. Schaefer, *The School as a Center of Inquiry* (New York: Harper & Row, 1967), p. 36.]

54. Main, *The Social Structure of Revolutionary America*, pp. 201–202.

55. In this connection, see S. Haber, "The Professions and Higher Education: A Historical View," in M. S. Gordon (ed.), *Higher Education and the Labor Market* (New York: McGraw-Hill, 1974), pp. 237–280.

56. As quoted in R. H. Shryock, *Medicine in America: Historical Essays* (Baltimore: Johns Hopkins University Press, 1966), pp. 150–151.

57. As quoted in Ludmerer, *Learning to Heal*, p. 27.

58. Ludmerer, *Learning to Heal,* p. 27.

59. See, for example, G. S. Counts, "The Social Status of Occupations: A Problem in Vocational Guidance," *School Review,* Jan. 1925, *33,* 16–27; G. W. Hartmann, "The Prestige of Occupations: A Comparison of Educational Occupations and Others," *Personnel Journal,* Oct. 1934, *13,* 144–152; A. Inkeles and P. H. Rossi, "National Comparisons of Occupational Prestige," *American Journal of Sociology,* Jan. 1956, *61,* 329–339; R. W. Hodge, P. M. Siegel, and P. H. Rossi, "Occupational Prestige in the United States, 1925–63," *American Journal of Sociology,* 1964, *70,* 289–302.

60. Shryock, *Medicine in America,* chap. 8.

61. S. J. Kunitz, "Professionalism and Social Control in the Progressive Era: The Case of the Flexner Report," *Social Problems;* 1974, *22* (1), p. 25.

62. S. Jarcho, "Medical Education in the United States—1910–1956," *Journal of the Mount Sinai Hospital,* 1959, *26,* 342–343.

63. A. Flexner, *Medical Education in the United States and Canada,* Bulletin no. 4 (New York: Carnegie Foundation for the Advancement of Teaching, 1910).

64. See, for example, M. Schudson, "The Flexner Report and the Reed Report: Notes on the History of Professional Education in the United States," *Social Science Quarterly,* 1974, *55,* 374–361.

65. The literature pertaining to Flexner and the reform of medical education is extensive and well worth consulting. In addition to sources previously cited, see D. H. Banta, "Medical Education, Abraham Flexner—A Reappraisal," *Social Science and Medicine,* 1971 *5,* 655–661; L. F. Barker, "Medicine and the Universities," *American Medicine,* 1902, *4,* 143–147; C. B. Chapman, "The Flexner Report by Abraham Flexner," *Daedalus,* Winter 1974, pp. 105–117; D. Fox, "Abraham Flexner's Unpublished Report: Foundations and Medical Education, 1909–1928," *Bulletin of the History of Medicine,* Winter 1980, *54,* 475–496; R. P. Hudson, "Abraham Flexner in Perspective: American Medical Education, 1865–1910," *Bulletin of the History of Medicine,* Sept.–Oct. 1972, *46,* 545–561; S. Jonas,

Medical Mystery: The Training of Doctors in the United States (New York: Norton, 1978); M. Kaufman, *American Medical Education: The Formative Years, 1765-1910* (Westport, Conn.: Greenwood Press, 1976); R. A. Kessel, "The A.M.A. and the Supply of Physicians," Symposium on Health Care, part 1, *Law and Contemporary Problems,* Spring 1970, *35,* 267-283; L. S. King, "Clinical Science Gets Enthroned: Part II," *Journal of the American Medical Association,* 1983, *250,* 1847-1850; L. S. King, "The Flexner Report of 1910," *Journal of the American Medical Association,* 1984, *251,* 1079-1086; E. C. Lagemann, *Private Power for the Public Good: A History of the Carnegie Foundation for the Advancement of Teaching* (Middletown, Conn.: Wesleyan University Press, 1983); C. E. Odegaard, "A Description of the Role of the University in Modern Society Together with Encouragement to the Medical School to Turn Its Flirtation with the University into a Full Blown Romance," *California Medicine,* May 1967, *106,* 337-345; G. Stevens, *The Structure of American Medical Practice, 1875-1941* (Philadelphia: University of Pennsylvania Press, 1983); R. Stevens, *American Medicine and the Public Interest* (New Haven, Conn.: Yale University Press, 1971); M. R. Walsh, *Doctors Wanted: No Women Need Apply* (New Haven, Conn.: Yale University Press, 1977); J. R. Woodworth, "Some Influences on the Reform of Schools of Law and Medicine, 1890-1930," *Sociological Quarterly,* Autumn 1973, *14,* 496-516.

66. G. E. Markowitz and D. K. Rosner, "Doctors in Crisis: A Study of the Use of Medical Education Reform to Establish Modern Professional Elitism in Medicine," *American Quarterly,* Mar. 1973, *25,* 83-107.

67. See, for example, H. S. Berliner, "A Larger Perspective on the Flexner Report," *International Journal of Health Services,* Sept. 1975, *5,* 573-592; H. S. Berliner, "New Light on the Flexner Report: Notes on the AMA-Carnegie Foundation Background," *Bulletin of the History of Medicine,* 1977, *51,* 603-609; E. R. Brown, *Rockefeller Medicine Men: Medical Care and Capitalism in America* (Berkeley: University of California Press, 1979).

68. Larson, *The Rise of Professionalism,* chaps. 3-4. See also D. H. Kerr, *Barriers to Integrity: Modern Modes of Knowledge Utilization* (Boulder, Colo.: Westview Press, 1984), chap. 3.

69. Starr, *The Social Transformation of American Medicine.* See especially pp. 58-59, 71-80, 137-142, 230-231.

70. Starr, *The Social Transformation of American Medicine,* p. 144.

71. Starr, *The Social Transformation of American Medicine,* p. 80.

72. Johnson, *Professions and Power,* p. 43.

73. In this connection, see Veysey, "Plural Organized Worlds of the Humanities."

74. Johnson, *Professions and Power,* p. 45.

75. The probability of developing a new technology is low. Even if a new technology did emerge, there would remain the critical matter of teacher acceptance. If past behavior is any indicator, the odds for acceptance are not good: Teachers have tended to view almost every technological development to date as a threat to their "professionalism."

76. There have been, of course, interesting and possibly useful advances in educational psychology over the past several decades; these advances, some have argued, provide a reasonable basis for claiming that teaching has become a science. See, for example, N. L. Gage, "What Do We Know About Teaching Effectiveness," *Phi Delta Kappan,* Oct. 1984, *66,* 87-93. But these advances, while perhaps edifying to the cognoscente, have not, and most likely will not, produce manifestly efficacious and universal outcomes.

77. As was suggested in an address by Chester Finn, assistant to the secretary of education, at the annual meeting of the American Association of Colleges for Teacher Education, Chicago, Mar. 1986.

78. For a penetrating discussion of the nature and implications of rhetoric, see R. Weaver, *The Ethics of Rhetoric* (Chicago: Regnery, 1953). Particularly germane are chap. 3, "Edmund Burke and the Argument from Circumstance," and chap 4, "Abraham Lincoln and the Argument from Definition." The implications of sources of argument are treated with extraor-

dinary insight by J. B. White in *When Words Lose Their Meaning: Constitutions and Reconstitutions of Language, Character, and Community* (Chicago: University of Chicago Press, 1984) and *Heracles' Bow: Essays on the Rhetoric and Poetics of the Law* (Madison: University of Wisconsin Press, 1985).

79.   A. Etzioni, *The Active Society* (New York: Free Press, 1968), chap. 21.

80.   G. Bateson, *Steps to an Ecology of Mind* (New York: Ballantine, 1972), p. 65. See also the essays on double-bind theory in Part Three of this volume.

81.   R. Laing, *The Politics of the Family* (New York: Vintage Books, 1972), p. 44.

82.   H. S. Becker, "The Nature of a Profession," in N. Henry (ed.), *Education for the Professions,* Sixty-First Yearbook (Part II) of the National Society for the Study of Education (Chicago: University of Chicago Press, 1962), pp. 26–46.

83.   R. Soder and R. L. Andrews, "The Moral Imperatives of Compulsory Schooling," *Curriculum in Context,* Summer 1985, pp. 6–9, 12.

84.   See, for example, Goodlad, *A Place Called School;* C. Boyer, *High School* (New York: Harper & Row, 1983); T. R. Sizer, *Horace's Compromise* (Boston: Houghton Mifflin, 1984).

3

The Limits
of Teacher
Professionalization

Barry L. Bull

Teaching has become a central focus of contemporary concern about the improvement of schooling. Much of the most thoughtful recent literature on teaching argues for increased professionalism in teaching, professionalism that includes considerably more autonomy for teachers than they have enjoyed in the past.[1] In this chapter, I consider whether truly professional autonomy for teachers can be justified and develop a conception of legitimate teacher autonomy that may be useful in the reform and restructuring of the teaching career now under way. Of course, these are normative tasks; that is, they involve a consideration of what teaching should be in our society. Clearly, this inquiry depends on what Americans think about how schools should operate and what they should accomplish.

Americans today, however, often evince what appears to be a self-contradictory attitude toward public schools. On the one hand, we expect schools to discipline the nation's children vigorously—to constrain their thoughts and especially their behavior for the present and to produce loyal citizens and willing workers for the future. On the other hand, we want children (especially our own) to have the chance to express and develop their individual potential in school and to emerge with a personal strength of character and a

Note: A presentation based on an earlier draft of this chapter was made at the annual meeting of the American Educational Research Association, New Orleans, 1988.

freedom of intelligence that will enable them to lead rich and independent adult lives.

This dual attitude is hardly a new arrival on the American educational scene. In 1837, Horace Mann's first annual report on education in Massachusetts complained both of the public's apathy toward education, which allowed public school students to be treated "as so many male and female automata," and of many parents' deep commitment to and high aspirations for their own children's education that led them to abandon public schools altogether.[2] John Dewey, in 1916, contrasted two common American conceptions of education—first, as a form of social control of the individual and, second, as the unconstrained and natural growth of the individual's physical and intellectual powers.[3] Since World War II, we have seen the momentum of school reform shift from education for social adjustment to education for personal liberation and back again.

Our attitudes toward schools are closely related to our vision of the moral purpose of government. After all, how public schools—which are agencies of the state—are to treat our youngest citizens and what they may legitimately expect our children to become as adults logically depend on our beliefs about the moral authority and responsibilities of government. It is tempting, therefore, to view the public's dual attitude toward schools as arising from different and competing visions of legitimate government. Thus, one might suppose that those with an authoritarian conception of government expect schools to enforce on all children a particular way of life deemed on religious or ideological grounds to be morally best; those with a laissez-faire conception of government expect public schools, if they are necessary at all, simply to enable children to develop strictly according to their own lights. On this account, some Americans see schoolteaching as the systematic enculturation of children; others see it as the protection of children from any such collective enculturation. Thus, this explanation suggests that the American public holds no coherent view of the moral responsibilities of teachers and, therefore, that the effort to assess the moral justification of professional autonomy for teachers is futile.

This view of Americans' dual attitude toward schools as the result of ideological conflict is inadequate for two reasons. First, that attitude implies not just that some Americans believe one thing about schools and others believe something else but that the same individuals include both constraint and independence in their conceptions of the purpose of schooling. Second, the contending authoritarian and laissez-faire conceptions of government are not representative of Americans' historical or contemporary beliefs about government. A brief consideration of American history can help us identify a more representative conception of government.

From this country's inception, diversity has posed a practical and philosophical challenge to the very idea of a United States of America, even when the diversity that mattered excluded non-Europeans. Precisely what common cause could compel Puritan Massachusetts, Roman Catholic Maryland, and Anglican Virginia; the Yankee trader, the Pennsylvania farmer, and the southern plantation owner; or the urban guildsman and the rural agriculturalist to join together in rebellion against the British Crown and to continue their cooperation once independence had been secured? To meet this challenge, Thomas Jefferson reached back ninety years to the political philosophy of John Locke, which had played an important role in the resolution of the decades of turmoil of the English Civil War.

Locke argued that agreement on a single vision of the good life or the political ascendancy of one such vision over its competitors is not required for the establishment and maintenance of a civil government.[4] Instead, the legitimate function of such a government lies with the protection of all individuals' natural rights to life, liberty, and property (or, in the words of Jefferson's Declaration of Independence, to life, liberty, and the pursuit of happiness).[5] Thus, unity in diversity—or *e pluribus unum,* as it is expressed on the official seal of the United States—not only is possible but imposes on citizens a common moral obligation to provide for and to preserve one another's opportunities to choose and pursue their own visions of the good.

Locke's and Jefferson's conception of government is one of a family of conceptions that philosophers and political theorists label political liberalism.[6] In the most general terms, liberalism prescribes one basic purpose for government—to facilitate the realization of each citizen's vision of the good life, whatever that vision turns out to be.[7] Liberalism contrasts with authoritarianism, which

prescribes for all a particular vision of the good life, and with the
extreme laissez-faire conception of government, which denies altogether the existence of common, enforceable moral obligations.
Liberalism is thus simultaneously a doctrine of freedom and of
responsibility—the freedom for each to choose and pursue a personal vision of the good and the responsibility to enable others to do
likewise.

A liberal society's educational goals, in the broadest terms,
are simultaneously to promote each person's independence in the
formation of his or her vision of the good and to promote a common
recognition of one's obligation to respect and secure a similar independence for others. These implications are, I suggest, a more plausible and historically realistic interpretation and explanation of
Americans' dual expectation that schools should both liberate and
constrain students than that provided by the competing-ideologies
view. Therefore, political liberalism is a useful starting place in our
exploration of teachers' moral responsibilities and their justified
autonomy.[8] As I show in more detail later, schoolteaching in a
liberal society *is* legitimately a form of enculturation—one, however, that shares little with that required by authoritarianism. At
this point, though, I will consider the place of individual freedom
in liberal political theory in preparation for our assessment of the
claim that teachers deserve a special sort of freedom—namely, professional autonomy.

Liberalism and Freedom

Liberalism's central commitment to facilitating the realization of each person's vision of the good life, whatever that vision
turns out to be, has traditionally been taken to require a liberal
society to guarantee each citizen's freedom to act as his or her view
of the good dictates. However, because individuals' views of the
good may differ, one person's acting freely in pursuit of her good
may impede another's freedom to pursue his good. Since liberalism
is committed to all people's pursuit of their goods, any liberal theory must specify the morally legitimate limits of each person's
freedom.

The basic reason to limit someone's freedom under liberalism is that its exercise would unreasonably interfere with others' pursuit of their goods. Ideally, these limits to freedom should fall equally on all members of society, since a liberal society cannot prefer one person's vision of the good over another's. Thus, some freedoms—such as the freedom to buy and sell other people—cannot or will not be used in a way that does not impair others' pursuit of their goods and so should be denied equally to all members of society. Conversely, those freedoms—such as the freedom to hold religious beliefs—that cannot or will not be used unreasonably should be extended equally to all members of society. These considerations can be thought of as defining, at least in part, the basic liberties that are to be guaranteed to and protected for each member of a liberal society.

Unfortunately, it is not always possible to treat freedoms in this evenhanded way. There are two broad categories of freedoms that are especially problematic. The first might be called self-defeating freedoms—those freedoms the equal exercise of which by all members of society frustrates the very purpose of the freedoms themselves. The freedom to enforce one's own basic liberties is often argued to fall into this self-defeating category.[9] All people have a legitimate interest, based on their visions of the good life, in defending their basic freedoms against those who might violate or usurp them. If, however, all were granted the freedom to defend those basic freedoms, they would, it is argued, enjoy little if any real security against violation or usurpation. In other words, the social chaos that might result from each person's having the freedom to be his or her own police force, judge, jury, jailor, and executioner would militate against the very security of the person that this freedom is supposed to promote. If so, the freedom of self-defense would be self-defeating.

Similarly, modern economists have argued that giving all individuals the freedom to pursue certain economic goods—what are called public goods—may actually prevent individuals from securing those goods.[10] A lighthouse is the classic example of such a public good. Once a lighthouse has been built, its use cannot be denied to anyone. In a free market, each person can reason that paying a share of the cost of building the lighthouse would not enhance the benefit he or she would receive from its construction.

Because each can reason in this way, no one will voluntarily pay a share, and the lighthouse will not be built. Thus, the individual freedom to participate in the market for lighthouses is self-defeating, since it frustrates the very purpose of that freedom—the erection of individually and collectively cost-beneficial lighthouses.

The second category of problematic freedoms might be called risk-laden freedoms—freedoms to engage in actions that may or may not unreasonably impair others' chances to pursue their goods, depending on the manner and circumstances in which the actions are taken. Although most human freedoms might qualify as risk-laden in this sense, the freedom to perform surgery on others is an especially salient example. In the current state of medical technology, surgery can be an effective means by which both the surgeon and the patient can pursue their own visions of the good. Successful surgery depends, however, on levels of skill and knowledge not found in the general population.

Equal disposition of self-defeating and risk-laden freedoms is inconsistent with a liberal society's central commitment to facilitating each person's pursuit of his or her good. To deny the freedom to purchase lighthouses or perform surgery to all people would be to forgo potentially significant means of self-fulfillment for many individuals. Granting such freedoms to all, however, either would be ineffective in bringing about the desired types of self-fulfillment or would allow some citizens to impose unreasonable risks on others.

There are, therefore, reasons both to permit the exercise of self-defeating and risk-laden freedoms and to reject the presumption of equality for those freedoms. To meet these problems, a liberal society may establish institutions that enable some but not all members of society to exercise those freedoms. Let us briefly consider what sorts of institutions might be appropriate to this end and what ethical principles should govern these institutions.

Self-Defeating Freedoms. To deal successfully with self-defeating freedoms, a liberal society must overcome an embarrassment of riches. Unless those freedoms are restricted, the goods of the society's citizens will not be achieved. However, the number of individuals who are able and willing to exercise those freedoms exceeds the number required to achieve the goal of a liberal society.

To solve this problem, a liberal society may create public offices and procedures for selecting citizens to fill those offices. The selected officeholders, then, would be permitted to exercise the otherwise self-defeating freedom in the interests of achieving the purpose of the freedom. A restricted freedom of this sort is a kind of power over other members of the society, since it allows some individuals to grant or withhold conditions necessary to the fulfillment of others' goals. The danger, of course, is that the officeholder may abuse the freedom he or she has been granted. Thus, in filling public offices, a liberal society must choose procedures that will ensure that officeholders will fulfill the intended purpose of their office. There are many different office-filling procedures that a liberal society has at its disposal.

Of course, democratic election is the procedure that springs immediately to mind. Election provides a means whereby non-officeholders can consent directly to an officeholder's exercising particular restricted freedoms and can withdraw their consent if they believe the freedom to have been abused. Election is, however, relatively costly, and other procedures may be just as effective. Appointment by elected officials, employment through a civil service system, and even selection by random lottery (as in the case of jury duty and, at times, military service) are among the nonelective alternatives available.

Public professions,[11] among which the practice of law and certified public accountancy might be counted, are a special case of the use of nonelective mechanisms for filling public office. Although the members of public professions serve crucial public functions (note, for instance, that lawyers are "officers of the court"), they are neither elected to office nor typically held accountable to the electorate through appointment by a public agency. Why might such professions be justified in a liberal state? Obviously, the freedoms that public professionals enjoy must be self-defeating, but there must also be plausible reasons why the usual mechanisms of public accountability are inappropriate or ineffective.

To find these reasons, it is necessary to make explicit the liberal ethics of office that have been implicit in the discussion thus far. Democratic elections and public agencies are ways of ensuring that the actions of state officials meet the expectations of the voting public. Liberal societies, however, do not have an absolute commitment to the moral rightness of all of the majority's expectations or desires. It is not right, for example, for liberal governments to violate some citizens' basic liberties even if a political majority wishes it. Thus, the ethical principle that is to govern the actions of the officers of a liberal state is that they should do what the public has a right to expect. I will, adapting Ronald Dworkin's terminology, call this the principle of liberal integrity.[12]

The basic reason for establishing a public profession, then, is that there is a difference between what the public expects and what it has a right to expect of an officeholder. Such a difference exists most clearly in the enforcement of criminal laws. The public has a right to expect that suspects who are found to have actually broken the law be convicted and that those who have not be released. In practice, the public's desire for conviction may often make it difficult for a publicly accountable defense attorney to defend a suspect adequately. This gap between what the public often expects and what it has a right to expect justifies insulating defense attorneys from direct public accountability. The gap between the public's actual and its legitimate expectations is most serious when public officers' actions affect individuals' basic freedoms in some relatively permanent way.

There is, however, one additional condition that must be met before a public profession may be justified in a liberal society. For elective and bureaucratic offices, democratic election and accountability to elected officials can enforce the principle of integrity for officeholders. Those procedures are, however, inappropriate for offices justifiably filled by members of public professions. Thus, before the creation of these offices can be justified, it must be possible to devise effective alternative mechanisms by which the public can be protected against the fundamental vice of public office, malfeasance. Thus, public professions must be governed by an appropriate and effective code of ethical conduct.

In sum, liberal societies may legitimately authorize restricted spheres of autonomy by creating public offices in which some members of the society are permitted to exercise freedoms that facilitate the pursuit of individuals' goods but that would be self-defeating if everyone exercised them. When the public's expectations for the exercise of these freedoms diverge from what it should legitimately expect, some of these offices, constituting what I have called the public professions, may need to be filled through non-democratically accountable procedures. In creating these offices, however, a liberal society must ensure that those permitted to exercise such restricted autonomy will be governed by the principle of liberal integrity.

Risk-Laden Freedoms. A risk-laden freedom is one that, depending on how it is exercised, may either enhance or impair individuals' pursuit of their own goods. The problem of risk-laden freedoms for liberal societies is that the demand for the exercise of a risk-laden freedom, from those whose vision of the good requires them either to exercise the freedom or to receive the benefits from another's exercising it, exceeds the supply of those who are capable of exercising the freedom reasonably. The problem for the liberal society here is twofold: to whom to restrict the exercise of risk-laden freedoms and to whom to distribute the benefits of that restricted exercise.

It may be tempting to suppose that the solution to these problems is straightforward—simply restrict exercise to the competent and permit the free market to distribute the benefits to those to whom they are worth the most. Unfortunately, the fundamental liberal commitment to facilitating individuals' pursuit of their goods does not permit such easy solutions.

Competence is not an all-or-nothing affair; rather, it is a matter of degree. People are better or worse automobile mechanics rather than absolutely incompetent or absolutely competent at car repair. To exercise a risk-laden freedom, a society must, then, establish a definition of minimum competence somewhere along the continuum of performance. Because individuals in a liberal society have differing conceptions of the good, some might be satisfied with a level of performance that falls below the established minimum. In regulating the exercise of risk-laden freedoms, therefore, a liberal society inevitably limits access to certain benefits even when the beneficiaries themselves would be perfectly satisfied with the quality of those benefits. In general, then, a liberal society should allow everyone to exercise risk-laden freedoms.

The argument for the free exercise of risk-laden freedoms assumes that one of three things is true—that the ordinary person is generally skillful enough to exercise that freedom competently, that the risks imposed on others are not so severe that the ordinary person would not be able to compensate others for the damage caused by the incompetent exercise of the freedom, or that those on whom the risks are imposed have the opportunity and the ability to assess those risks before they permit another to exercise a freedom that would have an effect on them. Licensing is permitted, then, only when all three of those assumptions are false. Thus, the licensure of risk-laden freedoms requires the satisfaction of both of these criteria:

> *The competence criterion:* Successful exercise of the freedom depends on clearly definable skills that require special ability or training or both.
> *The severity criterion:* The risks that the exercise of a freedom imposes on others are so severe that their prior consent should be obtained.

and at least one of these two criteria:

> *The opportunity criterion:* Those on whom the risks are imposed generally do not have the opportunity to consent to the imposition of those risks.
> *The ability criterion:* Those on whom the risks are imposed generally are unable to evaluate those risks rationally.

These criteria imply, for example, that a liberal society may legitimately license the freedom to drive a car, since the successful exercise of that freedom requires special training, driving can impose serious risks on others, and the other drivers and pedestrians on whom those risks are imposed do not usually have the opportunity in advance to consent specifically to one's exercising that freedom. The freedom to perform surgery may also be licensed, because it, too, requires skill and imposes severe risks and because those whom it affects usually do not have the ability to assess the competence of surgeons (and thus the risks they run by allowing a particular surgeon to operate) even though they generally have the opportunity to do so.

To license a risk-laden freedom, a liberal society must give certain individuals the power to grant or withhold the license. Election or democratically accountable procedures are most often used to accomplish this licensing function. In some cases, however, determining who is a competent practitioner may be so complex that it can be done reliably only by skilled practitioners themselves. In these extraordinary cases—which I will call the licensed professions—a liberal society must invest the power to license in qualified professionals. As a result, the licensed professions are self-regulating, and their practitioners are not fully publicly accountable in the exercise of the restricted freedoms they have been granted. The licensed professions, like the public professions, therefore, must effectively enforce a code of ethical professional conduct in order to serve the legitimate purposes of a liberal society.

This code of conduct will have two aspects, one for each of the major ethical problems that risk-laden freedoms pose to a liberal society. On the one hand, a liberal society aims to bring the potentially beneficial or harmful consequences of risk-laden freedoms under the control of those to whom they may accrue so that individuals may pursue their goods reasonably in light of the risks involved. Those to whom a liberal society grants such a freedom have a moral obligation, then, to exercise it in a way that minimizes its risks to others. In other words, licensed professionals are obliged to practice competently. On the other hand, that the risks of a freedom are minimized does not imply that they do not exist. Those remaining risks may, according to some people's view of the good, still be unacceptable. Thus, licensed professionals have a further obligation to inform their clients of the risks that attach to competent practice and to permit them to decide whether to run those risks. In sum, the members of licensed professions are morally committed to providing those affected by certain risk-laden freedoms with competent, or risk-minimizing, practice and informed consent.

Individual risk management is not the only problem that risk-laden freedoms impose on liberal societies. Because such societies are committed to facilitating their members' pursuit of their goods, they must be concerned about individuals' access to the instrumentalities that are required by that pursuit, including the beneficial consequences of risk-laden freedoms. Ordinarily, liberal societies establish labor and commodity markets in which individuals can freely negotiate with one another for access to the instrumentalities they require. On the assumption that the economic power that individuals bring to those markets is justly distributed, free markets give the members of society fair access to the means of fulfilling their visions of the good. Restrictions on the exercise of risk-laden freedoms vitiate markets' potential to provide such fair access, because those restrictions artificially limit the available supply and variety of the beneficial consequences of those freedoms. When licensure of a freedom is justified, therefore, a liberal society must seek to ensure a just distribution of those beneficial consequences. Another condition a liberal society may legitimately impose on those who exercise a licensed risk-laden freedom, then, is that citizens be given fair access to the beneficial consequences of that exercise.

A liberal society may be justified in authorizing restricted spheres of autonomy by licensing some individuals to exercise certain risk-laden freedoms that are forbidden to others. In some of these restricted practices, the licensed professions, the licensing decision can appropriately be made only by those who are already qualified to exercise the freedom in question. In licensing such professions, however, a liberal society must protect itself against two threats to its commitment to facilitating its members' pursuit of their own goods—the failure of licensed professionals to exercise the risk-laden freedom competently and in accord with others' informed consent (or malpractice) and the failure to give others fair access to the beneficial effects of the risk-laden freedom (or maldistribution).

Professional Autonomy for Teachers?

This discussion of how a liberal society can justify permitting some citizens to exercise freedoms forbidden to others has prepared us to clarify the nature of teacher autonomy in three ways. We have seen, first, that there are two different bases for granting restricted autonomy in a liberal society—that the freedoms in question are self-defeating or that they are risk-laden. The validity of the claim that teachers should exercise a special sphere of autonomy, thus, depends on whether the practices in which teachers engage fall into either or both of these categories. Second, we have seen that there are two different types of procedures by which a liberal society may determine who is to be allowed to exercise the freedoms that are justifiably restricted—procedures in which that determination is directly or indirectly accountable to the will of the majority and procedures in which that determination is made by the authorized practitioners themselves. The validity of the claim that the autonomy that teachers should exercise is professional in nature, thus, depends on whether the procedures for determining admission to and retention in the practice of teaching are justifiably of the second type. Finally, we have seen that a liberal society is justified in authorizing limited spheres of autonomy only in order to achieve its fundamental commitment to facilitating its members' pursuit of their own goods. Those who are permitted a limited sphere of autonomy must, therefore, exercise their restricted freedoms according to ethical principles derived from the fundamental liberal commitment. The nature of teacher autonomy, should such autonomy prove to be justified, will be defined by the ethical principles associated with the exercise of the freedoms that it includes.

The Case for Teaching as a Public Office and a Public Profession. In liberal societies, public officeholders are allowed to exercise self-defeating freedoms—such as the freedom to enforce one's own basic rights—whose generally beneficial purposes would be frustrated if everyone were permitted to exercise them. If teaching is legitimately a public office, it must involve the exercise of such a self-defeating freedom. To show that the freedom to teach has this character, we need to establish, first, that teaching has a purpose that is applicable to all members of a liberal society and, second, that giving everyone the freedom to teach would defeat the achievement of that purpose.

Teaching can have as many different purposes as there are visions of the good in a society. One might teach in order to promote the greater glory of God, the perpetuation of a particular art form, or the flourishing of a particular community. To the extent that any of these purposes cannot be shared by all members of a

liberal society no matter what their vision of the good turns out to
be, the freedom to teach for that purpose cannot be recognized by
the society as self-defeating and thus be restricted to those who hold
a particular public office.

It is, however, generally important in a liberal society that its
members come to hold some vision of the good that they have
chosen for themselves. Thus, while the development of each person's specific potential to become, say, a Buddhist monk to the
exclusion of other possibilities cannot be a legitimate purpose of a
liberal society, the development of each person's more general potential to choose and hold some vision of the good, including that of
the Buddhist monk, can be a legitimate liberal purpose. Because
teaching may be necessary to develop that general potential, the
freedom to teach for that purpose is a legitimate candidate for a self-
defeating freedom.

But is the freedom to teach for this purpose in fact self-
defeating? Is it true, in other words, that if everyone were granted
the freedom to teach for this purpose, people would not actually
develop the general capacities to choose and hold a vision of the
good at which that freedom aims?[13] Having one's own vision of the
good does not require that each person invent his or her vision from
scratch or that it be wholly idiosyncratic. By and large, one's vision
of the good will result from one's exposure to the various human
possibilities that others' experiences make available. In the long
run, having one's own vision of the good depends on one's having
access to others' understandings and experiences of the world. But it
also depends on one's having the abilities to comprehend and assess
the possibilities that others exemplify, to understand oneself, and to
create a coherent life from among the available possibilities. These
and perhaps other abilities constitute the general capacity to choose
and hold a vision of the good.

It is important to make two general observations about these
abilities. First, they are matters of degree. The more languages one
can speak, the more value systems one understands, the more one
has experienced one's own talents and proclivities, and so on, the
more capable one is to choose and hold a view of the good. But,
second, it does not seem to be psychologically or developmentally
possible for the infant to learn all human languages or value sys-

tems simultaneously. Thus, for children to develop robust capacities to choose and hold a vision of the good in the long run, it seems initially necessary for them to develop a rather narrow range of abilities—such as how to speak one or two languages, to interact successfully with the members of one's immediate community, to make judgments of fact and value compatible with one's language and community, and so on.

In light of these observations, let us consider a society in which everyone enjoys the freedom to teach anyone else whatever he or she pleases and to determine, according to his or her own interests, from whom to accept such instruction. Among adults with reasonably well-established visions of the good, this arrangement seems eminently sensible, for these freedoms are important means to the continued evolution and expression of their visions of the good. When exercised among adults, then, the freedoms to learn from and to teach others are consistent with the fundamental commitments of a liberal society.

For very young children, however, who lack not only a vision of the good but even the general capacity to choose and hold such a vision, these freedoms are problematic. These children need to establish in some systematic way a coherent cultural foundation that will enable them eventually to develop a genuinely self-chosen vision of the good. If taught indiscriminately by all and any adults, however, children may fail to develop any systematic foundation for becoming their own persons. Unrestricted freedoms to teach and learn from others, which are important for adults' being and becoming their own persons, can actually impede children's development toward that very goal.

In short, everyone's having the freedom to teach anyone and everyone else will defeat its legitimate liberal purpose when those who are taught have very limited capacities to choose and hold a vision of the good. As these capacities grow more robust, the self-defeating character of the freedom to teach dissipates. Therefore, a liberal society's justification for creating a public office of teacher is strongest for the development in the very young of the initial abilities that will enable them to choose and hold their own visions of the good.

In general, liberal societies recognize two types of "public office" for the exercise of the freedom to teach the young—those of parent and of schoolteacher. The office of parent can be seen in part as a liberal society's attempt to make the freedom to teach the young widely available even though that freedom must be restricted because it is self-defeating. Although the freedom to teach any child is inconsistent with the fundamental commitments of a liberal society, parenthood provides nearly everyone with the opportunity to exercise the freedom to teach some particular child and thereby to realize, to some extent at least, that part of each person's vision of the good that may require the exercise of that freedom.

Let us recall, however, that liberal societies distinguish two different categories of teaching—that done with the purpose of advancing a particular view of the good and that done with the purpose of developing the general capacity to choose and hold a vision of the good. As we have noted, the freedom to engage in personal-good-advancing instruction may not be restricted to public office, nor may public office be utilized to advance some personal goods to the exclusion of others. Rather, it is the freedom to engage in general capacity-developing instruction that may legitimately be restricted to and exercised by public office holders.

Now, these two categories of teaching are not mutually exclusive. For instance, teaching to advance one's own good, even when one's purpose is not to develop others' general capacities, may willy-nilly serve that purpose when it provides the initial cultural foundation that children need for the development of those capacities. Thus, parents who, for example, socialize their children to particular religious or political beliefs also contribute to their children's general development by teaching them a language, patterns of social interaction, and so on. As that foundation becomes effectively established, however, such personal-good-advancing instruction gradually ceases to serve the purpose of general capacity development. At this point, children need, for example, to develop the abilities to understand and evaluate their parents' and others' visions of the good life. As a result, it may be necessary for a liberal society to establish a second office for the exercise of the freedom to teach for general capacity development, the office of schoolteacher.

The freedom to teach for general capacity development should, on the lines I have suggested, be distributed in a liberal

society as follows. As an individual's general capacities to choose
and hold a view of the good become developed, restricting the freedom to teach that individual for that purpose to the holders of
public office becomes harder to justify. Similarly, as the teaching of
a parent ceases to contribute to the development of a child's general
capacities, the justification for the parent's continuing to exercise
exclusive control over the child's development also grows weaker.
The role of the schoolteacher, then, is to exercise the freedom to
develop a child's general capacities from the point where parental
exercise is no longer exclusive to the point at which the general
public's exercise of that freedom becomes justified. In other words,
whether a liberal society should create the public office of schoolteacher depends on whether there is a gap between parents' legitimately diminishing and the general public's legitimately increasing
freedom to teach children for the purpose of general capacity
development.

Does such a gap exist in contemporary American society?
Two considerations suggest that it does. A society is liberal to the
extent that its members' sense of justice includes a commitment to
liberal principles and that that sense of justice is regulative of its
members' actions.[11] Even when a liberal sense of justice is generally
regulative of citizens' interactions, the very circumstances of parenthood can make the sense of justice ineffective or, perhaps, inappropriate among the members of a family. Thus, liberal justice
requires one to respect and tolerate others' holding and living by
visions of the good that are incompatible with one's own. But such
tolerance does not require one to associate intimately with those
whose visions are radically different. It is probable, therefore, that
parents often impose expectations on their children that their sense
of justice would not permit them to impose on their fellow citizens
with whom they are less intimately related. Even in a reasonably
just society, then, the educative relationships between parents and
children are likely to fall short of the liberal ideal.

A similar argument can be made about the cultural diversity
and technical complexity of a society. When the range of options
from which an individual can fashion a view of the good is large
and when the skills necessary to understand and assess the options
are complex, the time it will take individuals to develop reasonably

robust capacities to choose and hold a view of the good will be increased. In such a society, moreover, parents are unlikely on their own to be able to develop their children's capacities to choose and hold a vision of the good, because they lack the requisite knowledge or ability. Since American society is both diverse and technically advanced, the justification for the public office of schoolteacher will be strong.

At this point, then, we have determined that the freedom to teach for general development is self-defeating and that there is a plausible case in contemporary American society for creating an office of schoolteacher to which the exercise of that freedom may legitimately be restricted during at least part of each individual's childhood. Let me point out here, as has been suggested elsewhere in this volume, that, according to this argument, schoolteaching is morally distinguishable from the other sorts of teaching that go on in a liberal society—parents teaching their children and adults teaching one another—for the legitimate purposes of parents' freedom to teach their children and adults' freedom to teach one another can be accomplished even if they are not explicitly concerned about how their teaching affects others' general capacities to choose and hold a vision of the good. As we will see, this is simply not the case for schoolteaching. But, first, let us consider whether schoolteaching in a liberal society should be considered a public profession.

The usual way of filling public offices is through democratic election or appointment by a democratically accountable public agency. In many rural communities until the early part of this century, something much like election was used to select teachers. Teachers were chosen by community consensus, often from among the older daughters of local families. Today, however, state and local bureaucracies control the filling of these public offices. The case for professionalizing teaching depends on the inadequacy of democratically accountable procedures for determining who may, in this case, exercise the self-defeating freedom to teach for general capacity development.

As I have argued, there are two criteria for creating a public profession in a liberal society:

1. What the public actually expects of the conduct of a pub-

lic officer is significantly different from what it has a right to expect, particularly when those expectations may have a relatively permanent effect on individuals' exercise of their basic freedoms.

2. There exist effective nondemocratic mechanisms for enforcing upon these officeholders the ethic of liberal integrity in the exercise of the restricted freedoms they have been granted.

By imposing on their students expectations concerning the development of their capacities to choose and hold views of the good, schoolteachers do affect others' abilities to exercise their basic freedoms as adults. When teachers are selected by democratically accountable procedures, those expectations are determined directly or indirectly by the will of the majority. If there is a significant difference between what the majority actually expects in this regard and what it has a right to expect on the basis of fundamental liberal commitments, a liberal society might, according to the first criterion, need to make the practice of schoolteaching a public profession.

As we have seen, if a liberal sense of justice does not govern parents' relationships with their children, or if parents are unable to foster the general capacity development required by liberalism, a liberal society is justified in making schoolteaching a public office. Filling that office through professional rather than democratic means requires one of two far stronger claims—namely, either that a majority of citizens do not possess a regulative sense of liberal justice with regard to the general capacity development of others' children or that publicly accountable mechanisms for admitting individuals to the practice of schoolteaching are very likely to be subverted by an unjust minority. If the first claim is true, democratically accountable selection procedures will result in the imposition on students of the majority's illiberal expectations for general capacity development. If the second claim is true, these expectations will be determined by an illiberal subversive minority. Though I cannot fully assess these claims here, I will note that they are inconsistent with the popular belief that the United States has an active and viable democratic tradition. As a result, these claims require clear substantiation before we act on them. As we shall see, there are other reasons for public control of schoolteaching even though it may threaten some illiberal consequences.

There is, I believe, no reason to suppose that schoolteaching will have any more difficulty in meeting the second criterion for public professions than law or public accounting. Indeed, the mechanisms whereby those professions enforce liberal integrity on their members—long and explicit socialization processes, admission-to-practice examinations, boards of professional practice, and so on—are widely regarded as plausible models for teaching.[15] What has received less attention, however, is the set of standards that those mechanisms are supposed to enforce—the standards of liberal integrity in teaching. It would be useful, then, to sketch the meaning of liberal integrity implied in the recognition of schoolteaching as a public profession.

Liberal integrity for schoolteachers, as for all other office-holders, is the carrying out of the legitimate function of their office. As we have seen, the liberal function of the office of schoolteacher is to develop students' capacities to choose and hold visions of the good in ways that prepare them to participate in and benefit from an adult society in which they themselves will enjoy the general autonomy of the liberal citizen. In other words, schoolteachers' basic duty is to enable their students to exercise the citizen's basic freedoms responsibly. These freedoms allow one to pursue one's own good in a way that also permits others to fairly pursue theirs. Therefore, to exercise these freedoms, one first needs to be one's own person—that is, to possess a strength of personality, an independence of judgment, and a degree of self-understanding that permit one to use those freedoms for one's own purposes. One thus also needs to have purposes that can reasonably be regarded as one's own. These purposes need not be invented ex nihilo, but they can and, in most cases, will be chosen freely from among those implicit in the various visions of the good available within one's civilization. For this choice to count as free, however, it must be made in light of a reasonable understanding of the range of possibilities before one. Finally, to exercise these general freedoms responsibly, one needs a sense of justice consistent with the fundamental commitments of a liberal society and regulative of one's own actions. The point of these freedoms is not to enable one to advance one's own good without regard to the costs one imposes on others but to pursue one's good within a scheme of cooperation that permits others a fair opportunity to do likewise.

Liberal integrity, therefore, commits the schoolteacher to treat students so that they become their own persons, develop their own purposes, and achieve an appropriate sense of justice. The first thing to note about these commitments is that the outcomes they specify are matters of degree. One can be more or less one's own person depending on how strong one's personality is, how penetrating and discriminating one's judgment, and how acute one's self-understanding. One's purposes can be more or less one's own depending on how broad is the range of possibilities from which they are chosen and how deep one's understanding of those possibilities. One's sense of justice can be more or less regulative of one's actions according to the extent to which one is willing to forgo the advancement of one's own good in order to treat others fairly.

Second, these commitments require that one's teaching has a content, but they do not specify precisely what that content should be. For instance, a student's independent judgment might include a command of deductive or inductive argument, esthetic discrimination and appreciation, the methods of inquiry for particular disciplines, and so on. A student's understanding of the range of possible goods available in his or her culture may or may not include specific knowledge of Roman Catholicism or automobile racing, for example. Or a student's sense of justice might consist of a commitment to Locke's natural rights or Mill's utilitarian principles or Rawls's contract theory. In short, the ethics of liberal integrity is to some extent indeterminate of the content and the level of student achievement toward which instruction should aim.

This indeterminacy might seem to mark off the legitimate sphere of autonomy of the schoolteacher. All of these alternatives of content and level for achievement apparently satisfy the general ethical requirements of liberal integrity for those who hold the public office of teacher. Since any choice a teacher might make from among those alternatives would seem to satisfy the ethics of teaching, the teacher, it might be argued, should be free to make those choices.

While this picture of teacher autonomy does agree with liberalism's general account of legitimate freedom, it is based on the false premise that liberalism is neutral as to the specific quality of judgment, range of experience, or sense of justice a teacher is to cultivate in students in the same way that it is neutral to one's aspiring to be a mountain climber or a car mechanic. But liberalism is indeterminate about these instructional matters not because in principle it does not distinguish among them but only because we are uncertain about how it should do so. It is not as if liberals do not or should not care about the judgment, experience, or sense of justice that the young acquire; rather, these are issues that have not yet been satisfactorily resolved in liberal thought.

It is, for example, a matter of some controversy whether and in what way basic good judgment includes the ability to make particular esthetic discriminations. Is the ability to distinguish the esthetic value of popular music from that of grand opera, say, a matter of general good judgment that all citizens should share or simply a matter of taste derived from various conceptions of the good to which a liberal society should be neutral? While we may not currently be able to answer such a question decisively, a liberal society is not at all neutral as to whatever may prove to be the best answer to it, for, in the long run, our ability to fulfill our obligations to develop others' capacities to choose and hold a vision of the good clearly depends on our success in finding that answer.

The real autonomy of the schoolteacher, then, cannot consist of the freedom to make these choices. Rather, it must be the freedom to prevent other adults or the public at large from imposing on the young a form of instruction that is not a plausible, if controversial, interpretation of the development of their general capacities to choose and hold views of the good. It is the freedom to protect the young from manipulation or propaganda—from those who seek to distort children's judgment by teaching them implausible and magical theories of natural causation, to impoverish their experience by depriving them of contact with significant cultural traditions within our society, or to corrupt their moral sense by promoting patently authoritarian political views.

We can now more fully understand the threat against which the professionalization of the office of schoolteacher might defend. If requiring teachers to be democratically accountable to the public will lead to these forms of distortion, impoverishment, and corruption of the young, the case for professonalization is strong. But the price that such professionalization exacts is very high. Professional autonomy over the content and quality of student achievement confers on teachers not only the freedom to rule out what is patently unjustified but also the freedom to choose from among what may or may not be justified. In other words, professionalization moves the debate over and the decision about the best interpretation of liberal commitments for instruction out of the public arena and into an officially restricted sphere. A public that has lost its opportunity to participate in these debates has been deprived of an important means of deepening its understanding of and commitment to liberalism itself. I suggest, then, that even when the dangers of democratic control of the office of schoolteacher are significant, the cost of professionalization to the society at large may still make it necessary to risk those dangers.

This discussion has also revealed schoolteaching in a liberal society to be a very special and limited form of enculturation. Such teaching clearly involves developing in students particular modes of judgment, introducing them to cultural alternatives available within our civilization, and inducting them into the political morality and conventions of a liberal society. The purpose of this enculturation, however, is to enable students to be their own persons and to live their own lives within that society; it is specifically not to promote some particular conception of the good life that the authoritarian might prescribe. In practice, liberal enculturation often weakens the student's commitment to what Bruce Ackerman describes as the child's primary culture—the family.[16]

The Case for Teaching as a Licensed Occupation or Profession. In liberal societies, licensing is a means for determining who should exercise certain risk-laden freedoms, freedoms whose exercise may impair others' pursuit of their goods, when those who bear the risks do not have the opportunity or the ability to assess them and when the risks are at least partially competence-dependent and sufficiently severe. In order to clarify the meanings of self-defeating and risk-laden freedoms, I have until now treated them independently. Nothing in these concepts, however, prevents a particular freedom from being both self-defeating and risk-laden. Thus, my argument that the freedom to teach for the purpose of developing young people's capacities to choose and hold views of the good is self-defeating leaves open the possibility that that freedom is also risk-laden and subject to licensing.

Teaching may fail in at least two ways. First, one's teaching may be ineffective; that is, a teacher may fail to develop in a student the behavior or belief at which the teacher aims. Second, one's teaching may be unsound; that is, though a teacher may succeed in developing in students the behavior or belief intended, the behavior may turn out to be inappropriate or the belief to be unwarranted. A person who has been taught ineffectively or unsoundly may be disadvantaged in his or her pursuit of the good in several ways: The student may fail to acquire the general characteristics that are fundamental to one's choosing, holding, or pursuing any view of the good; the student may adopt a view of the good that is poorly understood and, therefore, proves ultimately unsatisfactory; or the student may fail to acquire the knowledge or skill required to advance his or her view of the good. Moreover, ineffective or unsound teaching can disadvantage others who expect the student to have the knowledge or ability that the teaching is to effect. Since it appears that any act of teaching is subject to failure, and those failures can have adverse effects on individuals' pursuit of their goods, teaching seems to be inherently risk-laden.

A liberal society, however, is justified in licensing a risk-laden freedom only when, in the first place, the attendant risks to others are so severe that they must be assessed before someone exercises the freedom. I suggest that the severity of the risks of teaching varies along two dimensions—how fundamental are the consequences of the teaching for the student's pursuit of the good and how limited is the student's access to teaching that has the desired consequences. Thus, if what is to be learned is basic to having a view of the good or is central to fulfilling one's view of the good, the consequences of failed teaching are potentially severe. This potential is realized, however, only when one's other opportunities to benefit from successful teaching are limited. That is, even if someone fails to teach me something that is of central importance to my life, the risks attached to that teacher's failure are unacceptable only if I do not have other reasonable chances to learn elsewhere what I need.

This consideration implies that in liberal societies there is a general presumption against restricting the freedom to teach even though it is risk-laden, for, in doing so, a society limits the alternative opportunities available for its citizens to learn what may be central to the pursuit of their goods. This presumption may be overridden in special circumstances—specifically when, by taking advantage of one opportunity to learn what is needed, one thereby forecloses chances for other opportunities to do so . If someone's trying to teach me something results in my being unable to take advantage of others' efforts to teach me that thing, others' having the freedom to teach gives me no protection against the possibility that my teacher's teaching may fail. In other words, the presumption against restricting the freedom to teach can be overridden when that freedom is self-limiting.

We can now see that the severity criterion for licensing the freedom to teach is most likely to be met in the case of teaching the young. First, the young are learning to be their own persons—something that is fundamental to everyone's pursuit of his or her good. Second, the freedom to teach the young is likely to be self-limiting. Learning to be one's own person is—unlike learning to ride a bicycle or to make a soufflé—a long-term, perhaps even a lifelong endeavor. Substantial early failures in that learning process, while perhaps not wholly irremediable, are in practical terms often difficult to correct in adulthood. For example, the ability to read is, in our society, one of the general skills on which full adult independence most clearly rests. It is such a relatively long-term undertaking that early failure to teach a child to read imposes on him or her a chronic, if not incurable, disadvantage as an adult. Indeed, this disadvantage has been the basis of several, though generally unsuccessful, suits for educational malpractice.[17] Thus, the freedom to teach the young to be their own persons tends to be self-limiting. The importance of learning to be one's own person and the probability that early failures of teaching can seriously affect prospects for such learning imply that the risks of the freedom to teach the young for this purpose are severe enough to require their assessment before the exercise of that freedom is permitted.

Even when the harm attendant on the exercise of a risk-laden freedom is serious enough to meet the severity criterion, a society is not necessarily justified in licensing its exercise. As we have seen, giving those who bear the potential risks a realistic opportunity to assess those risks and to decide whether to allow the exercise of the freedom is, when feasible, more likely to satisfy a liberal society's commitment to facilitate its members' pursuit of their goods than is licensing. Thus, licensing must be based on the claim that such prior risk assessment is not feasible, because those who bear the risks lack either the opportunity or the ability to assess them.

Almost by definition, those who are not yet significantly their own persons lack the ability to assess and even the grounds for assessing risks of any kind. As noted, part of being one's own person includes understanding one's own aspirations, motivations, potential, and possibilities. This self-understanding is the foundation on which risk assessment is based, for the potential harms and benefits to be considered are measured against the view of one's own good. Young children are in no position to tell, for example, how seriously an adult's failure to teach them to read will interfere with their pursuit of their eventual visions of the good life. Thus, children's inability to assess the risks of someone's exercise of the freedom to teach supports the case for licensing that freedom. However, the justification for teacher licensing becomes weaker as the young become sufficiently their own persons to assess the risks of teaching against their developing sense of their own good. Thus, the ability criterion, like the severity criterion, implies that licensing the freedom to teach is age specific.

Finally, we have seen that licensing is appropriate when the risks that attach to a freedom depend on the competence with which it is exercised. Competence is relevant to teaching as a safeguard against the two types of failure that can impose risks on those who are taught—ineffectiveness and unsoundness. Teaching the young to be their own persons is likely to be unsound when the teacher lacks a reasonable understanding of what being one's own person requires—an understanding of the general capacities necessary for choosing, holding, and pursuing one's own good. Teaching is likely to be ineffective when the teacher lacks a reasonable understanding of the instructional strategies, methods, or arrangements that are likely to allow individual youths to develop the capacities necessary for being their own persons.

This liberal conception of competence in teaching the young coincides with the general expectation that the good teacher knows both his or her subject matter and how to get students to understand it, but it goes beyond that view in important ways. Soundness in teaching the young implies that what the teacher intends the students to learn will make a legitimate contribution to their becoming their own persons. Effectiveness in teaching the young implies that teachers' methods of teaching are also consistent with students' becoming their own persons. Thus, competent teaching of the young means not only that the teacher tries and succeeds in teaching subject matter that—in some narrow sense—is correct but also that the subject matter and the manner in which it is taught are consistent with the developing moral independence of students.[18] Knowing one's subject and communicating it understandably may be sufficient for competence in teaching adults whose general capacities to choose and hold a vision of the good are well developed, but they are only part of what is required for teaching the young. Here, again, is evidence that schoolteaching is a special case of teaching. In short, a liberal society that licenses the freedom to teach the young must be concerned with prospective teachers' understanding of their legitimate purposes and the nature of human development toward independence as well as with their command of subject matter and their pedagogical skill.

But even this broader formulation is somewhat misleading, because it represents the four elements of competence—ethical understanding, developmental understanding, subject matter mastery, and pedagogical skill—as being independent of one another. However, what instructional methods are considered to be effective, for instance, depends on their conduciveness to moral independence. Thus, one cannot determine whether behavior modification techniques meet the requirement for instructional effectiveness in a liberal society without knowing their consequences for the evolving moral independence of children at various ages or stages of development. Just as Lee Shulman argues that it makes little sense to conceive of pedagogical skill entirely apart from knowledge of subject matter, I suggest that it is just as inappropriate to divorce either the content or the method of teaching from its ethical purpose when one is concerned with the nature of teaching competence to be licensed in a liberal society.[19]

Conceptualizing the competence on which the successful exercise of a risk-laden freedom depends is only part of what the competence criterion for licensing requires. We must also understand competence well enough to determine reliably whether a candidate for a teaching license possesses it to an adequate degree. It strikes me that our understanding of soundness and effectiveness in teaching the young to be their own persons is in a surprisingly primitive state. I do not mean to minimize the very real advances in the quality and value of research on teaching made over the past twenty years or so. For example, we now have fairly good evidence of the relationship between certain teacher behaviors and students' scores on standardized tests.[20] Nevertheless, we still have little systematic understanding of the connection, if any, between those scores and students' moral independence. According to researchers themselves, our knowledge of the empirical effects of teachers' understanding of subject matter and their more complex behavior is limited.[21]

Our ignorance of teaching soundness and effectiveness is significantly conceptual and political, as well as empirical. For even with a reasonably complete knowledge of the relationship between teacher performance and student development, we would still need to specify what forms of development count as contributions to students' moral independence. We have already noted the controversy over the place and nature of esthetic judgment in the general intellectual capacities that all children should develop. The continuing controversy over the relative contributions of skill and content mastery to literacy is but one other indication of our lack of philosophical and political consensus on many important issues of educational content and method.[22]

Despite our collective uncertainty about teacher competence we may still have a reasonable, if incomplete, understanding of teacher incompetence. Thus, we have empirical evidence and conceptual and political agreement that a person who is grossly stupid, cruel, careless, exploitive, or mentally unstable is unable to teach the young soundly and effectively to be their own persons even though we lack a detailed understanding of the constructive qualities of teaching competence. The seriousness of the risks that the freedom to teach imposes on the young and their inability to assess those risks imply that a liberal society is justified in what might be called the negative licensing of this freedom—that is, restricting the freedom on the grounds of clear incompetence.

This consideration of the legitimate grounds for licensing the teaching of the young in a liberal society has put the issues of teacher professionalization in a perspective somewhat at odds with contemporary accounts. In agreement with those accounts, we have seen that licensure of teachers does depend on the existence of a reliable knowledge base for teaching. The requisite knowledge base includes, however, the subject matter and pedagogical techniques relevant not simply to children's learning in general but rather to their learning to be their own persons. Unfortunately, this knowledge base is at best incomplete because of the lack of pertinent empirical research and, more important, because of the limited political and conceptual agreement about the nature of moral independence. The agreement that does exist justifies a kind of negative licensing designed to exclude the incompetent. In this way, teaching the young to be their own persons is legitimately a licensed occupation.

Licensed *professions* are those occupations in which the licensing decision is appropriately reserved to qualified practitioners because ordinary citizens are unable to make those decisions even with the advice of experts. Defining and detecting incompetence in teaching are not, however, matters that can be accomplished only by those who are licensed to teach. Thus, given the current state of the knowledge base for teaching the young, there is little reason for granting professional status to that occupation. Moreover, restricting the licensing decision to practitioners at this time is likely to impede the development of the knowledge base on which the recognition of teaching as a licensed profession might eventually be justified. As I have suggested before, to close off public debate over the implications of liberal theory for instruction by removing the selection of those who are to hold the public office of schoolteacher from the sphere of democratic control is to deprive the public of the opportunity to attain rational consensus about the meaning of moral independence. To limit public participation in the licensing decision will, I suggest, have a similar effect. In the absence of a more detailed and comprehensive consensus about the nature of moral independence in a liberal society, the ideological foundation on which the knowledge base for teaching must be built is slender; without that knowledge base, the case for teaching as a licensed profession cannot succeed.

As a licensed occupation, teaching has a code of ethics analogous but not identical to those of licensed professions. Licensed professionals are obliged to practice competently. Teachers are obliged to avoid the forms of incompetence about which there is societal consensus. Beyond that, teaching competence is subject to democratic determination in a way that professional competence is not. Because the risks of teaching the young to be morally independent are neither clearly defined nor well understood, democratically accountable political authorities have a legitimate role in defining teaching practice that might be inappropriate in, for example, medicine.

Licensed professionals are obliged to inform their clients of the risks of competent practice in order to permit them to assess those risks according to their own visions of the good. Such an obligation for teachers makes little sense on two counts: The risks are not well defined, and their clients do not have a firmly established vision of the good against which the risks may be evaluated. Instead, teachers are obliged to bring to the public debate over teaching competence what is known about the effects of the various curricula and instructional techniques that may be included in the polity's evolving conception of competent practice. Teachers and the general public thus have a shared responsibility to ensure that decisions about teaching competence are informed.

Finally, licensed professionals are obliged to provide fair access to the beneficial effects of the freedoms they are permitted to exercise. In granting a restricted freedom to professionals, a liberal society gives them a potentially significant power over their fellow citizens that is not subject to democratic control—a power that to be legitimate must be governed by a liberal society's commitment to facilitating all citizens' pursuit of their goods. Teaching practice, however, should be subject to democratic control; therefore, the obligation for fair access to the benefits of competent teaching falls significantly on the public as well as on licensed practitioners.

Thus, while the principle of access to teaching may be similar to that for medicine—that no one in need should be turned away—the responsibility for meeting the requirement of that principle is shared by teachers and the public. The public can meet its part of this obligation by supporting a sufficient number of teachers; teachers can meet their part of the obligation by the fair treatment of their own students.

Teacher Autonomy: Summary and Implications

Contemporary discussions of teaching almost without exception speak of the need for enhanced teacher autonomy. The freedom sought is not simply that of the ordinary citizen, important as that may be. It is, rather, a special sort of freedom in teaching for which some but not all citizens may qualify. In a society committed to facilitating its members' pursuit of their visions of the good, no matter what they may be, the claim that some but not all citizens should enjoy a particular freedom must be carefully justified. I have argued that the freedom to teach the young to be their own persons may legitimately be restricted in such a society because it is both self-defeating and risk-laden. Because this freedom is self-defeating, it may be restricted to those who hold the public office of schoolteacher, and because it is risk-laden (and for other specified reasons), holding that office may legitimately be limited to the qualified members of the licensed occupation of teaching.

The full professionalization of teaching the young either as a public office or as a licensed practice is not, however, justified. An office or a practice is professionalized when the selection of office-holders or the making of licensing decisions is accomplished by the members of the profession themselves, rather than by those who are directly or indirectly accountable to the citizens of a democratic polity. There is not, in the first place, a sufficient difference between what the public expects and what it has a right to expect (as there may be in law, for example) to justify professionalizing the selection of those who hold the office of schoolteacher. Nor is the knowledge base of teaching competence secure enough empirically, conceptually, or politically to justify the professionalization of teacher licensure. Indeed, professionalization of either selection or licensing is

likely to stifle the public debate on which depends the public's
understanding of what it has a right to expect and that may one day
lead to the conceptual clarity and political consensus necessary to
justify professional licensure. At least for the immediate future,
teaching the young to be their own persons is neither a public nor a
licensed profession.

Those who teach the young to be morally independent deserve a degree of restricted autonomy, although not the fully self-
regulating autonomy of the professions. Like all forms of autonomy, the autonomy of schoolteachers includes both freedom and
responsibility. The basic freedom, of course, is that of instructing
the young when parents no longer have an exclusive right to do so
and all members of the general public do not yet have that right.
Teachers' basic responsibility is to achieve the morally legitimate
purpose of their office—to develop children's capacities to choose,
hold, and pursue their own visions of the good. Liberal integrity
requires teachers, first, to develop in children the characteristics,
abilities, and understandings that the democratic polity determines
to be necessary for their moral independence and, second, to resist
the polity's directives that cannot plausibly be construed as relevant
to this central liberal purpose of education.

Not only as holders of public office but also as members of a
licensed occupation, teachers have a responsibility to practice competently. That responsibility lies, in part, in avoiding the forms of
incompetence about which there is general consensus. In addition,
teachers are responsible for adhering to the evolving standards of
competence determined by political majorities as the public debate
over the meaning of moral independence continues. That debate
has implications for both what should be taught and how instruction should be conducted.

Teachers also have an important role and responsibility in
the public determination of competence in teaching. Soundness and
effectiveness in teaching have empirical as well as conceptual and
political dimensions. Through their experience and education,
teachers have access to the empirical knowledge necessary to the
public's making informed decisions about competence. As a result,
teachers have a responsibility to make that empirical knowledge
available to the public just as the public has a responsibility to seek

out and utilize that knowledge in its deliberations. Here, too, teachers and members of the democratic polity have mutual and interlocking responsibilities for informed decision making.

Finally, teachers and the public have a shared responsibility for providing children with fair access to the opportunities to develop the capacities necessary to be their own persons. The public's part of this responsibility lies in providing an adequate quantity of and structured access to appropriate teaching. The role of teachers in meeting this responsibility lies in the fair treatment of their students.

Teacher autonomy in a liberal society consists, in sum, of the freedom to teach the young to be their own persons in accordance with the principles of integrity, competent practice, informed decision making, and fair access. The ethical responsibilities implied by these principles are shared by teachers and the members of the democratic polity. In this light, the reform of teaching must be seen as the search for institutional arrangements most likely to ensure that these shared responsibilities are fulfilled. In the remainder of this chapter, I consider the implications of this account of the moral nature of schoolteaching for three widely discussed aspects of the institutions that govern its practice—admission to practice, teacher education, and the structure and organization of schools.

Admission to Practice. In being admitted to practice as a schoolteacher, one becomes both a public officeholder and a member of a licensed occupation. In designing an institutional mechanism for determining who may hold that office and practice that occupation, three questions must be confronted: Who should be required to be admitted to practice, who should make that judgment, and on what grounds should the judgment be made?

In the liberal tradition I have described, the answer in principle to the first question is straightforward—absolutely everyone permitted to exercise the freedom to develop the young's capacities for moral independence, once the primary foundation for such development has been laid by parents, should be admitted to the practice of schoolteaching, whether they are public or private schoolteachers or parents engaged in home instruction. A liberal society owes its children the chance to acquire the forms of judgment, the breadth of experience, and the understanding of the citizen's obligation to treat others justly on which moral independence in that society depends. Thus, whoever has the responsibility for children's educational development toward moral independence beyond the period of primary enculturation by parents must be able to meet those obligations.

At present, most states do not require private schoolteachers to be licensed, and few view their procedures for evaluating parents' requests for home instruction as a form of teacher licensure (although most count a parent's being appropriately certified as supporting such a request).[23] Often these policies are represented as a necessary response to parents' rights to choose a private school or to rear their children as their conscience dictates. In a liberal society, parents, like all citizens have the fundamental right to pursue their own visions of the good, whatever they happen to be. But this right carries with it the responsibility not to pursue one's good in a way that prevents others from doing likewise. In principle, then, parents have no more right to hinder or distort their own child's development toward moral independence than they have to do so for any other child.

To be sure, there may be a number of practical, legal, and even moral difficulties in putting this principle of universal licensure of schoolteachers into practice. It may, for instance, be expensive to evaluate all parents' requests for home instruction in the way required, and the licensing of private schoolteachers might involve an unconstitutional entanglement of church and state. Nevertheless, the obligation to license all schoolteachers to every extent practical is clear.

The answer to the second question—Who should admit schoolteachers to practice?—is equally straightforward. My arguments against the professionalization of teaching imply that licensing decisions should be delegated neither to teachers themselves nor to any other body not effectively accountable to the public. The active public consideration of the meaning of moral independence and its implications for soundness and effectiveness in teaching is at present an important stimulus to the public commitment to and understanding of liberalism. Thus, the public should be involved in licensing decisions even though considerations of efficiency may require the use of a publicly accountable agency for this purpose. As a result, current proposals for national or state licensing authorities that are insulated from the political process are, although perhaps superficially attractive, morally unjustifiable.[24]

The relatively easy answers I have proposed for the first two questions about admission to practice make answering the third question—On what basis should licensing decisions be made?—harder than it may seem. It has been generally supposed, especially in recent discussions of raising teacher certification standards, that the public has a right to establish whatever requirements for admission to practice it wants and thinks it can afford. This supposition is based on a confusion between licensing standards and employment requirements.

Most schoolteachers teach in public schools, and in most states only they must be licensed by the state. Thus, when the public wants to change the character of the public schoolteaching corps, it is natural to seek to do so by changing licensing requirements. But a license should, as I have argued, be required of any schoolteacher, public or private. Thus, licensing standards are conceptually different from the requirements for employment in public schools; they are the minimum qualifications that apply to anyone who wishes to teach children. Licensing applies to those qualifications that are widely accepted as necessary for promoting children's moral independence. If a political majority wishes to establish additional requirements for employment in public schools, it may establish higher minimum job qualifications. Requiring independent national or state board certification, then, might be one way to impose these higher qualifications for employment in public schools.

There are also good reasons not to adopt such independent certification as a mandatory, statewide public school employment requirement. First, the uniform adoption of such requirements will significantly foreclose healthy local debate about soundness and effectiveness in teaching. Second, as we have already noted, soundness and effectiveness are qualities about which there is much conceptual, political, and empirical uncertainty. In general, uniformity is a poor response to uncertainty. When, for example, we do not understand the cause of a particular kind of cancer, it is important to have a corps of researchers working on the problem from a variety of different theoretical perspectives. It would be foolish to constrain all researchers to use the same approach even if at the moment one approach seems more promising than others. It would be equally foolish to adopt one detailed and uniform conception of teaching competence in the teeth of our current uncertainty about teaching soundness and effectiveness in a liberal society, for to do so would be to limit our prospects for clarifying and dispelling that uncertainty in the long run. Therefore, while the public has a right to determine the qualifications of its employees, it would be unwise to adopt at the state level (and certainly at the national level) uniform employment qualifications that significantly exceed minimum licensing standards.

What, then, should those licensing standards be? Because the precise content of those standards is to be the prerogative of political authorities, I can do no more than indicate the general categories to be covered by such standards and the questions that those authorities should ask themselves as they seek to establish the standards.

Because schoolteaching is a public office, the minimum qualifications for admission to practice include an understanding of, a commitment to, and a disposition to meet the moral responsibilities of office. The primary duty of liberal integrity requires that schoolteachers recognize as the basic purpose of teaching the development of children's capacities for moral independence. That duty implies, on the one hand, an ability to recognize and resist clearly illiberal expectations that may be imposed by school authorities and, on the other, the ability and willingness to carry out the legitimate expectations of the public in a way that is consistent with the principles of competent practice, informed consent, and fair distribution. Admission to practice should not be taken as an opportunity to impose on teachers a narrow political orthodoxy. However, licensing authorities must seek to exclude those whose practice is not guided by the most basic moral commitments of a liberal society.

Furthermore, in the discussion of schoolteaching as a risk-laden freedom, we found that the negative licensure of teachers is justified in order to ensure that children's development will not be impaired by clearly identifiable teaching incompetence. This perspective on licensing is another reminder that the task of licensing authorities is to establish minimum and not what they believe to be optimum qualifications. As noted, teaching competence consists in an understanding of the purposes of teaching, subject matter, instructional strategies, and children's development toward moral independence. The question that licensing authorities should ask themselves is, thus, at what point a candidate's understanding of these matters is so defective as to pose a clear threat to children's psychological, intellectual, and moral development. This approach permits age- and subject-specific licensing and constrains licensing authorities from setting inappropriate standards. Thus, even if such authorities were convinced that elementary teachers with a command of calculus would have a marginally salutary effect on children's mathematical achievement, they would be unjustified in establishing an understanding of calculus as a minimum requirement for the elementary schoolteaching license even if they believe that an adequate supply of such teachers is available. Licensing, once again, aims not at the maximization of children's achievement but at their protection against incompetence.

Teacher Education. Over the past twenty-five years, the relationship between state licensing authorities and university teacher education programs has changed dramatically.[25] Today, most states will certify any graduate of a teacher education program that has been approved by the state, although an increasing number of states are now requiring program graduates to pass paper-and-pencil tests as well. The approval of these university programs entails significant state regulation of the content and processes of teacher education. Some of the current reform proposals in education seek even more systematic control of teacher education by state or national accrediting agencies.[26] Our discussion of teacher licensing calls into question many of these current practices and reform efforts, for, as now practiced, program approval tends to establish standards for licensing far in excess of those justified minimums just considered. As a result, program approval produces a kind of uniformity in the available teaching corps that I have argued is not only morally unjustified but also pragmatically unwise.

Program approval is not inherently inconsistent with legitimate licensing. Indeed, much of what licensing authorities have a need to know about a candidate's character, beliefs, and abilities can best be ascertained by program faculty that over a significant period of time have observed the candidate's academic abilities, interactions with children, and pedagogical practice. Thus, the testimony of program faculties is often the most reliable evidence that candidates have an appropriate understanding of the moral purpose of teaching and that, in the context of teaching, they do not evince those forms of incompetence that threaten children's development. However, program standards, either as written by approval authorities or as enforced by visiting approval teams, often require candidates to understand subject matter in a particular way, to utilize particular instructional techniques, or to adhere to a detailed "philosophy of teaching." Indeed, in the plethora of specific program requirements, some of the public's most fundamental licensing concerns are ignored or traded off for other, less central matters. As a result, program approval standards should focus directly on legitimate licensing concerns—candidates' clear understanding of the moral purpose and responsibilities of teaching and the detection of incompetence—and should leave other matters to program faculties and administrators.

The purpose of this discretion is not, however, to grant to universities the final authority to determine the nature of teaching in a liberal society but to permit them to respond and contribute to the diversity of such conceptions that the public debate about teaching competence generates in public and private schools. Schools do have some effect on program design as a result of their role in the student-teaching component of preparation programs and their decisions to hire program graduates. This effect is probably too indirect to keep universities in vital contact with the public debate about teaching. Therefore, program approval should also require the systematic involvement of school officials and teachers in the design and modification of program curricula and the involvement of university faculty members in schools' efforts to confront and resolve the educational problems they face. The purpose of this mutual involvement is not to turn teacher education over to the schools or the operation of the schools over to the universities. Rather, it is to open a line of communication between the public, whose deliberations about schools are crucial to the development and definition of liberally justified education, and university faculty members, who can contribute to those deliberations and whose task is to educate teachers who can play an intelligent and morally legitimate role in the schools.

These changes in the program approval standards would require teacher education programs to be similar in some ways but would encourage them to be diverse in many others. All programs would lay a common foundation for prospective teachers' conception of their moral role in society—the freedoms they will be granted, the purpose of those freedoms, and their consequent moral responsibilities—and all would screen candidates for incompetence. But outside of these commonalities, prospective teachers' specific understanding of subject matter, the pedagogical approaches and skills they have mastered, their detailed conceptions of moral independence, and their understanding of children's development toward independence may legitimately take a wide variety of forms. Through meaningful involvement with schools, these aspects of program content will be shaped by the educational alternatives to which vital public debate over schooling may lead.

Structure and Organization of Schools. The discussion of teacher licensing and education has assumed the existence of widespread public debate about and involvement in schools and active educational experimentation by schools. Neither assumption seems especially descriptive of the current situation. At least one important reason for this lack of involvement and diversity is the tight administrative control over schools exercised by districts and, to an increasing extent, by states. Such control means that public debate is restricted largely to the district and state levels and that the opportunity for school-level experimentation is severely curtailed.[27] I submit that the moral purposes and responsibilities of teaching in a liberal society imply that much of the authority over schooling should at present be decentralized to the school level.

School-based management has become a popular element in contemporary school reform. The meaning and especially the justification of this reform vary considerably. Some argue that such decentralization of school authority will return to parents their legitimate right to control their own children's education.[28] Others claim that school-based management will allow teachers to practice in a fully professional manner.[29] Neither of these justifications is consistent with political liberalism, for schoolteaching in a liberal society is justified precisely because, once children reach a sufficient level of development, parents no longer have an exclusive right to control their education. As we have seen, teachers in a liberal society are not justified in exercising fully professional autonomy. Therefore, decentralization of school authority must be justified on other grounds, and, as a result, it will take a form somewhat different from what others may have in mind.

The moral responsibilities that attach to schoolteaching are shared by the public and teachers. However, the current highly centralized system of school control militates against the direct acknowledgment and sharing of these responsibilities by teachers and members of the public. First, the bureaucratic distance between state and local boards of education, on the one hand, and schools and teachers, on the other, diminishes teachers' awareness and understanding of the public's expectations. To be sure, boards' decisions do trickle down to schools in the form of directives and regulations, but the purposes of those policies are often obscure, and teachers rarely have a full sense of the issues and the debate that stimulated their adoption. Second, centralized control systems diminish and discourage broad participation in the debate about school policy by reducing the number of channels available for meaningful public discussion and placing them at a psychologically forbidding or geographically inconvenient distance from most members of the public. As a result, few citizens have direct opportunities to formulate and express their own expectations and to confront those of others.

Decentralizing decision-making authority to school-level boards of education is one way to overcome these problems. The point of decentralizing is to permit members of the public and teachers to undertake in a meaningful way their shared moral responsibilities for schooling in a liberal society. The direct assumption of these responsibilities will deepen teachers' and the public's understanding of and commitment to the legitimate moral purposes of schooling. The diversity of approaches to achieving those purposes taken in various schools can serve as a social laboratory for clarifying the meaning of moral independence for children and improving our understanding of how to promote it in schools.

These comments on teacher licensing, teaching education, and school organization are indications of the general directions in which our common political heritage should take us in the reshaping of our schooling system. Obviously, a wide variety of practical and moral questions still need to be addressed: How can we ensure a fair distribution of educational resources in a decentralized system? How can we enable teachers to fulfill their moral obligation to resist illiberal public expectations? These are serious and difficult questions for which I offer no clear answers in this chapter. I hope, however, that I have succeeded in clarifying the kinds of questions we need to consider as we attempt to fashion the schools that our children deserve.

Notes

1. Teacher autonomy is, to a greater or lesser extent, important in most of the recent reports on teaching, but especially in the Holmes Group, *Tomorrow's Teachers* (East Lansing, Mich.: Holmes Group, 1986); Carnegie Task Force on Teaching as a Profession, *A Nation Prepared: Schools for the 21st Century* (New York: Carnegie Forum on Education and the Economy, 1986).

2. H. Mann, *The Republic and the School* (L. Cremin, ed.) (New York: Teachers College Press, 1957), p. 30.

3. J. Dewey, *Democracy and Education* (New York: Free Press, 1966), pp. 23–53.

4. J. Locke, *Two Treatises of Government*, rev. ed. (New York: New American Library, 1965).

5. T. Jefferson, "Declaration of Independence," in A. Koch and W. Peden (eds.), *The Life and Selected Writings of Thomas Jefferson* (New York: Modern Library, 1944), pp. 22–28.

6. Political liberalism should not be confused with the liberalism that is contrasted with conservatism in contemporary American politics. Indeed, most aspects of what is encompassed by both liberalism and conservatism in the United States are simply alternative interpretations of political liberalism.

7. This treatment of the basis of liberalism is adapted from R.

Dworkin, "Liberalism," in S. Hampshire (ed.), *Public and Private Morality* (Cambridge, England: Cambridge University Press, 1978), pp. 113–143.

8. Several philosophers have recently articulated persuasive, if different, defenses of political liberalism, including J. Rawls, *A Theory of Justice* (Cambridge, Mass.: Harvard University Press, 1971); R. Dworkin, *Taking Rights Seriously* (Cambridge, Mass.: Harvard University Press, 1977); and B. Ackerman, *Social Justice and the Liberal State* (New Haven, Conn.: Yale University Press, 1980).

9. Liberal theorists who have advanced various versions of this argument include Thomas Hobbes in *Leviathan* (New York: Bobbs-Merrill, 1958); John Locke in *Two Treatises of Government;* and, more recently, Robert Nozick in *Anarchy, State, and Utopia* (New York: Basic Books, 1975).

10. This argument was formally presented by Paul Samuelson in "The Pure Theory of Public Expenditure," *Review of Economics and Statistics*, Nov. 1954, *36*, 387–390, and developed further by Mancur Olson in *The Logic of Collective Action* (Cambridge, Mass.: Harvard University Press, 1965).

11. I owe this phrase to Pat Stone.

12. R. Dworkin, *Law's Empire* (Cambridge, Mass.: Harvard University Press, 1986), particularly pp. 164–167.

13. The argument here closely follows Ackerman, *Social Justice in the Liberal State*, pp. 139–167.

14. Rawls, *A Theory of Justice*, p. 454.

15. For example, Carnegie Task Force on Teaching as a Profession, *A Nation Prepared*, pp. 63–78.

16. Ackerman, *Social Justice in the Liberal State*, pp. 140–143.

17. For example, *Peter W.* v. *San Francisco Unified School District*, 131 Cal. Rptr. 854 (1976), and *Donohue* v. *Copaique Union Free School District*, 410 N.Y.S.2d 99 (1978).

18. Compare R. S. Peters, *Ethics and Education* (London: Allen & Unwin, 1966), pp. 24–45; and I. Scheffler, "Philosophical Models of Teaching," in I. Scheffler, *Reason and Teaching* (New York: Bobbs-Merrill, 1973), pp. 67–81.

19. L. Shulman, "Those Who Understand: Knowledge Growth in Teaching," *Educational Researcher*, 1986, *15* (2), 4–14.

20. J. Brophy and T. Good, "Teacher Behavior and Student Achievement," in M. C. Wittrock (ed.), *Handbook of Research on Teaching,* 3rd ed. (New York: Macmillan, 1986), pp. 328–375.

21. For example, L. Shulman, "Knowledge and Teaching: Foundations of the New Reform," *Harvard Education Review,* 1987, *57* (1), 1–22; D. Berliner, "In Pursuit of the Expert Pedagogue," *Educational Research,* 1986, *15* (7), 5–13.

22. E. D. Hirsch, Jr., *Cultural Literacy: What Every American Should Know* (Boston: Houghton Mifflin, 1987).

23. M. Yudof, D. Kirp, T. van Geel, and B. Levin, *Educational Policy and the Law,* 2nd ed. (Berkeley, Calif.: McCutchan, 1982), pp. 46, 52–60.

24. The states of Oregon and California seem to come closest to having a licensure system of this independent type. N. L. Zimpher, "Certification and Teacher Licensing," in M. J. Dunkin (ed.), *International Encyclopaedia of Teaching and Teacher Education* (Elmsford, N.Y.: Pergamon Press, 1987), p. 659. The nation's governors are sympathetic to national board certification as proposed by the Carnegie Task Force on Teaching as a Profession, *A Nation Prepared.* See National Governors' Association, *Time for Results: The Governors' 1991 Report on Education* (Washington, D.C.: National Governors' Association, 1986), p. 40.

25. J. M. Cronin, "State Regulation of Teacher Preparation," in L. Shulman and G. Sykes (eds.), *Handbook of Teaching and Policy* (New York: Longman, 1983), pp. 171–191.

26. Cronin, "State Regulation of Teacher Preparation."

27. A. E. Wise, *Legislated Learning: The Bureaucratization of the American Classroom* (Berkeley: University of California Press, 1979).

28. B. Bull, "Liberty and the New Localism," *Educational Theory,* 1984, *34* (1), pp. 75–94.

29. Carnegie Task Force on Teaching as a Profession, *A Nation Prepared,* pp. 57–63.

4

Some Moral Considerations on Teaching as a Profession

Gary D Fenstermacher

One month before he left office, Chester Finn, who served in the closing years of the Reagan administration as assistant secretary for educational research and improvement, was interviewed about his accomplishments and his views of the current state of American education. No less direct and candid than his boss, Secretary of Education William Bennett, Finn made an interesting observation about the road ahead:

> Well, the big tussle now is going to be over who is in charge. Five years ago, something remarkable happened. . . . Governors and legislators and business leaders began to make the big decisions about what was going to happen in American education. . . . But what is happening is that the profession is fighting back and trying to retrieve control, and it is doing so under the heading of professionalization and decentralization and autonomy and school site management, and I think it's a very sophisticated campaign by the profession to put itself back in the driver's seat. It carries with it the suggestion that the lay policy makers should butt out. And I think that would be a horrendous blunder for this country.[1]

There is something of a war going on over control of the occupation of teaching. As Finn describes it, the teaching profession

itself is on one side, while policymakers, particularly state legislators and governors, are on the other side. As one examines the battles that have occurred in the last few years, an uneasy feeling begins
to emerge. It may be best if neither side wins this war, for neither
side appears to have a morally grounded sense of the meaning of
teaching.

As the teaching profession confronts the policymakers, the
discussion often centers on the so-called knowledge base for teaching. Teachers argue that good teaching requires complex and sophisticated skills, built on a knowledge base that has undergone an
enormous expansion in the last fifteen years.[2] Lawmakers respond
that the dollars expended on education are inadequately justified by
the results. Too few students, they argue, have the requisite skills
and values for productive work and citizenship. The teachers do not
deny the lawmakers' description of the problem, but they decry the
proposed solutions. More testing, more accountability, and more
standardization, say the teachers, will not produce the results that
lawmakers seek. Rather than more rules, laws, and data analyses,
teachers claim that they need more support, more autonomy, better
working conditions, and more opportunity to use the professional
knowledge available to them.

In the midst of these claims and counterclaims, very little is
heard about the fundamental purposes of teaching. It is as if that
matter were somehow settled or obvious, and now the issue is
simply what means are needed to achieve the obvious ends. Yet, as
one looks closely at the rhetoric in the debate, one sees that it is not
about the enlightenment of the young, the emancipation of the
mind and soul, or the development of human virtue. The rhetoric is
about the status and prestige of teachers in society, about the testing
of teachers and learners, about models for career advancement,
about measuring competence and effectiveness, and about restructuring schools in ways that "optimize" performance and results.

Much of this rhetoric is found in what might be called the
"professionalization literature" in teaching.[3] This literature encom-
passes arguments and exhortations intended to resolve the issue of
whether teaching is a trade, a craft, or a true profession. That part of
the literature favoring professional status for teaching describes
how the occupation of teaching can be developed as a profession. As

one examines this literature, it does not take long to discover that it is nearly devoid of talk about the moral nature of teaching, the moral duties and obligations of teachers, and the profound importance of teachers to the moral development of students. It is as if the moral dimensions of teaching were lost, forgotten about, or—to put the best possible light on the matter—simply taken for granted.

How can that be? How is it possible to define or stipulate the occupational nature of teaching without reference to the moral nature of the enterprise? Imagine law with its grand principles of jurisprudence, its cases and precedents, but without its canons of legal practice. Imagine medicine with its extraordinary knowledge base but without its Hippocratic oath. It seems nearly impossible to imagine the field of medicine without a profound moral commitment to relief from pain and suffering and the preservation of life. If the moral ends of medicine were stripped away, the value and uses of what remains would be most difficult to ascertain. There would be medical tools and technologies, physicians with skills, and a knowledge base. But for what purpose? Of what value would the knowledge and skill of the physician be without any moral commitment to relieve suffering and preserve life?

In the same way, how is it possible to conceive of teaching disconnected from its moral underpinnings? Like medicine, teaching is a form of skilled practice, and also like medicine, teaching becomes nearly incomprehensible when disconnected from its fundamental moral purposes.[4] These purposes are rooted in the moral development of the young. Children do not enter the world compassionate, caring, fair, loving, and tolerant. Nor do these qualities emerge in due course like hair on the body or hormones in the endocrine system. Rather, moral qualities are learned—acquired in the course of lived experience. If there are no models for them, no obvious or even subtle pressure to adopt moral qualities, no hints, no homilies, no maxims, and no opportunity to imitate moral action, the moral virtues may be missed, perhaps never to be acquired.

The rhetoric of the professionalization of teaching is grounded primarily in the knowledge base of teaching, not the moral base. Therefore, it is a rhetoric that clusters around notions pertinent to knowledge, such as expertise, skill, competence, objectivity, validity, and assessment. Yet, as we have seen, these are not the concepts that capture the essential meaning of teaching. Without the specification of the moral principles and purposes of teaching, the concept amounts to little more than a technical performance to no particular point. Just as a physician who has no idea of why or to what end he or she practices medicine or a lawyer who lacks any sense of the rule of law in the just society, a teacher without moral purpose is aimless, as open to incivility and harm as to good.

Teaching as a Moral Activity

Although it should require no defense to establish that teaching is a highly moral undertaking, the present controversy over the next stage in the evolution of the teaching occupation clearly shows that the moral dimensions of teaching are often ignored or forgotten.[5] What makes teaching a moral endeavor is that it is, quite centrally, human action undertaken in regard to other human beings. Thus, matters of what is fair, right, just, and virtuous are always present. Whenever a teacher asks a student to share something with another student, decides between combatants in a schoolyard dispute, sets procedures for who will go first, second, third, and so on, or discusses the welfare of a student with another teacher, moral considerations are present. The teacher's conduct, at all times and in all ways, is a moral matter. For that reason alone, teaching is a profoundly moral activity.

This observation that there are moral qualities to a teacher's actions would amount to little more than a platitude if it were not for the fact that the morality of the teacher may have a considerable impact on the morality of the student. The teacher is a model for the students, such that the particular and concrete meaning of such traits as honesty, fair play, consideration of others, tolerance, and sharing are "picked up," as it were, by observing, imitating, and discussing what teachers do in classrooms. This point has seldom been made better than by Gilbert Ryle, in his classic article "Can Virtue Be Taught?":

> What will help to make us self-controlled, fair-minded
> or hard-working are good examples set by others, and

then ourselves practising and failing, and practising
again, and failing again, but not quite so soon and so
on. In matters of morals, as in the skills and arts, we
learn first by being shown by others, then by being
trained by others, naturally with some worded homily,
praise and rebuke, and lastly by being trained by
ourselves.[6]

There are several different ways teachers serve as both moral
agents and moral educators. They can be quite directive, teaching
morality outright—a form of instruction often called didactic instruction. When it becomes heavy-handed or highly ideological, it is
often considered indoctrination. Rather than specific instruction in
morality, teachers can teach *about* morality, as might be the case in
courses on world religions, philosophy, civics, or sex education. A
third way to undertake moral education is to act morally, holding
oneself up as a possible model—at first a model to be imitated, later
a model that will be influential in guiding the conduct of one's
students.

The first two forms of moral education are generally well
known and much discussed. Depending on the teacher and the content, these two forms of moral education can be powerful influences
on certain children at certain times in their development. Neither of
the first two forms, however, has the potential to shape and influence student conduct in such educationally productive ways as the
third form. Here the teacher acts justly while assisting and expect-
ing just conduct from students; the teacher shows compassion and
caring, seeking these traits from his or her students; the teacher
models tolerance while showing students how to be tolerant. Nearly
everything that a teacher does while in contact with students carries
moral weight. Every response to a question, every assignment
handed out, every discussion on issues, every resolution of a dispute,
every grade given to a student carries with it the moral character of
the teacher. This moral character can be thought of as the *manner* of
the teacher.

Manner is an accompaniment to everything teachers do in
their classrooms. Chemistry can be taught in myriad ways, but however it is taught, the teacher will always be giving directions, ex-

plaining, demonstrating, checking, adjudicating, motivating, reprimanding, and in all these activities displaying the manner that marks him or her as morally well developed or not. Teachers who understand their impact as moral educators take their manner quite seriously. They understand that they cannot expect honesty without being honest or generosity without being generous or diligence without themselves being diligent. Just as we understand that teachers must engage in critical thinking with students if they expect students to think critically in their presence, they must exemplify moral principles and virtues in order to elicit them from students. Indeed, there is more to this third form of moral education than merely exemplifying moral principles. Teachers must also, as Ryle states, draw attention to what they are doing and why, hold it up for the students to see and understand, and, by suggestion and demeanor, call on the students to follow along. There must then be support for those students who try to model the teacher and some sense of safety for those who are not yet ready to do so.

Just as teachers possess a manner that defines the moral character of their teaching, so learners have a manner that identifies their moral development. The manner of the learner is within and without school; while within school, it is encouraged through engagement with the teacher and the subject matter. Teaching is a moral activity not simply because teachers exercise authority and control over those in their care. Perhaps more important, it is a moral activity because teachers have a specific responsibility for the proper and appropriate moral development of their students. If the students are to develop in morally appropriate ways, they too must experience a degree of autonomy in their work. They too must be given the latitude and flexibility to try actions based on new or different ideas, to assess the consequences of these actions, to ponder the goodness and rightness of what they are doing or contemplate doing, and to jointly reflect on their thought and action in concert with other students and teachers.

Thus, the teacher as moral educator is conscious of his or her manner, expanding and acting critically on it, striving whenever and wherever possible to be a more moral person and a better moral educator. Teachers' manners as moral persons are as vital to their work as teachers as their mastery of the subjects they teach and their skill as instructors in the classroom. Yet one seldom hears about improving one's moral actions, one's manner, in the furor over who will gain hegemony over the occupation of teaching. Instead, much is heard of the parallels between knowledge development in medicine, for example, and knowledge development in teaching, leading many to believe in parallels between the professionalization of medicine and law as occupations and the professionalization of teaching. There are dangers in these parallels, dangers for maintaining any sense of teaching as a moral endeavor.

Professionalizing Teaching

There are at least three important differences between the practice of teaching and the ways that law and medicine are typically practiced. These differences are (1) the mystification of knowledge, (2) social distance, and (3) reciprocity of effort.[7] Each of these will be described in turn.

One of the ways that physicians have succeeded in garnering the status and income they presently enjoy is to "lock up" or mystify their knowledge. Until quite recently, it was extremely difficult to receive any diagnostic instruction from a physician. For example, diagnosing an earache or elevated blood pressure is not a difficult process. However, for the longest time, the medical profession insisted that only a doctor could use an otoscope or sphygmomanometer properly. Physicians saw themselves not as giving their knowledge to the patient but rather as being responsible for making the patient well. Teaching, at least what most of us would regard as good teaching, requires that the teacher give his or her knowledge away to the learner—both knowledge of the subject under study and knowledge of how to learn that subject. Eventually, the good teacher must also give most of his or her knowledge of teaching away to learners, in the hopes that they will learn to be teachers of themselves.

The second difference between the practice of medicine and law and the practice of teaching is the nature of social distance. Physicians seem to delight in introducing themselves as "Dr. So-and-so." In their time with patients, they frequently confine themselves to the specific ailments described by the patient. In order to meet the demands for their services or of their preferred life-styles, they may have three or four patients in different waiting rooms at one time. For what they regard as good professional reasons, they typically do not get close to the broader lives of their patients. Lawyers may be a bit less distant, depending on whether they are attempting to absolve the client of a crime or planning a tax and estate program, although they, too, are inclined by their rules of practice and by preference to remain as remote as possible from the parts of their clients' lives that are not pertinent to the business at hand.

Teachers may also at times wish for social distance from the complex, tangled, and sometimes destructive lives of their students, but they cannot both teach well and ignore the many dimensions of the lives of their students. Teaching well requires as broad and deep an understanding of the learner as possible, a concern for how what is taught relates to the life experience of the learner, and a willingness to engage the learner in the context of the learner's own intentions, interests, and desires. Social distance of the variety favored by many physicians inhibits the capacity of teachers to do their job well. If teachers were to think of themselves professionally, as many physicians and lawyers think of themselves professionally, they would be ill-served by adopting the same concept of social distance that characterizes much of the practice of law and medicine.

Finally, there is the matter of reciprocity of effort. A visit to a physician often ends with "You have bumbumitis. Fill this prescription and take one tablet three times a day." There is nothing else for you to do but take the pills. The surgeon says, "You have rottennottis. Let's schedule surgery for next month. Don't eat or drink for twenty-four hours before that." You have nothing to do; as a matter of fact, you are going to be sound asleep when the surgeon does the cutting. The lawyer visits the jail to talk to the client. "Don't say anything to anybody," she says. "I'll handle everything. The only person you need to talk to is me." Once again, you are completely in the hands of the professional. There is little for you to do but trust her judgment and skill.

Not so with teaching. The point of teaching is student learning. In order to learn, students must expend effort; they must work. A reciprocity of effort is required, with the teacher doing certain things and stipulating that the students must also do certain things, be it drill and practice, extended reading, analytical essays, or workbook assignments. The teacher cannot accomplish this task by giving pills, putting the learner in some sort of trance, or telling the learner not to talk to anyone.

There has been something of decline in the notion of reciprocity of effort in teaching and learning over the last decade. It may be explained by the increasing presence of teacher accountability, wherein we hold the teacher accountable for what the student learns without examining the level and quality of effort expended by the student. There is a saying that when a European reader does not understand a book, he or she accepts the blame as the reader; when an American reader does not understand a book, it is the author who is blamed. This saying seems to describe the state of teaching in America today: When the learner does not learn, it is the teacher who is responsible. Such a condemnation misses the critical importance of reciprocity of effort, wherein the learner who expends no effort in learning must accept a major share of responsibility for the failure to learn.

These three features—mystification of knowledge, social distance, and reciprocity of effort—are critically important differences between medicine and law, on the one hand, and teaching, on the other. (Other critical differences are argued by Soder in Chapter Two.) If those who argue for the professionalization of teaching have medicine and law as models for the transformation, serious difficulties for teaching lie ahead. The capacity of the teacher for moral development is seriously impaired by the kind of professionalization that is so rooted in expertise and skilled practice that it increases the distance between teacher and student, hides needed knowledge from the student, and places the student in the role of passive recipient of skilled treatment.

The Professional as Expert

Perhaps in part because of the fascination with medicine and law, much of the discussion about professionalizing teaching is rooted in systemic reforms, such as requiring advanced degrees for promotion to higher career levels, developing a national certification examination for advanced teachers, installing elaborate testing programs designed to assess both students and teachers, and revising the standards for initial teacher preparation. These proposals aim at capitalizing on knowledge and skills by ensuring that those trained as teachers are truly experts in their field.

As mentioned earlier, many of the arguments on behalf of professionalizing teaching rest on the emergence of what is called a knowledge base for the field. This base is the result of nearly twenty years of intensive, high-quality research on teaching. Although there has been considerable debate over the validity and power of the various methods for studying teaching, the field itself has benefited greatly from the results of many different kinds of studies and from attempts to synthesize these results into a series of incisive, illuminating, and generally quite effective understandings about teaching. There can be little doubt that much progress has been made in the last two decades. However, in the desire to celebrate this remarkable epistemic accomplishment, we may too easily lose sight of the fact that teaching is defined not by the technical skills of its practitioners but by the educative intentions and moral purpose with which they undertake their work. Thus, the knowledge base helps teachers teach more effectively than they could before, but it does not clarify what it is that teachers ought to teach or at what purposes this improved teaching is aimed.

One way to gain perspective on the matter of expertise is to consider modern aviation. Thirty to forty years ago, much of what is known as general (that is, not commercial or military) aviation was a matter of skill with stick and rudder, dead-reckoning navigation, and carefully nurtured seat-of-the-pants instincts. These relatively simple skills and instincts still form the core of flying, but no one can fly in heavily trafficked airways with just these skills. The crowding of modern airports, the amount of airplane traffic, and the horrible consequences of aviation accidents have resulted in the development of complex requirements and skills for flying. Aviation electronics alone (radio, navigation, and radar equipment) can cost more than the airplane itself, and their use requires as much time to learn as any other aspect of flying.

The bearing of modern aviation on modern teaching is this: More planes, bigger planes and more flights have made flying ex-

tremely complex and have led to the need for more and more expertise on the part of the pilot. More diverse populations of students, a
desire for more education, a need to educate with reasonable economy, expanding knowledge, and changing social and cultural practices have made teaching far more complex and have led to the need
for more expertise on the part of the teacher.

Flying itself has not changed; it is still a matter of moving
from one point to another in three-dimensional space. What has
changed are the demands that must be met in order to fly well in the
air traffic system of today. Neither has teaching changed in fundamental ways; it is still a matter of instructing and assisting students
so that they acquire the knowledge, understanding, traits of character, and conduct required for a personally rewarding life, productive
employment, and effective citizenship. But teaching under the conditions of modern schooling is vastly more complex than it was
thirty or forty years ago. Good practice under conditions of complexity requires expertise.

The problems with notions of expertise begin when we lose
sight of the fact that expertise is largely a response to the great
increase in complexity of modern schooling and is not the result of
some fundamental revision in the meaning of teaching. An expanded knowledge base does indeed permit teachers to practice ex-
pertly under the conditions of modern schooling, but it does not
change what we *mean* by teaching. If, however, we begin to allow
conceptions of expertise to drive our view of the occupation of
teaching, the consequences can be inimical to the very education we
are trying to achieve. Some scholars have already noted the consequences for universities as they became driven almost exclusively by
a concern for knowledge production and technical application:

> It is interesting that many professors in universities no
> longer think of themselves as intellectuals. Rather
> they think of themselves as academics, as people who
> have become technically proficient in a subject. . . . It
> is generally a compliment when we refer to someone
> as a "real academic," for we usually mean such a per-
> son is a "professional." By "professional," however,
> we do not mean one who has committed his or her life

to pursuing tasks for a good commonly held; rather, we mean someone . . . whose expertise gives power over others. When teaching becomes solely a matter of expertise, the very nature of scholarship is perverted.[8]

The knowledge base should not be the sole place to look when thinking about the forms that the occupation of teaching might take, for if one looks only there, a preoccupation with expertise over all else is the likely conclusion to the search. Expertise alone is not the best foundation if one's intent is to educate as broadly as possible.

Rethinking the Occupation of Teaching

Thus far, we have examined the moral nature of teaching, how the teacher serves as moral educator, some distinctions between teaching and other professions, and how the notion of expertise so prominently figures into conceptions of professional practice. If these contentions have merit, there should be a growing skepticism about the rectitude of professionalizing the occupation of teaching, at least in ways analogous to other professions. A skeptical attitude should not, however, keep us from understanding how teaching might be conceived as a highly professional undertaking, although without the trappings typically connected with professionalization.

One feature of the occupational character of teaching seems very clear: The moral and intellectual development of the learner is sustained best when the finest practitioners remain as close to and as involved with the learner as possible. In short, we are most advantaged in the moral development of the young when the finest exemplars of moral practice remain as close to learners as possible for as long as possible. This imperative is at odds with the professionalization agendas contained in many of the recent reform initiatives, wherein the better teachers are "promoted" to higher levels of the organization, becoming increasingly distant from the learners they supposedly serve. For example, both the Carnegie and the Holmes reports[9] call for hierarchical differentiation in the teaching occupation, beginning with, in the case of the Holmes report, the position of instructor, moving through professional teacher to the top level of career professional. Although it is not always required by the higher positions, it is frequently the case that as teachers move up the career ladder, they move out of the classroom.

In the course of examining the education of "at risk" learners, Richardson, Casanova, Placier, and Guilfoyle studied a school that was restructuring along the lines suggested in the Holmes and Carnegie reports.[10] Desert View Elementary School is located in a lower- to middle-class suburb of an urban center in the American Southwest. Nearly 80 percent of its students are of limited English proficiency or bilingual. The school had been engaged in the restructuring effort for two years before the study began. The teachers and principal worked closely together on the reform effort, exercising considerable control over its pace and direction. The school district's adoption of a career-ladder plan a few years earlier provided the basis for the school staff's reorganization efforts.

The investigators found that, as the teachers reorganized their work along the lines suggested in the Holmes and Carnegie reports, a major portion of their time shifted from working with students in classrooms to dealing with what the researchers called "the systemics of schooling." Among the systemic activities were collective planning sessions, team meetings to design instructional interventions for problem learners, staff development and teacher mentoring activities, and providing leadership to teams of teachers. The complexities of scheduling classes and special sessions increased quite dramatically. The most needy students found themselves with the most fragmented schedule and the greatest number of changes in teachers and workrooms during the day.

The difficulties inherent in this scheme are not hard to detect. For the teacher, status and prestige increase as one gains in responsibility and authority. But the gain in authority here is not in expanded responsibility for learners but in expanded responsibility for other teachers and their classrooms. This expansion in responsibility creates a distance between the promoted teacher and the students and thus reduces the learner's opportunities to gain in moral development from contact with the best teachers. Perhaps the departure of the best teachers is not so destructive as suggested here, for there may be benefit in having these excellent teachers serve as guides, tutors, and mentors to less experienced or less capable teachers. If that were all that was involved, the hierarchical differentiation of the teaching occupation might be considered a most reasonable and needed reform.

The problem is with the social and cultural context in which the proposed hierarchical differentiation is set. Within the organizational norms of our culture, status and prestige are linked to moving up the organizational ladder. Salary increases usually accompany jumps to the next higher level in the organization, thereby enhancing the status and prestige of the promoted employee. This structure has worked reasonably well for American industry and government so long as the hierarchy generally reflects the skill and competence necessary to perform at a certain level. That is, the lower the position on the hierarchy, the less skill, training, and competence usually required to do the assigned job. As one moves up the hierarchy, the increased complexity and challenge of the work, requiring increased training and skill to perform it successfully, usually justify the increased salary and augmented status.

Not so, however, in teaching. The complexity of classroom teaching, the training and skill required to do it well, are among the most demanding tasks in the entire system of schooling. True, the hours required of administrators and supervisors may be longer, and the workaday problems they encounter may be more dramatic in the short run. But no argument of which I am aware establishes that the successful performance of classroom teaching demands less skill, training, exercise of intelligence, and competence than the successful performance of any other professional role in institutions of formal education.

The strength of this contention grows as the realities of our contemporary culture are confronted. Classrooms contain children of enormous diversity in language, culture, family background, and preparation for school activities, as well as tremendous variation in both readiness and ability to learn.[11] This alone accounts for great challenge to the teacher. However, the systemics of schooling are also more complex, with a multitude of curriculum requirements, tests, accountability standards, and legal requirements at the local, state, and federal levels. Combine these forms of complexity with the lessening of a unifying and civilizing cultural consensus in modern American society, then imagine the predicament of a teacher charged with teaching a skill or subject to every learner in what is essentially the same type of classroom and school environment that existed fifty or one hundred years ago. This classroom environment is now vastly more complex, filled with far more variation and difference, and is constantly on the brink of disarray for lack of common purpose and respected cultural norms to regulate human communication and exchange.

One way to confront the conditions of the contemporary classroom is to argue that this nation is unlikely ever to produce enough people of sufficient talent, motivation, and commitment to cover all the classrooms of America. We therefore need to think of a differentiated work force, wherein the best and brightest—of whom, on this line of reasoning, we have too few—are given educational duties that closely correspond to their talent and qualifications. Among these duties is the supervision of the many who are something less than the best and the brightest and the preparation of the few who will become the best and the brightest. Unfortunately, to perform these duties, the best and the brightest are given assignments that are likely to take them out of the classroom, thus removing them from students.

The challenge before us is to design career opportunities for the best and the brightest that *retain* them in the classroom and that keep them close to their students, in career paths that do not require moving out in order to move up. The career path should be constructed in a way that does not derail the finest teachers into the systemics of the school but permits them to focus their talent and skill on student learning. In order to construct such a career path, the autonomy of the teacher is essential. The classroom teacher must be able to formulate her or his own plans, act on these plans, assess them, and act again. In other words, the teacher must be regarded as a professional, without the occupation of teaching itself falling heir to stereotypical, conventional conceptions of professionalization.

Although teaching is indeed a skilled activity, one that requires intelligence on the part of the practitioner and a sustained period of training, the acknowledgment of this fact does not mean that the occupation of teaching should now follow the historical path of medicine and law. Mitchell and Kerchner have studied the work of teaching, examining the type of labor performed and the ways in which teaching is organized to perform that labor.[12,13] Mitchell contends that teaching involves elements of four different types of labor: (1) industrial labor, (2) skilled craft, (3) artistic performance, and (4) professional practice. He argues that "teaching involves elements of all four of the basic work types."[14] Therefore, "what is needed is a system that links support for craft, artistic and professional aspects of teaching to the present system that gives too much attention to its laboring aspects."[15]

To achieve this balanced view of teacher labor, Mitchell and Kerchner argue for what they call "policy trust agreements." Contending that education is simply too complex to structure teacher work on such a simple instrument as a collective bargaining contract, Mitchell states that the labor relations system that covers teaching must "permit teachers to develop personally effective means of working on problems and support the expectation that constant revision and improvement are necessary."[16] Policy trust agreements strive for joint planning to develop shared goals rather than specifying work performance rules. Policy trust agreements require teachers and administrators to agree on common goals and the resources necessary to attain these goals and to provide for regular and continual revision of terms, in relation to progress being made toward attainment of shared goals—in marked contrast with the formal grievance procedures so often required in collective bargaining contracts.

One important benefit of the policy trust agreement is that it permits some fundamental alterations in the way the work and labor relations of teachers are viewed, without also carrying the trappings of bureaucratic hierarchy and complex structural adaptations. Policy trust agreements permit the treatment of teachers as autonomous agents in the classroom and school, without necessitating such things as career-ladder schemes or teacher promotion models based on national screening examinations, advanced graduate degrees, or standardized district or state teacher evaluation systems.

Of course, career-ladder or teacher-ranking programs may be built into policy trust agreements as part of the specification of the implementation process used to allocate resources to the identified goals. However, the trust agreement does not require teacher hierarchies in order to provide for teacher autonomy. Policy trust agreements thus provide an example of how teachers may be treated as autonomous agents in classrooms without the adoption of schemes that would increase the physical and social distance between them and their students.

Finding a resolution for the problem of autonomy does not resolve all of the issues that make up the current debate about the professionalization of teaching. However, this resolution does suggest how the occupation of teaching can be considered a highly professional endeavor without the imposition on it of the features of professionalization that have characterized fields such as law and medicine. Furthermore, there clearly are ways of acknowledging the need for the autonomy and professional status for teachers that do not require removing them from the classroom or instituting bureaucratic ladders for them to ascend in the search for status and prestige. These considerations suggest that teaching may be an occupation quite different from those with which we may be tempted to compare it.

The Unique Nature of Teaching as a Profession

In the opening chapter of this book, Goodlad argues that teaching in public schools is a special case of teaching, writ large, as well as a special case among comparable occupations or professions. Along with Goodlad, I believe that teaching is best understood as unique among the human service professions. It is unique in the sense of what it demands from its practitioners and the purposes its practitioners serve in the larger society.

The first characteristic of uniqueness is the demand that the best practitioners remain closest to the learners. In medicine, law, and many other professions, we have observed expertise and specialization driving the professional further and further from the patient or client. The sick or accused are increasingly served by paramedics or paralegals, by aides, and by others of less skill or training than the exalted professional. This hierarchical differentiation is a consequence of increasing specialization and demands for remuneration and status that are often justified as the price of expertise.

In contrast, the need for teachers who are enlightened moral

agents and moral educators calls for close, caring, connected association between teachers and students. If expertise and specialization
lead, as they so often do, to calls for enhanced status and remuneration, then the most highly competent teachers will be driven far
from learners. The nation will simply not be able to afford enough
of them to keep them closely associated with all children in schools.

The options remaining are not many. One is to reduce the
complexity of the modern school and classroom so that the level of
expertise required of a teacher does not elevate salaries to the point
where communities can afford only novices and the less competent
for daily close association with schoolchildren. This sounds similar
to a proposal to simplify the nation's air traffic control system by
reducing the number of planes, passengers, and flights to the point
where an exponential reduction in the complexity of piloting and
air control becomes possible. Yet it might be possible to diminish a
significant share of the complexity of modern schooling by altering
the working conditions of teachers, the regulatory and assessment
environments that surround the schools, and the structure and organization of the school setting. If the complexity of schooling
could be reduced, it might be possible to diminish the demands for
expertise placed on teachers, thus restraining salary demands that
would restrict the quality and competence of those who deal most
directly with learners.

In fact, the likelihood of simplifying the school environment
is very low. The struggle between the teaching profession and the
state policy apparatus mentioned at the outset of this chapter is one
reason why little attention is likely to be paid to fundamentally
rethinking the character of schooling in the United States. It seems
that there are only a few who care to consider the possibility of
simplification. Indeed, it may be in error to suggest that it is feasible
even if it were to prove politically possible. Another alternative is to
radically alter the salary structures of nonclassroom personnel,
thereby infusing more funds into the salaries of those who serve the
classroom. For example, current proposals for school-site-level
management may diminish the need for central office administration, thus freeing up scarce dollars to support teacher salaries.

Although interesting to contemplate, these alternatives are
unlikely to yield funds sufficient to keep good teachers in classrooms if the professionalization characteristics mentioned earlier

are widely adopted. To avoid this consequence, it is necessary to recast the professionalization agenda in such a way that a value is placed on teacher competence and teacher autonomy but not on the kind of hierarchical differentiation that entices the best teachers to leave direct contact with children for higher status, higher pay, and greater control. To accomplish this goal, teaching must be conceived as an egalitarian, nonelitist occupation, wherein many are considered fit to serve and all might gain in competence and effectiveness by remaining in close association with peers as well as students.

In such a setting, expertise is viewed as a commodity of the group, as the property of the cadre of teachers in the school. No one person is perceived as entitled to more control, status, or salary than another solely by virtue of advanced degrees, specialization, or expertise. The organization of the profession of classroom teachers thus remains quite flat. However, it is a profession, in the sense that it does require specialized skill, highly developed moral qualities, and advanced knowledge. As members of a profession, its practitioners possess the right and privilege of autonomous action in the classroom.

The picture is of a profession quite different from those with which we are familiar. It is a popular profession in that its practice is open to all who wish to struggle to achieve its ideals and master its requirements for competent practice. It is an egalitarian profession in that its practitioners use expertise and specialization not as instruments of status and control but as a shared resource of the group. It is a demanding profession in that it requires the reflective exercise of knowledge and skill, while being intensely engaged in the complex, perhaps greatly disadvantaged lives of one's students. It is—must be—a profession different from any of which we are immediately aware. To think of teaching in this way is to think of it as a fundamentally moral undertaking.

Notes

1. "Exclusive Interview: Chester E. Finn, Jr., Department of Education." *Education Reports* (National Center for Education Information), Sept. 12, 1988, pp. 2–6.
2. A number of examples of the expanded knowledge base for

teaching stand as testimony to the claims of the teaching profession. Three examples illustrate the point. The first is the technical treatment found in M. C. Wittrock (ed.), *The Handbook of Research on Teaching*, 3rd ed. (New York: Macmillan, 1986); the second, an attempt to present the empirical evidence and expanded theory to practicing teachers, is V. Richardson-Koehler (ed.), *Educator's Handbook: A Research Perspective* (New York: Longman, 1987); the third, M. C. Reynolds (ed.), *Knowledge Base for the Beginning Teacher* (New York: Pergamon Press, 1989), is intended for use in preparing new teachers.

3. The professionalization literature can be quite vast, depending on how broadly one wishes to search. Among the sources of immediate relevance to the argument in this chapter are P. Gordon, H. Perkin, H. Sockett, and E. Hoyle, *Is Teaching a Profession?*, 2nd ed. (London: Institute of Education, University of London, 1985); B. A. Kimball, "The Problem of Teachers' Authority in Light of the Structural Analysis of Professions," *Educational Theory*, Winter 1988; *38*, 1–9; W. P. Metzger, "A Spectre Is Haunting American Scholars: The Spectre of 'Professionalism,'" *Educational Researcher*, Aug.–Sept. 1987, pp. 10–19; V. Richardson-Koehler and G. Fenstermacher, "Graduate Programs of Teacher Education and the Professionalization of Teaching," in A. E. Woolfolk (ed.), *Research Perspectives on the Graduate Preparation of Teachers* (Englewood Cliffs, N.J.: Prentice Hall, 1989), pp. 153–168; R. Soder, "Studying the Education of Educators: What We Can Learn from Other Professions," *Phi Delta Kappan*, Dec. 1988, pp. 299–305; J. F. Soltis (ed.), *Reform Teacher Education: The Impact of the Holmes Group Report* (New York: Teachers College Press, 1987); A. E. Wise, "Graduate Teacher Education and Teacher Professionalism," *Journal of Teacher Education*, 1986, *37* (5), 36–40.

4. The literature on the moral dimensions of teaching is extensive, and much of it is cited in other chapters in this book. Works of special interest to the topic of this chapter include J. M. Atherton, "Virtues in Moral Education: Objections and Replies," *Educational Theory*, Summer 1988, *38*, 299–310; I. Pritchard, *Education and Character* (Washington, D.C.: Of-

fice of Research, U.S. Department of Education, 1988); K. Ryan, "Teacher Education and Moral Education," *Journal of Teacher Education,* Sept.-Oct. 1988, *39,* 18-23. H. T. Sockett, "Education and Will: Aspects of Personal Capability," *American Journal of Education,* Feb. 1988, *96,* 195-214; A. R. Tom, *Teaching as a Moral Craft* (New York: Longman, 1984).

5. See, for example, H. T. Sockett, "Has Shulman Got the Strategy Right?" *Harvard Education Review,* May 1987, *57,* 208-219.

6. G. Ryle, "Can Virtue Be Taught?" in R. F. Dearden, P. H. Hirst, and R. S. Peters (eds.), *Education and the Development of Reason,* Part 3: *Education and Reason* (London: Routledge & Kegan Paul, 1975), pp. 46-47. On this same idea, see also H. Howe II, "Can Schools Teach Values?" *Teachers College Record,* Fall 1987, *89,* 55-68.

7. This section is critical of the way medicine and law are often practiced, as observed by patients and clients. It is not intended to be critical of the best practitioners of law and medicine. Indeed, it may be appropriate for law, medicine, and teaching to become more alike than different on the three categories discussed here. On this point, see Association of American Medical Colleges, *Physicians for the Twenty-First Century: The GPEP Report* (Washington, D.C.: Association of American Medical Colleges, 1984).

8. S. M. Hauerwas, "The Morality of Teaching," in A. L. De-Neef, C. D. Goodwin, and E.S. McCrate (eds.), *The Academic's Handbook* (Durham, N.C.: Duke University Press, n.d.), p. 24.

9. Carnegie Task Force on Teaching as a Profession, *A Nation Prepared: Teachers for the 21st Century* (New York: Carnegie Forum on Education and the Economy, 1986); Holmes Group, *Tomorrow's Teachers* (East Lansing, Mich.: Holmes Group, 1986).

10. V. Richardson, U. Casanova, P. Placier, and K. Guilfoyle, *School Children at Risk* (London: Falmer Press, 1989).

11. H. L. Hodgkinson, *All One System: Demographics of Education: Kindergarten Through Graduate School* (Washington, D.C.: Institute for Educational Leadership, 1985).

12. D. E. Mitchell, "A New Approach to Collective Bargaining,"
     Policy Briefs (Far West Laboratory), Winter 1986, pp. 1-6.
13. C. E. Kerchner, "Teacher Professionalism Through Labor Re-
     lations," *Policy Briefs* (Far West Laboratory), Winter 1986,
     pp. 6-8.
14. Mitchell, "A New Approach to Collective Bargaining," p. 3.
15. Mitchell, "A New Approach to Collective Bargaining," p. 4.
16. Mitchell, "A New Approach to Collective Bargaining," p. 4

PART TWO

The Moral Mission of Education and Implications for the Teaching Profession

5

The Moral
Responsibility
of Public Schools

Walter Feinberg

This chapter explores the recent history of educational ideas in light of contemporary challenges to the moral and intellectual foundations of public education. It examines different moral visions that have guided compulsory public education and shows why past conceptions are no longer adequate. It then turns to recent works that attempt to recapture the moral mission of American education and evaluates them in light of the new American pluralism. It concludes by offering a conception of a public that is consistent with a wide-ranging pluralism and proposes this conception as a way to renew the moral basis of public education.

The Problem

We are witnessing a remarkable change in the circumstances of public schoolteaching. The moral foundations of compulsory education are being questioned as people of many different political and educational persuasions challenge its legitimacy. Alternative schools grow more popular, proposals for vouchers and tuition tax credits receive sympathetic hearings, home schooling appeals to more people, and the public schools' moral authority continues to diminish. Unless a new moral conception of public education is developed, public schools may stand as meaningless institutional shells, reminders of once larger purposes. Moreover, without such a

conception, teachers, other educators, and policymakers will have
little guidance to help them evaluate the merits of the many con-
flicting proposals for public education that have been offered in
recent times.

Development of Compulsory Public Education

The development of compulsory public education is closely
associated with the dramatic changes that occurred in American
society between the Civil War and the end of the First World War,
and especially with the spectacular rise in urbanization, industrialization, and immigration that occurred during this period. Compulsory schooling was initiated to ameliorate the social, political, cultural, and personal tensions caused by industrial development. The
purpose of schooling was to maintain a compliant work force and
to provide the human resources required by the new age. It was also
to correct inequities in market capitalism by providing new avenues
for upward mobility.

The reasons for compulsory public education arose from
many different sources. Pressure to Americanize the immigrant and
to develop an accommodating work force was one important factor.
The concern to eliminate the unhealthy effect of the sweatshop by
using compulsory schooling to control child labor was another.[1]
The vague belief, even in some rural areas, that compulsory schooling was the progressive thing to do provided an additional factor
accounting for the slow but uneven spread of compulsory attendance laws throughout the country. (Massachusetts enacted the first
such law in 1852, but it took a number of years before other states
followed. "Nearly one half of the states enacted compulsory attendance laws between 1870 and 1890, and within thirty years after the
latter date the other half had slowly and somewhat reluctantly followed their example."[2]) Compulsory schooling is most commonly
associated, however, with the rise in technology and increasing levels of industrialization. The guiding principle of technology was
efficiency, and this principle brought people and machines together
in urban areas, accelerated physical mobility, altered the nature and
place of work, and threatened to dislodge the extended family. Com-

pulsory public education developed in response to these events as a way to address problems that technology created.

At the turn of the century, educational reformers argued that traditional agents of socialization were no longer adequate for rearing children and that the school must become the principal avenue for enculturation. This argument provided an important reason for the advance of compulsory attendance laws in one state after another. Compulsory schooling became the symbol of a progressive state, one in which business would feel comfortable and a steady supply of acceptable labor could be ensured. Compulsory schooling was also a symbol of fairness and of the belief that differences of background and wealth could be overcome by hard work and talent. Of course, not everyone shared these visions. The working class sometimes opposed compulsory schooling on the grounds that it was an imposition on the poor by the rich,[3] and Catholics often chose to establish their own school system rather than conform to what they saw as the disguised sectarianism of the "secularized" Protestant. Whatever the merits of these oppositional movements, the development of public schooling was advanced by the capturing of the images of progress and fairness, and these images guided the most important debates about school reform.

Three themes are especially prominent in the historical debate about the purpose of compulsory public education. In the first, the professional theme, the teacher is viewed as an expert motivated by the interest of the individual child. Compulsory public education was said to be important because the socializing function of the traditional family could no longer be counted on to provide the attitudes and the skills required by a complex technological society. The second theme is social; it fits a bureaucratic model of school reform. It speaks to the role of the teacher in extending the principles of American industry and democracy and in maintaining America's prominence and strength. The third theme emphasizes fairness. The school is important because it provides equal opportunity and maintains fair access to social status and reward. These thematic structures provide models for understanding the historical continuities in American educational reform.

Moral and Philosophical Continuities
in American Educational Reform

The Professional Model

The Teacher as Expert. The professional model holds that teachers, like other professionals, must possess a high level of expertise based on a special body of knowledge that takes intelligence and hard work to acquire. It holds that rigorous education and sacrifice should be required for one to become a teacher and that, in return, teachers should be provided the same status and rewards as other professionals.

The professional model has been most successfully developed in medicine and is expressed forcefully in the work of Abraham Flexner in the early part of this century. Flexner and other advocates of the professionalization of medicine were successful because they could draw on a developing consensus that social progress would fly on the wings of science and technology.

Flexner argued that by linking medical practice with scientific research and by holding both together through affiliation with universities, the science of medicine could advance for the benefit of all humankind. Progress required that the best students be admitted for training into medical schools and that inferior institutions, of which there were many, be closed. The result was a steady increase in the income and the prestige of the medical profession and a growing belief that improvement in health care was due to the changes that had occurred in the education of physicians.

The Scientific Basis of the Profession of Teaching. The idea of a science of education is not new. It parallels, although with less success, the idea of a science of medicine. As early as 1825, James G. Carter, who has been given the title of "the Father of the Normal School," declared that a science of education was self-evident.[4] However, nineteenth-century works that spoke about a "science of education" were significantly different from their twentieth-century counterparts, being little more than treatises on ethical rules mixed with some theology and a generous portion of commonsense principles about classroom management and child psychology. The moral role of the teacher was to build character, maintain republican virtues, and develop national consciousness.

However, as the nineteenth century was coming to a close, the connection between the ethics of education and the science of education became more tenuous. In the nineteenth century, educators accepted the idea of a stable universe of values, and the task of educational theorists was simply to elaborate the implications of these values for classroom procedures. In the twentieth century, the belief grew that there was indeed a special scientific basis for teaching. At the same time, questions were raised about the idea that Americans were bound together by a set of shared values.

Until the end of the nineteenth century, many communities did not require any special knowledge or training to enter teaching, and many teachers were chosen directly out of the ranks of the high school graduates. As Krug notes, by the 1890s the requirements varied considerably from state to state. In Wisconsin, only half of the high school teachers were college graduates, while in neighboring Minnesota, two-thirds had graduated from college.[5] The drive to make teaching a profession was accompanied by more stringent educational requirements and by the development of four-year teachers' colleges, many of which were to become universities. It was no longer sufficient for the teacher to simply represent the "moral consensus" of the community.

The argument that teaching is a true profession on a par with law and medicine is a continuing theme for teachers and teacher educators. A common lament at meetings of professional associates is "Why can't someone do for education what Flexner did for medicine?" Most recently, the model has been used by the Holmes Group, which consists of deans of colleges of education from many of the country's major research universities, to argue that teacher certification should require both a broad liberal education and specific graduate-level training to encompass the complex responsibilities of the profession.

The professional model provides practitioners with a number of important prerogatives. In the first place, it holds that professionals should be able to control their own numbers and to police their own members. This follows from the fact that the knowledge required for professional practice is special and difficult

to acquire and that, therefore, only other professionals are capable
of judging whether a person is performing at a sufficiently high
level. Moreover, professionals are judged by their methods, not their
results. A doctor whose patient dies while undergoing a delicate
heart-lung transplant is judged not by the death but by the procedures used. Only other professionals can be the judges of
procedures.

Teaching's longing for professional status is understandable.
Professionals are more than problem solvers; they are need definers
as well, and as such they are granted a special moral authority.
Doctors do not just cure us of disease. They also tell us in what ways
we are sick, and in doing so they are granted a great deal of jurisdiction over otherwise private affairs. A psychiatrist can pronounce on
the capacity of a person to stand trial and can also advise about the
degree of responsibility a person exercises. Thus, if a group is
granted professional status, it is granted the right to define the needs
of others. In arguing that teachers have a right to this authority,
educational reformers have appealed to the authority granted by
knowledge of psychology and other behavioral sciences.[6] They argue that such knowledge provides the professional teacher with a
special understanding of different kinds of children and with the
ability to define and limit their educational risk.

The Bureaucratic Model: The School in the Service of the Nation

What the professional model gives with one hand the bureaucratic model takes away with the other. While teachers
struggled to achieve some degree of professional recognition, some
reformers argued for a more bureaucratically controlled educational
system—one that would address goals and purposes determined by
interests outside the school. These reformers argued that schools
exist to service the changing manpower needs that industrialization
requires and that, therefore, the activities of teachers must be rationalized and directed by outside interests and goals.

In the early and middle parts of the twentieth century, elaborate testing, placement, and training procedures developed to check
the teacher's judgment and to ensure an "objective" placement of

children. The basic goal was to service American industry, while industry itself would dictate the kind of product the schools were to produce. As Franklin Bobbitt, an instructor in education at the University of Chicago, put it in 1913, "A school system can no more find the standard of performance within itself than a steel plant can find the proper height or weight per yard of steel rails from the activities within the plant."[7] Bobbitt argued that it was the responsibility of the business community to set standards for the school. Business needed to determine the kind of labor that the nation's industry required and the level of proficiency to which it should be trained. The psychologists were to develop tests that would determine which students were most appropriate for different levels of training that a diversified labor force required; curriculum specialists would ensure that the training programs matched industrial needs; administrators were to find the most efficient ways of processing children through the system; and teachers would carry out the plan. Thus, in contrast to the professional model, wherein the teacher defines the nature of the child's need, here the primary need is determined by other agencies, and the teacher serves as but a conduit functioning between the planner and the child.

The bureaucratic model has been influential in different areas. In addition to serving industrial needs, the education system also developed the appropriate skills and attitudes in the personnel required for national expansion and development. By the end of the century, an aggressive tone was heard as the schools became agents in a developing international competition. "Either educate your people in the common school," warned William Torrey Harris, the U.S. commissioner of education from 1889 to 1906, "or your labor will not compete with other nations in the matter and use of machinery. If you cannot compete with other people in the matter of the use of machinery, you must recede from the front ranks of nations in every respect."[8] Harris argued that civilization was measured by the level of knowledge, technology, and industry of a culture and that countries with higher levels of science, technology, and power were justified in their imperial expansion. As Harris declared in articulating an educational policy for the United States' new possessions in 1899:

The white man proves his civilization to be superior
to other civilizations just by this very influence which
he exercises over the people that have lower forms of
civilizations, forms that do not permit them to con-
quer nature and to make the elements into ministers of
human power.[9]

The distinctive factor about the bureaucratic model is its
vision that the schools must be rationalized to serve as a primary
weapon in the maintenance or extension of American political and
economic ideals and institutions. This purpose often cuts across
otherwise important pedagogical differences. For example, in the
1940s and 1950s, there was a significant conflict between life-adjustment educators, who advocated a child-centered approach to education, and those who wanted to stress academic subjects. The life-
adjustment educators wanted to infuse the curriculum with material on how to cope with modern life and with practical courses
such as driver education and home economics. Their opponents
argued for more rigorous academic work in science, mathematics,
and languages. Yet each side justified its proposals on the basis of
bureaucratic, political, and even military needs that were remarkably similar. For example, Arthur Bestor, one of the foremost critics
of life adjustment, observed that "It is a curious ostrich-like way of
meeting life needs to de-emphasize mathematics at precisely the
time when the nation's security has come to depend on Einstein's
equation $E = MC^2$."[10] Yet the life-adjustment movement was also
anxious to justify itself as good for national defense. Advocates of
life adjustment argued on behalf of their program: "The improvement of education for all . . . guarantees a continuous flow of competent soldiers, sailors, and airmen to man the weapons of modern
war."[11]

The idea that the school should be used to enhance the position of the United States in the competition among nations is a
persistent theme in the educational reform literature. It was, for
example, one of the critical concerns that motivated the work of
James Conant in the late 1950s and the early 1960s as Americans
worried about Soviet achievements in space. It is also an important
motive behind the recent educational reform movements spirited by

the 1983 report of the National Commission on Excellence in Education, entitled *A Nation at Risk*.[12] The authors of this report were concerned about the ability of U.S. schools to meet the economic challenge arising from Japan and other Pacific Rim nations. The report warned of a rising tide of educational mediocrity and proposed that more attention be paid to academic subjects such as science and math. Much like Bestor, the authors of this report believed that national strength required a well-schooled population, and they argued that it was the obligation of teachers to meet this need.

The Fairness Model

The fairness model views the school as a distribution mechanism: The schools' role is to identify and develop talent and to help ensure that income and status are distributed on the basis of ability and motivation. The school thus serves as the ultimate guarantor of equality of opportunity and is an essential corrective to the inevitable distortions of market capitalism. Because schooling provides opportunities otherwise afforded only by family wealth and privilege, it is essential to the goal of democratic equality. It helps remove structural roadblocks to advancement, such as gender, race, and religion as well as lack of family status and wealth, and allows each individual to rise as far as his or her talents will allow. If the ideal were achieved, then a talented, motivated person from even a humble background could gain wealth and status equal to any other's. The fairness model provided the moral vision behind many of the early efforts to extend compulsory public education to new groups of American children during the early days of industrialization, and it also provided much of the moral force behind the arguments that were used to challenge the segregation of schools in mid-century.

Withering Rationales

While there is some tension among these different visions, in practice they have existed side by side without a great deal of noticeable strain. Granted, teachers have not received the professional authority that some have wanted, but licensing provided a quasi-professional status, and comfort could be taken from the fact that the schools were serving important individual and national purposes. More recently, each of these themes has been seriously questioned, and the moral foundation of teaching has been placed in doubt.

Declining Faith in Science and Professionalism

Faith in science has diminished, and even the prestige of medicine has suffered as a result. The existing consensus about the significance of medical education is being challenged by a new view that argues against the claim that changes in medical education account for most of the improvements in health in this century. Critics argue that changes in medical education helped to increase the prestige of the medical profession, but health improved because of increases in the standard of living and improvements in nutrition and sanitation. Most critics admit that science was helpful—vaccinations and antibiotics were important discoveries—but constructive changes had occurred prior to their development, and the administration of these innovations is routine and does not require years of medical training.

This changing understanding of the relationship between medical training and improved health has been accompanied by a reevaluation of the relation of a public to the professions. Critics of medicine argue that improvement in health was more a function of the increased level of public knowledge than a matter of the improving competence of the experts. Indeed, it was not until well into the second half of the twentieth century, with the development of transplant techniques and other intricate surgical procedures, that a credible link was developed between the rigorous selection and training procedures used by medical schools and the improvement of health for a significant segment of the population.

There are even deeper concerns that challenge the scientific foundation of professionalism. Whereas Flexner drew on the common belief that progress would ride on the wings of the growth of scientific knowledge, modern sensitivities are more skeptical about the claims of science and technology, and there is a greater concern about their effects. These concerns have both theoretical and practical considerations. The authority of science itself has been challenged through a new examination of the epistemological foundations of the scientific enterprise and the emerging view that successful revolutions in science rest on somewhat arbitrary foundations.[13] While this challenge has taken place largely within academic circles, some religious groups have attempted to dispute the foundationalist view of science in order to advance the cause of creationism in the school. (Of course, they have done this by substituting the foundationalism of sacred texts for the foundationalism of science.)

Professionalism has been challenged by other groups as well. Some have suggested that the relationship between science and professional competence is much less significant than the relationship between professionalism and the monopolization of certain service markets, such as health care.[14] The important feature of medical education is that it provides to those who complete it much control over health care. For the most part, doctors are the only people who can prescribe medication, admit people into hospitals, cut people under the skin, or receive third-party payment. By making admission into medical school dependent on high grades and test scores, medicine has become a profession for the children of the upper middle class. By having the authority to control its own numbers and by convincing the public that there is a necessary link between the rigor of medical training and the improvement of public health, the members of the profession are assured of high income and status. Yet some critics see these as the results of good salesmanship rather than good science.

The Decline of the American Century and the Challenge to the Bureaucratic Model

The Conflict Between the Bureaucratic Model and Traditional American Values. The rationalization of education called for by the bureaucratic model rubs against basic political themes of American society. It is especially antagonistic to concerns about the importance of the individual, the value of spontaneity, and the right of self-expression. The testing and sorting of children according to scores on tests, the articulation of educational goals with industrial needs, and the intrusion of the state into the socialization activities of the family are difficult to reconcile with traditional ideas about the limits of state power and the importance of the individual. These ideals have been used by both the left and the right to challenge the authority of public education. While segments of the religious right and the political left (especially the anarchistic segment) reject the value of public education for different reasons, each gains credibility by drawing on aspects of the traditional liberal theory of the minimal state.

The Ideal of the Minimal State. The question of the legitimacy of compulsory education is a question about the proper scope and limits of state authority. Power, it is said, originates from the people, and it is unlikely that people would want to allow the state any more power than necessary. The use of state power to maintain order and commerce is legitimate, but anything more is often seen as usurping the rights of the individual. There are citizens who believe that the state should not even be able to compel people to act in their own self-interest. Nor should it have the right to tax one person for the benefit of another.

While many early opponents of compulsory schooling used the liberal view of the minimal state to advance their concern, their arguments were overwhelmed by the idea that America had a mission and that it would take an educated, industrially competent, pliable worker-citizen to accomplish it. It was the power of the idea that American civilization was unique and had a singular mission in the world that brought many in an otherwise skeptical population to accept (or at least acquiesce to) the level of social control that compulsory public education implied. Nevertheless, the minimal state is still a powerful symbol. It is used effectively by elements of both the religious right and the political left to express doubt and hesitation about the value of that mission. Moreover, as America's role in furthering democracy throughout the world is seriously questioned and its support of the undemocratic regimes in many areas of the world is revealed, many people find it increasingly difficult to accept the level of state intervention that compulsory education requires.

The Appeal to the Minimal State by the Religious Right.
While many people disagree with fundamentalist values, the idea of
a minimal state lends credibility to complaints against the public
school. One need not accept creationists' views of human development or believe that works such as *The Wizard of Oz* or *The Diary
of Anne Frank* are ungodly to feel that fundamentalist religious
groups are making an important point—the family ought to have
the ultimate say about what is and is not proper educational material for its child. The credibility of the stance is derived from a
minimalist view of the state and from the idea that the state should
have limited authority in matters regarding education. One need
not accept the charge advanced by some fundamentalist parents that
the school is advocating a form of secular humanism to be sympathetic to their concerns. One need only accept a minimalist view of
the state and be sympathetic to the charge that the state is usurping
the parents' right to determine what is in the best interest of the
child. One does not have to believe that the parents are possessed of
greater insight than the schoolteacher. Indeed, one may disagree
passionately with the parents' values. However, if one accepts a
minimalist view of the state, the first question is not *what* is really
in the best interest of the child. The first question is *who* has the
right to determine what is in the best interest of the child. The issue
is neither ethical nor psychological; it is jurisdictional. For the
minimalist, the state's role is severely limited.

The Appeal to the Minimal State by the Anarchist Left. The
anarchist left's critique of compulsory schooling also develops its
plausibility by drawing on sentiments that reflect a minimalist-state
point of view. The leading advocate of deschooling, Ivan Illich,
proposed that the first article "of a new bill of rights for a modern,
humanist society would correspond to the first amendment of the
U.S. Constitution: 'The State shall make no law with respect to the
establishment of education.' "[15] Arguing against compulsory education, Illich concludes that "Schoolteachers and ministers are the
only professionals who feel entitled to pry into the private affairs of
their clients at the same time as they preach to a captive audience."[16]
   Implicit in Illich's argument against schooling is an appeal
to rights of privacy that the teacher, as an agent of the state, appar-

ently violates whenever he or she probes the inner life of the student. Ironically, in equating the school with the church, Illich foreshadowed themes that were to be developed by the conservative fundamentalists in their attack on public schooling and secular humanism.

Despite the fact that the left and the right share common ground, there are important differences. Behind both is the belief that the state serves the interests of the ruling class and that the school, as an instrument of the state, provides the means for establishing ideological hegemony. Yet the concern of the left—that compulsory schooling serves to create passive, uncritical citizens—is not the same as the concern of the religious right. For the fundamentalist, the problem is that schools create prideful, ungodly individuals. The ideal is to create a person who will receive "God's words" humbly and uncritically.

For the advocates of deschooling on the left, compulsory education has become a fix—a kind of narcotics dispenser for people who crave one credential after another. For Ivan Illich, the only solution is to end compulsory education by deschooling society. Like the right, Illich, too, leans on a minimalist view of the state. His argument draws credibility from the suggestion that the state has gone beyond its legitimate function—although he is ambiguous about whether there can really be a legitimate function for the state.

The ambiguity is important. It provides a way for the advocates of deschooling to appeal to a publicly acknowledged set of values without committing themselves to the economic or religious positions that are often associated with these values. Privacy and strict limitations on administrative authority thus can be claimed by the left as well as the right. However, unlike the fundamentalist parents, whose criticism of schooling rests on a vision of a religious idea, the deschoolers have a secular vision in mind. The deschooling argument is based on a vision of a certain kind of learner—an active, spontaneous, critical person. Ultimately, according to this view, compulsory education fails not because it violates a fundamental political principle but because it discourages the development of an active, inquiring, and critical learner.

The Public Function of Appeals to the Minimal State. In its appeal to the authority of the family and, by implication, to the ideal of a minimal state, the religious right also makes use of a publicly sanctioned set of values. To make their case credible to those outside their own community, fundamentalist parents must reach beyond their own narrowly held vision of the good and do business on the basis of a more widely accepted currency. Even the question of objectivity and neutrality, which is used to argue the case for a curriculum more consistent with fundamentalist concerns, already signals a willingness to address Caesar on his own terms and to enter the arena of public symbols and discourse.

There is a significant difference, however, between the ground on which the legal battles are waged and the ground on which the fundamentalist parents hold their beliefs. The legal battle is about the school's neutrality or lack of neutrality. It is about the school's purported bias toward the secular and against the religious. Yet, from inside the religious fundamentalist's framework, the important issue is not whether the child is learning to be neutral and dispassionate. It is about whether teaching children to be dispassionate and objective about ultimate values is proper. As Geertz observes, the difference between the scientific and the religious attitude is the difference between detachment and analysis on the one side and commitment and encounter on the other.[17] In this respect, the fundamentalists who argue for including creationism in the curriculum as a way to balance the teaching of evolution have already gone beyond the sectarian values they are defending. They have acknowledged, perhaps reluctantly, a public set of values in which they and others must participate.

Like the fundamentalist, but for different reasons, the deschooler feels compelled to cite an established set of public values in order to provide the argument against compulsory education. Once these values are cited, the problem that remains for this element of the left is to *interpret* their counterpart on the right—to find a compatible explanation for an ultimately alien set of values. To do so, the right must become "sociologized"—made into an object for sociology. Once this operation is performed, the conflict can be seen as a class struggle between two distinct economic (and cultural) groups. As one observer explains:

> For many southerners, creationism is part of a developing rhetoric of resistance against the reigning ideology of the new South, just as religious revivalism provided popular release from the public demands of deference and servility in the old South. The site of the rebellion is public education because schools are the institutions where the new South ideology has worked most dramatically to marginalize working-class southern whites under the guise of meritocracy and equal opportunity.[18]

When the creationist is viewed as a member of the culture of the oppressed, the question of school practice becomes complicated. If one supports compulsory schooling and the evolutionist account that goes with it, one appears to be siding with the established powers against the oppressed. Yet if one supports the parents, failing to object to the creationist doctrine, one is facilitating the teaching of error and untruth.

   The dilemma arises because the analysis of schooling provided by the left, even that part of it not especially receptive to the deschooling argument, leaves little room to draw finer discriminations about practice. The left begins with a critique of the class system and with the view that the state functions to serve the interests of the ruling class. The state does this by serving as the instrument for determining and enforcing the rules by which power and control will be distributed. It monopolizes both the instruments of force and the instruments of thought. The school monopolizes the ideological message of the state, providing the framework through which experience is understood. Schooling is especially useful in teaching students to rationalize their ultimate place in the scheme of things and to understand how it is that they "wind up just where they belong." Thus, according to the left, the primary political function of compulsory schooling is to maintain the existing power relations by, first, providing everyone with the belief that they were given an equal opportunity to advance as far as their talents will take them and, second, by concealing the essentially arbitrary nature of the distribution of power.

The left's critiques of this political function are developed within a social science framework that is informed by a Marxist understanding of the relations of institutions to each other. However, the approach leaves little room for evaluating existing pedagogical practice except through a cynical lens where every pedagogical act is understood only in terms of its role in maintaining the existing relations of power. Thus, for example, in the words of Bourdieu and Passeron, displays of affection by primary school teachers for their students become ways to "gain possession of that subtle instrument of repression, the withdrawal of affection."[19] However, this cynicism is self-defeating, because there is nothing to inhibit it from reflecting back on the genuineness of the cynic. Ironically, the analysis from the left, carried to its extreme, undercuts not just the authority of the school but the authority of the left as well. As Bourdieu and Passeron write, seemingly unaware of how well the passage refers to their own critique of the educational system:

> The paradox of Epimenides the liar would appear in a new form: either you believe I'm not lying when I tell you education is violence and my teaching isn't legitimate, so you can't believe me; or you believe I'm lying and my teaching is legitimate, so you still can't believe what I say when I tell you it is violence.[20]

Thus, the thorough critique of practice leaves no room for either practice or critique.

By explicitly or implicitly appealing to the ideal of a minimal state, both the political right and the anarchistic left remind us of the importance of the individual and try to convince us that the state is usurping private initiative. Yet the appeal to the *idea* of the minimal state is not an appeal to the central values of their own traditions. Rather, it is an appeal to a public value—one that is acknowledged and accepted by different individuals with different ideologies for different reasons. For example, the religious right does not argue its case in the public arena by appealing to *God's* will. It does not speak in court of *God's* desire to have children taught Christian values. Rather, it argues the case on the grounds of its *beliefs* about God's will and of the *right* to have those beliefs respected. If a witness does speak about God's will, it is to demonstrate sincerity to the larger public that must decide the merits of the case. The appeal is not to the private communal values of the sect but to the public values of the society.[21]

The left has a similar relation to the publicly acknowledged value of the minimal state. It generates rhetorical force for a more equalitarian, spontaneous, communal society by gesturing toward the idea of eliminating compulsion and reducing the involvement of government in the educational process. Unresolved is the question of how the vast separation between the fundamentalist or the libertarian right and the equalitarian left might be resolved in any future nonmanipulative society with a minimum administrative and enforcement apparatus. Because the appeal to the minimal state is often implicit, this issue need not be addressed, and the left can leave unanswered questions about the ultimate value of the minimal state as it makes its appeal for creativity while gesturing to the support of a publicly sanctioned discourse.

The result is that both left and right, in their by-the-way appeal to individuality and the minimal state, implicitly acknowledge the importance of the sphere of public values as the basis for accommodating individual differences. Whether the acknowledgment of this sphere also entails compulsory education is an open question, but any system of education that is proposed will need to provide the means for the continuation of this public sphere.

The important issue is not whether the minimal state itself represents any ultimate public value. The point is that the appeal to notions of individuality, privacy, and the minimal state serves an important public function—it enables an argument to be carried on between otherwise incommensurate views. Appeals of this type implicitly acknowledge the important function that institutions intent on developing a space for public debate and dialogue serve in a pluralistic society.

Fairness Denied

Arguments for compulsory education have been based on the idea that the school is the only institution that can counter the accidents of birth, guarantee equality of opportunity and provide objective and fair ways to select and train talented individuals. With this idea in mind, Jewish groups successfully lobbied to have quotas removed from universities in the early part of the century; by mid-century, civil rights groups used the same idea to argue successfully against legal segregation.

Yet, by the middle of the 1960s, serious questions were raised about the school's role in providing equal opportunity. Some have argued that the school merely serves to reproduce an unequal labor force and, by providing the appearance of objectivity, legitimates the inequality. Others have challenged the objectivity of instruments such as IQ tests that have been used to determine individual selection and placement. Still others questioned the very concept of equality of opportunity because it applied only to individuals and obscured the otherwise obvious fact that entire groups were being discriminated against. This last argument is especially powerful. It proposes that the history of exclusion leads members of oppressed groups to overlook "opportunities" in desirable fields and to limit their horizons to areas that have been historically open to them. Hence, women "chose" to be nurses rather than doctors, and blacks "chose" to be mail carriers rather than lawyers. Yet, just because they got what they "wanted," it does not mean that they were operating under a system of equal opportunity. Rather, they were taught, by the schools and other institutions, to want what they could get. Thus, the whole conception of equal opportunity, as well as the school's role in furthering it, is now questioned.

In Search of a Renewed Moral Foundation

Two recent books are important because of their authors' attempts to develop a new moral foundation for education. These books are Allan Bloom's *The Closing of the American Mind*[22] and E. D. Hirsch, Jr.'s *Cultural Literacy*.[23] Bloom and Hirsch believe that the most serious educational problem is the failure to transmit a unifying culture to the young and that the most important educational task is to rebuild a fragmented culture.

Bloom: Unity Destroyed. Bloom's *The Closing of the American Mind* laments the disintegration of the student's "soul," a term that he uses to decry not only the splintered vocationalism found in the university but also the increasing isolation and separateness of life in America. Independence rather than initiation into a common normative enterprise has become the goal of growing up.[24] Today's emphasis on *self*-development, *self*-expression, and *individual* growth means the de-emphasis of communal norms. Because few communal sanctions are available, ethically problematic acts such as divorce and abortion become morally easy. Such acts increase the normlessness of the public order and contribute to children's growing sense of moral and intellectual arbitrariness.[25]

The focus of Bloom's remarks is the students at elite universities such as the University of Chicago and Cornell, but his discussion is intended as a commentary on American society itself and on its neglect of public, communal norms. The root of the problem, Bloom tells us, is the students' easy acceptance of moral relativism. The result is a blasé attitude and a deep admiration for the fanatic— the person who, recognizing the moral void, seizes the moment and carves out his or her own universe of values.[26]

Unfortunately, the university, reluctant to raise questions about personally held values, has submitted to this distemper and has failed to preserve the intellectual atmosphere required for the theoretical life. It is failing to fulfill its roles as envisaged by the theorists of the Enlightenment.

The Enlightenment thinkers intended the university to be a house for reasoned discourse where "knowledge is the goal: competence and reason are required of those who pursue it."[27] Bloom believes that this goal dictates the subjects that should be taught in the university: philosophy, mathematics, and the physical, biological, and political sciences. Engineering, law, and medicine, while "lower in dignity," are also allowed, because they provide respect for the sciences from people outside the university.[28] The contemporary "cafeteria" university has failed to meet Bloom's standards.

Yet, for all its appeal to reason, *The Closing of the American Mind* does not set out a rational argument. There are anecdotes about student culture, some of which ring true and some of which do not; there are some engaging discussions of the history of ideas; there is pop social science; there is a vindictive equating of the New Left with Hitler's Youth and an attack on some of the administrators and teachers at Cornell for kowtowing to the demands of the student demonstrations of the late 1960s.[29] There is a complaint about the careerism of students in the 1980s and the claim that this is the ironic and tragic legacy of the students of the 1960s; finally, there is the assurance that all of the problems of women and most of the problems of blacks have been resolved. There is passion in the name of reason but not reason itself. In the end, Bloom fails to provide the kind of coherent moral vision that could be used as the foundation for an educational renewal.

His vision of the moral foundation of education provides us with a prefabricated culture. It seems to claim that those at elite universities may assimilate this culture, but even they cannot participate in its creation. The laws of nature were discovered centuries ago, and we must follow them as best we can. When we break nature's laws, as women do when they follow the route of feminism and as universities do when they adopt the latest educational fad, we invite retribution. Children grow up scarred, and students graduate miseducated and with their "souls" impoverished.

Hirsch and the Requirements of Cultural Literacy. If Bloom's *Closing of the American Mind* speaks to the problems of educating the nation's elite, E. D. Hirsch, Jr.'s *Cultural Literacy* addresses the problem of teaching the nation's masses. Cultural literacy, he tells us, is "the only sure avenue of opportunity for disadvantaged children, the only reliable way of combatting the social determinism that now condemns them to remain in the same social and educational condition as their parents."[30] Hirsch blames the schools and their fragmented curriculum for the inability of poor children to break out of the cycle of poverty,[31] and he blames the fragmented curriculum on the theory that education is a process of natural development, a theory that Hirsch suggests originated with Rousseau and, according to him, was promulgated in this country by Dewey.[32]

Hirsch draws on work in cognitive psychology to support the view that cultural literacy is a prerequisite to reading.[33] The good reader actively engages the written material and is constantly drawing inferences from the text by applying relevant prior knowledge to it. Hirsch argues that differences in reading arise from different levels of background information. Literacy is a problem because the background information of many students is seriously inadequate.

As an argument about reading, there is very little that is unusual about Hirsch's views, unless one is committed to a radical phonics approach. To say that background knowledge contributes to one's reading comprehension is not an exciting idea and hardly warrants the book a place on the best-seller list. What is somewhat different about Hirsch's approach is that he uses this commonplace insight to argue that the decline in reading ability speaks to the need for a national core of items that each and every student should be able to identify, and he concludes his book with a sixty-three-page, double-column list of such items.[34] The list has attracted significant attention, but it is less important than the view of the moral mission of education that lies behind it. What Hirsch wants is a common set of cultural references similar to that once provided by the Bible. Hirsch's argument is only minimally about reading.

Considering the theoretical and empirical studies that Hirsch uses to support his ideas, there are very few implications that he should be drawing about a prescribed content. The only proper conclusion would be that students should be allowed to read passages that have familiar content. Of course, this could involve learning the thousands of items that Hirsch has on his list in some rote way and then reading about each of them. However, it could (as Paulo Freire's literacy programs do) involve the written coding of locally spoken language. While neither of these is sufficient in itself (Freire does recognize the need to move from local to global themes), cognitive psychology and schema theory alone do not tell us what the nature of the content should be. Indeed, the irony of Hirsch's appeal is that while he acknowledges an active theory of mind, he advocates a very passive pedagogy where students memorize the handed-down meanings of a huge list of words. (In an afterthought, Hirsch suggests that teaching should be *interesting*, by which he means nothing more than what the rest of us would mean by *entertaining*.[35]) The more important reason for Hirsch's proposal has little to do with the prerequisites for reading and a great deal to do with what Hirsch believes is necessary for the formation of a public in a modern nation like the United States.[36]

Hirsch tells us that modern nationalism is driven by economic and technical forces and that these forces inexorably lead to national standards for both language and culture. While standards are initially chosen arbitrarily, their change at a later date would be chaotic. It is to avoid such chaos that Hirsch believes that "Americans need to learn not just the grammar of their language but also their national vocabulary. They need to learn not only the associations of such words as "to run" but also such terms as "Teddy Roosevelt," "DNA," and "Hamlet" and, of course, the multitude of other words that appear on Hirsch's list.[37] Hirsch tells us that while the particular stories, songs, facts, myths, and legends may be arbitrarily chosen at first, they support a principle of national identity and cohesion that is not arbitrary. This principle transcends the interests of a particular region and class.[38] All of this serves as a warning to American society that the benefits gained from the peaceful adoption of the English language by the American colonies will be lost if the arguments for multilingualism gain favor in this country.[39] (Hirsch overlooks the fact that his reference to the American Revolution also shows that language is not the only issue that tears a society apart.)

Like Bloom, Hirsch provides an overinterpreted view of cultural transmission. He admits that there may be differences regarding the items in his list, and he grants that some of the items are more important than others. (Since the list includes Thomas Jefferson and Peter Piper, Hirsch is right.) He does not, however, specify which items to count as more and which to count as less significant. The mistake is more than one of merely confusing the important and the trivial. It involves the assumption that there are set associations that attach themselves to different items and that these can be taught as unproblematic. Yet what associations should we attach to, say, "Manifest Destiny"—the philosophy of westward expansion or the ideology of Native American genocide? Is, say, feminism the movement to provide women with equal rights or the cause of the moral decay of the American family? Was World War II a conflict between the Axis and the Allies that took place between 1939 and 1945, or was it a moment in a conflict that began in the early part of the last century and continues today over the flow of capital and raw materials throughout the world? The point is not that one or another of these answers is correct. It is that each of these and many of the other items on the list are in contention and the associations that adhere to a term are not settled. Becoming a member of a public does not involve learning the "proper" response to an item. Rather, it involves finding a way to enter the debate about which items are worth considering and how we should think about them.

The Limited Moral Vision. While Hirsch does not echo Bloom's cranky elitist tone, his and Bloom's view about the moral purpose of education are quite similar. Putting aside the fact that Bloom is addressing the education of the elite and Hirsch the schooling of the masses, each views the role of education as an induction into the heritage of American civilization. For Bloom, the proper initiation for the elite is an introduction to the great writings of Western civilization. For Hirsch, the masses must understand the basic vocabulary of the American tradition.

Yet both Bloom and Hirsch have a defective view of the nature of a democratic public and the way it is created. Each assumes that a public is created by the transmission of a body of fully interpreted cultural material to a new generation. This assumption mistakes the means for the end and provides little opportunity for new cultural interpretations to arise. The unstated consequence of their views is that each new generation is fated to accept the meaning of the old.

Both Bloom and Hirsch correctly identify the important role that schools play in creating a public. However, they fail to acknowledge the fact that a public is created in the debate over its own constitution and over the struggle to give meaning to the events of the past and in the self-conscious awareness that a common self-definition is at stake in the debate. The fact that different individuals happen to hold, in some isolated way, the same cultural material does not mean that they constitute a public. Rather, the development of a public involves entrance into a critical dialogue in which respect for the interpretations of others is a part of the rational inquiry.

What Hirsch and Bloom fail to see is that the moral foundation of education as an induction into the public involves an active engagement with the materials and symbols of a society. The encouragement of an active engagement requires that communal symbols be connected to meanings that are familiar and significant. A democratic public is always in the process of constituting itself, and the imposition of unexamined meanings retards the self-formative process. Certainly, the ability to identify significant people or events is important. However, it is important not because it is a prerequisite for reading or because the ability to identify such events is necessary or sufficient for the creation of a unified nation. It is important because the inability to identify certain events and people suggests that youngsters may be losing the will to actively participate in the cultural experience of their community and to develop the skills required to debate and guide its future conduct. For example, Israeli educators are said to be concerned because a disturbingly high percentage of Israeli youth cannot identify Adolf Hitler or give the years that the Holocaust took place.[40] The complaint sounds similar to Hirsch's concern that American students do not know when the Civil War was fought or who Benedict Arnold was. Yet it is quite different. The fact that Israeli students cannot identify Hitler or give the dates of the Holocaust is a symptom; it is not the problem. To teach the Holocaust as one item on a list of several thousand would be to teach it as dead knowledge and to misunderstand the significance of that event in the continuous formation and reformation of the Israeli public. The problem is to keep these events alive in the Israeli memory by allowing their significance to be continuously confronted and reinterpreted in light of modern concerns.

Moral Responsibility in an Age of Uncertainty

Culture and the Issue of Overinterpretation. While Bloom argues for a return to universal principles and natural law, and Hirsch builds his case on the foundation of relativism, each is driven by an impulse to rest education on a solid, uninterpretable base. This is what drives Bloom to appeal to the certainty of natural laws and to then use those laws to show how inadequate are contemporary movements such as feminism. (He does this, of course, without regard for the fact that much of feminism is concerned with the constricted historical application of the "laws" uncovered by Enlightenment thinkers.) It is this same impulse that moves Hirsch to make the preposterous suggestion that all that economically poor students must do to fulfill the American dream is to memorize his seemingly endless list of names, dates, places, and events.

The idea that drives both Hirsch and Bloom is the view that there is a preestablished standard that can be used to determine membership in the public and that it is the moral role of education to see that everyone is given the opportunity to learn to act in accordance with that ideal. By providing a world already interpreted, they hope to avoid the uncertainty of a world whose meaning must continually be negotiated.

Bloom and Hirsch are correct: Education does have a moral mission, and that mission has to do with the creation of a public in a democratic society. Unfortunately, they misunderstand both the nature of that mission and the character of a democratic public in the latter part of the twentieth century. Nevertheless, they do help us remember that the term *public* as used to modify *education* not only refers to the way schools are to be financed but also affirms the purpose of the enterprise. The major role of public education is to create a public.

What Is a Public? The meaning of *the public* can be understood on different levels. The term is most readily understood in contrast to that which is not public but is private. For example, the relationship entered into by two parties to a contract is essentially a private matter. When people choose to purchase an automobile from one dealer rather than another or to marry one person and not another, they have made a private decision. If we could write unambiguous contracts, if we could assume that all parties to a contract were impeccably honest, and if, after signing our names, we could erect an impenetrable wall around the signers, eliminating the effect of the contract on any innocent nonsigners, then the idea of a public might not be necessary at all. If I were able to appropriate a piece of land, build a factory, hire workers for a mutually agreeable wage, and sell my products to whoever wanted to buy them without affecting anyone outside the contract, then the idea of a public would be unnecessary. But then so, too, would the idea of a contract, for a contract is a private promise made binding by public enforcement.

The public—those not party to the initial contract—takes an

interest in my activity because the consequences are not confined to the parties directly involved. The land that I appropriate may be good farmland. By building a factory on it, I may reduce the amount of food available to the community. The workers may be brought from outside the community, placing a burden on housing and educational resources. The factory may emit dangerous fumes into the air. Because of these and other factors, the concept of a *public* begins to take shape. The public, as Dewey put it in *The Public and Its Problems,* arises because of the indirect consequences of private acts.[41] It is that group that suffers the indirect consequences of acts that are initiated in private quarters. Yet it is more than this.

While the above example provides an abstract idea of the meaning of *the public,* as the term stands here it is only a residual category. Here the concept of the *public* is formed in response to the acts of private parties. At this point, the public comprises everyone who is *left out* of the action and suggests only an aggregate of private interests acting in consort to contain the otherwise harmful effects of the direct action of other private individuals. If this were all that the public involved, then it would be merely a special arm of a shifting set of private interests and would have no special status of its own. Under this conception, people serving the public would really be serving their own or someone else's private interests. Moreover, under this conception of the public, there would be no other alternative, since any expressed public interest would be reducible to a collection of private interests.[42]

Thus, there is a second level on which the concept of the public must be understood. This involves the actions that are taken and the practices that develop to sustain the free flow of ideas about the general well-being. This means that in order for a public to come into existence, it must be aware of itself as an entity and it must have a general conception of its own well-being. This entails a level of collective self-consciousness and a collective understanding that the constitution of a public takes place through the very debates about its own nature. Under this conception, the role of public education is to create and recreate a public by giving voice to an otherwise inarticulate, uninformed mass. The idea of a public suggests, as Dewey well understood, a sense of shared experience and symbols for communicating the meaning of that experience to others.

Dewey sensed that the end of foundationalism was at hand and that many of the ethical guidelines that had served us in earlier times were no longer adequate for the world that was emerging. Yet Dewey held out the possibility that science, in the form of both a method and a community of inquiry, would serve as the modern world's substitute for foundationalism. Today, neither ethics nor science can give that kind of security, and there are neither first principles nor first methods that can provide the basis for establishing the responsibility of the teaching profession. Teachers are forced to develop moral guidelines without the certainty of science or first principles. Moreover, because teaching has as its goal the development of an informed public, it cannot model itself on professions such as medicine that insist on maintaining the gap between professional and everyday knowledge. The goal of creating a public requires that everyday knowledge be respected in its own right, even though it must often be informed by expert knowledge. The guidelines need to be developed from within the teaching profession itself and out of its task of constituting a public in an age of uncertainty.

Yet this public is unlike the public of Hirsch and Bloom, in which each individual is seeking to find the foundation for the correct interpretation of reality. Here the public is construed as searching for a way to enter a conversation about its own nature, knowing that in the process of interpreting its nature, it is also engaged in the process of constituting it. The responsibility of creating a public out of diverse voices requires that local interests, cultures, symbols, and issues be heard within the context of a larger discussion. Of course, the price of entry into the public-forming process is that local ideas and values are subjected to critical evaluation from other standpoints. From the local point of view, it is not sufficient, as Hirsch would have it, to list a local hero or event along with the other items that together are taken for a national culture. Local voices bring local interest and standards from which to reflect on other standpoints. However, it is also not sufficient to simply include the local perspective, as fundamentalists would propose, to "balance" other points of view. If it is included, then it must become a possible object of criticism from other standpoints and using other standards. To enter the public-forming process involves risks as well as benefits, and some cultures may find the risks too large.

From the point of view of the teacher, there are, of course, professional judgments that need to be made about the appropriateness of a certain course of study or subject matter for a certain group of students. Here, issues of individual development, of emotional and intellectual growth, enter the picture. A student may not yet be ready to enter into a deeply critical discussion of his or her own cultural roots, and, on considering the requirements of future intellectual and emotional growth, a teacher may decide that it is inappropriate to probe these matters at a certain time. Cultural pride has an important place in public education, as do cultural interpretation and critique.

There is another important role that teachers need to play in helping to constitute a public; this involves their collective ability to identify conditions that inhibit children from developing the skills needed to become participants in a self-forming public. This role involves the recognition that as important as the school may be in helping some youngsters enter the public conversation, ultimately it is but one agent in the process of public renewal. The quality of other institutions, such as the media, the courts, and the instruments of income distribution, have much to do with the quality of the public discussion. Thus, the responsibility of teachers must extend beyond the school to a collective critique of the institutions that contribute to the quality of the public-forming process.

Notes

1. E. A. Krug, *The Shaping of the American High School, 1880– 1920* (Madison: University of Wisconsin Press, 1964), p. 226.
2. H. G. Good and J. D. Teller, *A History of Western Education*, 3rd ed. (Toronto: Macmillan, 1969), p. 483.
3. M. Katz, *The Irony of Early School Reform: Educational Innovation in Mid-Nineteenth Century Massachusetts* (Cambridge, Mass.: Harvard University Press, 1968).
4. J. Robarts, "The Rise of Educational Science in America,"

unpublished doctoral dissertation, University of Illinois, Urbana, 1963.

5.   Krug, *The Shaping of the American High School*, p. 187.

6.   Holmes Group, *Tomorrow's Teachers* (East Lansing, Mich.: Holmes Group, 1986).

7.   R. E. Callahan, *Education and the Cult of Efficiency: A Study of the Social Forces That Have Shaped the Administration of the Public Schools* (Chicago: University of Chicago Press, 1962), p. 35. The treatment of Bobbitt here is drawn from Callahan's important study.

8.   W. T. Harris, "Educational Needs of Urban Civilization," *Education*, 1885, *5*, 447.

9.   W. T. Harris, "An Educational Policy of Our New Possessions," *Educational Review*, 1899, *18*, 115.

10. A. E. Bestor, *Educational Wastelands: The Retreat from Learning in Our Public Schools* (Urbana: University of Illinois Press, 1953); Good and Teller, *A History of Western Education*.

11. C. W. Sanford, H. C. Hand, and W. B. Spaulding (eds.), "The School and National Security," *Illinois Secondary School Curriculum Program Bulletin*, May 1951, *16*, 38.

12. National Commission on Excellence in Education, *A Nation at Risk: The Imperative for Educational Reform* (Washington, D.C.: U.S. Government Printing Office, 1983).

13. I. Lakatos and A. Musgrave, *Criticism and the Growth of Knowledge* (Cambridge, England: Cambridge University Press, 1970); T. S. Kuhn, *The Structure of Scientific Revolutions* (Chicago: University of Chicago Press, 1962).

14. I. Illich, *Medical Nemesis* (Toronto: Bantam Books, 1976).

15. I. Illich, *Deschooling Society* (New York: Harper & Row, 1971), p. 11

16. Illich, *Deschooling Society*, p. 31.

17. C. Geertz, *The Interpretation of Cultures* (New York: Basic Books, 1973), pp. 87–125.

18. G. Peller, "Creation, Evolution and the New South," *Tikkum*, Nov.–Dec. 1987, p. 72. This is intended as an example of

the issues involved in sociologizing. It is not intended to identify Peller with deschooling.

19. P. Bourdieu and J. Passeron, *Reproduction in Education, Society and Culture* (London: Sage, 1977), p. 17.

20. Bourdieu and Passeron, *Reproduction in Education, Society
and Culture*, p. 12.

21. I am drawing on a distinction made by Thomas Greene in a
number of presentations before the American Educational
Studies Association and the Philosophy of Education Society.

22. A. Bloom, *The Closing of the American Mind: How Higher
Education Has Failed Democracy and Impoverished the Souls
of Today's Students* (New York: Simon & Schuster, 1987).

23. E. D. Hirsch, Jr., *Cultural Literacy: What Every American
Needs to Know* (Boston: Houghton Mifflin, 1987).

24. Bloom, *The Closing of the American Mind*, pp. 83-137.

25. Bloom, *The Closing of the American Mind*, p. 119. Bloom
goes on to claim that children of divorced parents often lack
intellectual daring because of a lack of confidence in the future and hence make poor candidates for the liberal arts (p.
120).

26. Bloom, *The Closing of the American Mind*, pp. 142-143. It is
interesting to observe how Bloom assumes that when left to
formulate their own values, people become extremist and
fanatical, while saying little about the extent to which traditional values may be defended by the same behavior.

27. Bloom, *The Closing of the American Mind*, p. 261.

28. Bloom, *The Closing of the American Mind*, pp. 261-262.

29. Bloom, *The Closing of the American Mind*, pp. 314-315.

30. Hirsch, *Cultural Literacy*, p. xiii.

31. Hirsch, *Cultural Literacy*, p. xiii.

32. This extraordinary misrepresentation of Dewey appears to
come from Hirsch's reading of the first two chapters of
Schools of Tomorrow, in which Dewey and his daughter
sketch Rousseau's educational theory and describe a school
that attempts to exemplify it. Hirsch seems to accept this as a
statement of Dewey's own preference, although in the preface
Dewey made it clear that he was simply describing some at-

tempts to put education theory into practice. Indeed, had Hirsch read *Democracy and Education,* published only a year after *Schools of Tomorrow,* he would have found a searching criticism of Rousseau along the lines of his own objection to Dewey. Cremin puts Dewey's treatment of Rousseau in context when he correctly describes the chapter in *Schools of Tomorrow* by noting that Rousseau's pedagogy is not allowed to stand alone "but is soon incorporated into the larger social reformism that bears the earmarks of Dewey's own philosophy." L. A. Cremin, *The Transformation of the School: Progressivism in American Education, 1876–1957* (New York: Vintage, 1961), pp. 153–154.

33. Hirsch, *Cultural Literacy,* p. 12.

34. Of course, if anything is likely to provide the coup de grace to public education, it would be a nationwide attempt to take this list seriously; if Hirsch really wants his proposal to succeed, he should sell it to some prime-time TV game show.

35. In addition to the use of research studies from cognitive psychology, Hirsch attempts to support the use of the list in two other ways. The first is to shock readers by informing them of the ignorance of high school students. This approach is also inadequate. It is one thing to find out that a student does not know the dates of the Civil War; it is quite another to determine whether the school attempted to teach those dates. Hirsch attempts to deduce the latter from the former. Moreover, it is one thing to be disturbed by the fact that students do not know when the Civil War was fought; it is quite another to insist that they be able to identify "curriculum vitae" (p. 165) or know who said, "I never met a man I didn't like" (p. 179). Hirsch has succeeded in turning a popular and entertaining parlor game into a proposal that a lot of people, including some professionals who should know better, have taken as a serious suggestion about school reform.

36. Hirsch, *Cultural Literacy,* chap. 3.

37. Hirsch, *Cultural Literacy,* p. 84.

38. Hirsch, *Cultural Literacy,* pp. 82–83.

39. Hirsch, *Cultural Literacy,* p. 93.

40. *Christian Science Monitor,* Dec. 14, 1987, p. 12.
41. J. Dewey, *The Public and Its Problems* (Denver, Colo.: Alan Swallow, 1927), p. 12.
42. Dewey himself rejected this notion as he sought to develop an understanding of the public that was consistent with his ideal of the great community.

6

The Legal and Moral
Responsibility
of Teachers

Kenneth A. Strike

The law in many states requires that teachers be people of good moral character. Those who are found not to be of good character may be denied certification. Similarly, the law in many states permits the dismissal of teachers, even tenured teachers, for immorality. Such laws suggest that it is widely agreed that those who teach our children should be good and ethical individuals. Yet it is hard to imagine anything more controversial than an attempt to say what this means in detail and, having done so, to require that teachers live up to a specific ethical code.

Currently, the law sets only the most minimal of standards. For example, teachers may not be felons and may not sexually molest or physically abuse our children. May we not expect more? But attempts to specify more are likely to be problematic. They will quickly run afoul of the fact that in a pluralistic society, we are committed to respecting the private lives and civil liberties of our teachers.

I have performed the following experiment in several of my classes. One scenario is constructed in which a homosexual teaches a class of students that contains a number of fundamentalist children; another is constructed in which a member of the Ku Klux Klan teaches a class that contains a number of black children. In both cases, it is stipulated that the teacher does not use the position to promote personal views. Nor is there any evidence that teaching effectiveness is impaired unless simply by the students' reactions to the teacher. Then my students indicate whether they would be willing to dismiss either the homosexual teacher or the Klan member.

The results have become predictable. Almost no one is willing to dismiss the homosexual teacher; a majority of students are willing to dismiss the Klan member. Why? Generally, students claim that sexual preference is a private matter. Government has no right to interfere in matters of sexual preference. Besides, ethical standards are relative. We do not have a right to impose our personal ethical views on others.

These sentiments disappear for the Klan member. Students who extol privacy and proclaim ethical relativism about sexual preference nevertheless know that a teacher ought not be a bigot. Bigots are poor role models and are offensive to black children. Bigots, as such, harm children.

The law may afford more protection to the Klan member than to the homosexual. Freedom of association is clearly a constitutional right. One may not discharge a teacher for exercising his or her constitutional rights. But the legal status of sexual preference is less clear. It may involve a right to privacy, if there is one, but the law is unclear and is evolving.

What is noteworthy is the firm ethical sentiments of most students, despite the fact that many also claim to be ethical relativists. While firm, their views are less often consistent or coherent. At the same time, it is clear that one would not have to go far outside the halls of an Ivy League university to discover communities whose ethical sentiments are equally firm and equally confused, but also different. There is much that Americans disagree about. Even when people have strong feelings about ethical matters, they are often unable to articulate coherent reasons for their opinions.

What then should we expect our teachers to be? What kinds of ethical standards can we expect them to live up to, and to what extent can these ethical standards be legally enforced? How should we proceed to think about and discover appropriate ethical standards for teachers? How can we train or select people who have a suitable character or who will live up to appropriate ethical standards? It is hoped that we should expect more of our teachers than that they not be felons or abuse their students. But could we ever agree on more?

Legal Issues

In most states, legal issues about teacher morality center on two statutes: the denial or withdrawal of certificates from individuals who are deemed not to be persons of good character and the provision that school districts may discharge teachers for immorality. Before we examine the meaning of these statutes, two crucial points about their enforcement need to be made. First, teachers may not be discharged for exercising their constitutional rights, and, second, teachers may have significant rights of due process that must be respected in attempts to pursue a charge of immorality.

Consider the case of Marvin L. Pickering, who was charged under Illinois law with conduct "detrimental to the efficient operation and administration of the schools of the district."[1] His case has become the lead precedent concerning the constitutional rights of teachers. Pickering's misdeed consisted of a letter to a local newspaper that was critical of how the board of education had handled a bond issue and of the allocation of resources between the school's educational program and its athletic program. It was generally conceded that the statements were substantially incorrect and unfounded but were not made recklessly or with knowledge of their falsity. They were also largely ignored. In overturning Pickering's dismissal, the U.S. Supreme Court had this to say:

> The question whether a school system requires additional funds is a matter of legitimate public concern on which the judgment of the school administration, including the School Board, cannot, in a society that leaves such questions to popular vote, be taken as conclusive. On such a question free and open debate is vital to informed decision-making by the electorate. Teachers are, as a class, the members of a community most likely to have informed and definite opinions as to how funds allotted to the operation of the schools should be spent. Accordingly, it is essential that they be able to speak out freely on such questions without fear of retaliatory dismissal. . . .
> What we do have before us is a case in which a

teacher has made erroneous public statements upon issues then currently the subject of public attention, which are critical of his ultimate employer but which are neither shown nor can be presumed to have in any way either impeded the teacher's proper performance of his daily duties in the classroom or to have interfered with the regular operation of the schools generally. In these circumstances we conclude that the interest of the school administration in limiting teachers' opportunities to contribute to public debate is not significantly greater than its interest in limiting a similar contribution by any member of the general public.[2]

Pickering outlines the basic legal framework for considering any case where a teacher's dismissal is sought for actions that may be constitutionally protected. Teachers continue to have such constitutional rights as are available to all citizens; however, courts will consider the effects of the teacher's actions. Unless an adverse effect on the school program can be demonstrated, no action against the teacher is warranted. In short, courts will balance the rights of the teacher against the requirements of the efficient management of the school. While Pickering does not deal per se with immoral conduct, the same framework of analysis is likely to be followed, especially if there is any suggestion that the conduct in question is constitutionally protected.

A related aspect is that it is the effect of conduct on the welfare of the school program that counts, not the time or place of the conduct. A teacher whose out-of-school conduct adversely affects the school program will not be protected by the fact that the misconduct occurred away from school premises or on the teacher's own time.

In cases where teachers are charged with immorality, they may have significant rights of due process that must be respected. The Fourteenth Amendment requires that government must provide due process whenever life, liberty, or property is threatened by governmental action. Any action that threatens to restrict some constitutionally protected activity will thereby threaten a liberty. Teachers may also have a property right in their jobs, which the Supreme Court has defined as a reasonable expectation of continued employment.[3] The granting of tenure confers a property interest in a teaching position, although it can also be conferred in other ways. Tenured teachers thus are entitled to extensive rights of due process and, as a rule, cannot be dismissed for immorality or denied a license because of it without a rather extensive hearing on the matter.[4]

What, then, constitutes immorality or bad character, and how are state laws of the sort noted above applied? To address this question, it is pertinent to review some representative cases dealing both with denial or withdrawal of certification and with dismissal for immoral conduct.

In 1961, Dean Norman Bay was denied a teaching certificate by the state of Oregon because he had failed to show that he was a person of good moral character as required by Oregon law. He took his case to court, seeking to have the decision of the state board of education overturned. The circuit court of Union County agreed with Bay, holding that the board lacked competent evidence to make the decision. However, the Oregon Supreme Court reversed the circuit court and reinstated the decision of the board.[5] The board's grounds for holding that Bay had failed to provide evidence of good character were a 1953 conviction for breaking and entering and grand larceny. Bay had subsequently been paroled, completed college, and taught elementary school under a one-year emergency certificate.

Two factors are apparently significant in the decision of the Oregon Supreme Court. One has to do with standards of judicial review. The court noted that it was not within its power to review the evidence put before an administrative agency and to substitute its judgment for that of the agency. Instead, review was limited to determining whether the agency had acted impartially, had performed its duties faithfully, had stayed within its jurisdiction, had committed no errors of law, had not behaved capriciously, and had arrived at no judgment that was clearly wrong. It is the last of these factors that was at issue in this case. The court held that the board's judgment was not clearly wrong. That Bay had been guilty of burglary while occupying a position of trust was evidence of lack of good moral character. It was a matter of judgment as to whether this deficiency of character had been overcome. The court could not, therefore, find that the board was clearly wrong.

Compare this to a second case.[6] Iowa law permits the Board of Public Instruction to grant teaching certificates to those who are, among other things, morally fit to teach. Richard Erb had been certified since 1963 and had been an art teacher in the Nishna Valley Community School. His certificate was revoked by the state board after he was caught having sexual intercourse with a woman in the backseat of a car (the woman's husband was hiding in the trunk). The state board revoked Erb's certificate despite the fact that he had broken off his affair, that the local school board had declined to accept his resignation, that he was a highly rated teacher, and that he had been forgiven by his wife and by the student body. In reversing the state board's decision, the Iowa Supreme Court rejected the board's claim that committing adultery was sufficient to show that someone was unfit to teach. Allowing this decision to stand, they claimed, would permit the board to revoke the certificate of any teacher of whose private conduct they disapproved. Instead, they held that revocation of certificate for immorality requires a showing of reasonable likelihood that the teacher's retention in the profession would adversely affect the school community.[7] There was, they claimed, no such showing here.

The phrase "reasonable likelihood" is worth special note. The Iowa court does not seem to require any demonstration of actual harmful effect. Instead, it seems to require an argument that is more than speculative that harmful effects are likely. A stronger standard, one requiring some demonstration of actual harmful consequences, is possible.[8]

Nevertheless, courts generally require some evidence that "immoral conduct" affects teaching before they will uphold a discharge on the basis of immoral conduct. Consider three cases dealing with homosexuality.

In 1969, the California Supreme Court overturned the dismissal of Marc Morrison for immoral conduct.[9] Morrison was discharged as the result of a brief homosexual encounter with another teacher. In overturning his dismissal, the court noted that the homosexual encounter was brief and discrete and had not recurred. The court's primary concerns, however, were with the vagueness of the concept of immoral behavior and with its potential for permitting the personal moral convictions of administrators or public officials to become the standard of conduct for teachers. In insisting that charges of immoral conduct can be sustained only if they are job related, the court suggested the following standards for judging the fitness to teach:

> In determining whether the teacher's conduct thus indicates unfitness to teach the board may consider such matters as the likelihood that the conduct may have adversely affected students or fellow teachers, the degree of such adversity anticipated, the proximity or remoteness in time of the conduct, the type of teaching certificate held by the party involved, the extenuating or aggravating circumstances, if any, surrounding the conduct, the praiseworthiness or blameworthiness of the motives resulting in the conduct, the likelihood of the recurrence of the questioned conduct, and the extent to which disciplinary action may inflict an adverse impact or chilling effect upon the constitutional rights of the teacher involved or other teachers.[10]

Briefly summarized, this passage indicates that teachers may be dismissed for immoral conduct when that conduct might adversely affect students or the school program. The judgment of whether immoral conduct does have such effects depends very much on the circumstances.

There have been other cases where courts have ruled that homosexual conduct is grounds for dismissal. The same California court that reversed the dismissal of Marc Morrison upheld the discharge of Thomas Sarac for immorality.[11] Here the act in question involved a homosexual advance to a police officer on a public beach. Sarac pleaded guilty to criminal charges in connection with the incident. Similarly, the Supreme Court of Washington upheld the discharge of James Gaylord on the grounds of immorality because he was a known homosexual.[12] Several observations by the court are noteworthy. The court held that dismissal for immorality required a showing of actual or prospective adverse performance as a teacher.[13] In commenting on the grounds for believing that Gaylord's activity constituted grounds for dismissal under this standard, the court commented:

> After Gaylord's homosexual status became publicly known, it would and did impair his teaching efficiency. A teacher's efficiency is determined by his relationship with his students, their parents, the school administration and fellow teachers. If Gaylord had not been discharged after he became known as a homosexual, the result would be fear, confusion, suspicion, parental concern and pressure on the administration by students, parents and other teachers.[14]

The court later added that

> Gaylord's homosexual conduct must be considered in the context of his position of teaching high school students. Such students could treat the retention of the high school teacher by the school board as indicating adult approval of his homosexuality.[15]

Here the court insists that teachers cannot be dismissed because someone happens to believe that their behavior is immoral. Instead, there must be some showing of adverse effect on teaching performance. However, the standards for showing adverse effect are not strong. Prospective effect seems to count. That students might be influenced either because the teacher functions as a role model or because the failure to dismiss is treated as tacit approval by the school also counts. Thus, courts have generally not required demonstration of actual harmful effects or required any empirical demonstration of the reasoning used to show prospective harmful effect.

These cases are noteworthy because they are controversial and thus become the source of the refinement of judicial standards. There are other cases where judges routinely find that conduct is immoral and thus where there are clear grounds for dismissal.[16] Sexual misconduct involving students is the most obvious case and is likely to justify dismissal even if the conduct is off campus and after hours or even if it goes only as far as suggestive remarks.

Habitual public drunkenness and drug use are also grounds justifying dismissal. Felony convictions also qualify.

Four points are worth noting here. First, in judging a case of immoral conduct, courts are not likely to ask whether the conduct is genuinely immoral. That is not the role of a court. What is at stake is its effect on teaching. However, community moral standards do count in such judgments. The fact that the members of a given community believe that certain conduct is immoral contributes to its effects. Thus, conduct that will result in dismissal in some communities may pass without notice in others.[17] Second, it is the effect on the job that counts, not the time or place of the conduct. However, the publicness of the behavior in question does make a difference. Students are not adversely affected by behavior of which they are unaware. Third, a demonstration of actual adverse effects seems generally not to be required. Courts seem to insist only on a reasonable argument that adverse effects are possible and likely. Arguments that the teacher is a bad role model or that not dismissing the teacher conveys approval seem to count. Finally, these kinds of standards seem most likely to come into play where the issue is some form of sexual activity away from school. In cases where teachers become sexually involved with students or minors, courts are likely to find the actual or prospective harmful consequences to be self-evident.

We should gain two basic lessons from this brief legal review. First, the basic task faced by the courts is to distinguish some sphere of liberty regarding the teacher's life that the employer may rightfully control. This task is accomplished by balancing the interest of the teacher against the interests of the school's educational program. Courts will treat the teacher's constitutional rights as a strong interest and will require a substantial demonstration that an activity is detrimental to the school's program before they will allow the school to interfere with the teacher's conduct. At the other pole are activities that are illegal or involve some form of overt aggression against a student. Courts have little difficulty finding that these constitute immoral behavior. In the middle are activities that usually are not illegal and that may have some degree of legal protection as part of a right of privacy but that are found to be immoral or offensive by some part of the community. It is not surprising that various sexual activities head the list here and are the most difficult to resolve. There is no moral consensus about them, they may be held to be part of the individual's private sphere regardless of whether they are thought to be immoral, and their effects on students are difficult to ascertain. Courts will thus find it difficult to strike a principled balance about such matters.

Second, especially in this middle ground, courts must act in an area of great ignorance. We simply lack any very clear understanding about how the character or moral behavior of teachers affects the character or moral behavior of students. Even if we were clear about our goals concerning the moral education of students, which we are not, it is unclear how the accomplishment of these goals would be affected by a teacher's conduct or character. For example, role model arguments are a popular way to link teacher conduct or character to student conduct or character, but there is little empirical evidence to suggest that such claims are true. Moreover, it is quite possible to hold that student character is improved by an occasional bad example. In the absence of evidence, it is possible to argue almost anything. Thus, courts must rely on common sense and intuition in judging such matters. It is not surprising, therefore, that issues remain contested and ambiguous.

The Liberal Construction of the Law

The structure of law on teacher morality is readily recognizable. I shall characterize it as "liberal." Here I do not use *liberal* in opposition to *conservative* but rather to refer to that tradition in political philosophy that makes a central virtue of human freedom and seeks, for the sake of freedom, to restrict the power of government. One of the key tasks that any liberal theory must accomplish is to provide a principled way of distinguishing those areas of one's life over which government or society can exercise authority and those over which political or social authority cannot be rightfully exercised. How are we to distinguish between the public sphere wherein social authority can be exercised and the private sphere in which the individual is by right sovereign?

For illustrative purposes, consider two different liberal views on how this distinction is to be drawn. The first is that of J. S. Mill, who, in *On Liberty*, writes:

> The sole end for which mankind are warranted, individually or collectively, in interfering with the liberty of action of any of their number is self-protection. That the only purpose for which power can be rightfully exercised over any member of a civilized community, against his will, is to prevent harm to others. His own good, either physical or moral, is not a sufficient warrant. He cannot rightfully be compelled to do or forbear because it will be better for him to do so, because it will make him happier, because, in the opinions of others, to do so would be wise or even right. . . . The only part of the conduct of anyone for which he is amenable to society is that which concerns others. In the part which merely concerns himself, his independence is, of right, absolute. Over himself, over his own body and mind, the individual is sovereign.[18]

Mill's formulation makes the right to interfere in someone's life contingent on the consequences of that person's act. A government may interfere in someone else's behavior to the degree that that behavior affects the welfare of others.

A second response is suggested by Bruce Ackerman, whose starting point is that a liberal society is one in which claims to power over social resources must be justified by discussion and argument (conversations). However, not just any argument will do. One constraint on conversations that can be used to justify social authority is that they must be neutral. Ackerman writes:

> A power structure is illegitimate if it can be justified only through a conversation in which some person (or group) must assert that he is (or they are) the privileged moral authority:
> Neutrality. No reason is a good reason if it requires the holder to assert:

(a) that his conception of the good is better than that asserted by any of his fellow citizens, or
(b) that, regardless of his conception of the good, he is intrinsically superior to one or more of his fellow citizens.[19]

The point of Ackerman's view may be less evident than that of Mill's. Consider some examples of how it might be applied. Suppose, for example, that a principal proposed to deny a teaching position to someone because of race. To decide whether this use of power was illegal, we would have to ask for its justification. Suppose that the reason given was that the principal preferred a member of his own race. Clearly, this justification is not neutral. It violates part (b) of Ackerman's conception of neutrality in that it treats the welfare of the members of one race as inherently superior to that of others.

Suppose then that another principal proposed to dismiss a teacher because he spent all his spare time skiing, which the principal believed to be frivolous: Someone who devoted all of his spare time to the activity lacked the maturity of character to be a teacher. Is this a neutral justification? Not if the principal is merely expressing his view of skiing. Neutrality precludes justification of power that assumes that one view of what is good is inherently to be preferred to another. If, however, the principal has observed that during the skiing season the teacher is frequently absent, often late, and rarely prepared, the justification may be neutral. Presumably, the principal could explain why it was better for a teacher to show up regularly, be on time, and be prepared and would not be assuming that one vision of a good life is inherently preferred to another. But now the justification has lost its connection with skiing. The principal is no longer expressing a view about what goods are or are not inherently worth pursuing. The justification now has to do with the conditions for successful performance of the job. As long as the job itself can be defended with neutral arguments, the job-related argument does not violate neutrality.

There are some significant differences between Mill's and Ackerman's formulations that go to the heart of moral philosophy. For Mill, human beings are maximizers of satisfaction. The best and most just society is that which produces the greatest happiness for the greatest number. Mill thus tends to defend individual liberty in terms of its connection with the general social welfare. Freedom of expression is justified because truth is best sought by a process of free and open debate. A society that represses free expression cannot be progressive or have enlightened social policies. Freedom of life-style (which Mill calls "individuality") is justified for a variety of reasons. Each person is the best judge of his or her own happiness. Nonstandard life-styles are experiments in living. Societies that enforce conformity fail to progress, because they fail to learn. Ackerman, however, regards human beings as autonomous choosers of ends. People have a right to their own concepts of their own good and a prima facie equal claim on the resources required to support their own concepts of the good. Governments may not base their actions either on the assumption that some visions of a good life are inherently more worthy than others or on the assumption that the interests of some are inherently to be preferred over those of others.

The philosophical justifications of the views of Mill and Ackerman thus differ significantly. Nevertheless, their solutions to the question of the scope and limits of government authority have much in common. Both see intellectual liberty as highly protected. For Mill, freedom and debate are essential features of a progressive society; for Ackerman, it is essential to a liberal society that power be justified by rational dialogue. Mill and Ackerman also both provide for extensive freedom of life-style. In neither case is government entitled to a view about what is good for people. People are entitled to their own conception of their own good.

Moreover, for both Mill and Ackerman, governments may seek to promote justice and may generate a legal structure within the bounds of which people may pursue their own good. For Mill, government may act when the actions of individuals affect the welfare of others; for Ackerman, government may act so long as its actions can be given neutral justification. For both, the central point of government is to act so as to regulate and facilitate individual pursuit of the good without defining what that good will be and without preferring the interests of some to those of others. In short, for liberals, government may not tell us what we should or should not value, but it may enforce reasonable standards of justice that regulate the manner in which we pursue our own sense of our own good.

What we should note about the above discussion is that the law of teacher morality can be represented as solving the liberal problem in a liberal way. The task is to discover the limits of the authority of the state over the lives of teachers. If the solution to this problem is to be a liberal one, the teacher's intellectual liberty and freedom of life-style must be respected. The teacher may be interfered with only when the teacher's behavior harms someone else. Such regulations as may be appropriate for teachers must be neutral. They cannot regulate the teacher's conception of his or her own good, and they may not assume that the welfare of some people is inherently to be preferred to that of others. This problem is solved by insisting that attempts to regulate the moral life of a teacher be job related. We may not refuse to certify or dismiss a teacher merely because we disapprove of that teacher's views or life-style. We must show that the teacher's conduct affects his or her job performance.

Reasonable people may disagree, of course, about the nature of the job and about what counts as having a negative effect on it. As I have suggested, one pressing issue here is whether the teacher has any duty to be a role model and, if so, what power this gives the school over a teacher's behavior. Nevertheless, it should be clear that this has become a liberal debate. It is no longer sufficient to show that the teacher's conduct violates prevailing community standards; it must now be shown that the teacher's conduct harms job performance.

One important caveat to this discussion needs to be mentioned. A liberal view of schooling will require that neutrality be respected not only for teachers but also (especially) for students. Schools will not be entitled to impose orthodoxies on students or to impose any preordained view of a good life on students.[20] It may be claimed, however, that there is an inherent conflict between respecting the neutrality of students and respecting the neutrality of teachers. We must remember that students are compelled to attend school. Moreover, it may be argued that students, who are usually viewed as immature and therefore unusually impressionable, are likely to be influenced by a teacher's character or moral behavior, not just by what a teacher says about the subject matter being taught. It may also be argued that the very fact that schools fail to condemn a certain sort of behavior may be treated by students as a sign of its endorsement.[21] This is, of course, merely a variant on the role model argument. If it is true that a teacher's character or moral conduct influences students, then such freedoms of expression and life-style as are granted to teachers may be inconsistent with a similar degree of freedom for students and their parents, who are compelled to send them to school.

What I believe follows from this discussion is that both the structure of the law and its ambiguities can best be seen as resulting from the attempt to solve a characteristically liberal problem. The law must give expression to reasonable requirements for the behavior of teachers without unreasonably restricting their liberty. The debate about what this means is generally carried on against the background of liberal assumptions. The generally liberal orientation of the political philosophy of our society is one factor that must be taken into account if we are to have a coherent view of ethics for teachers.

Ethics for Teachers: Observations on Content

The law provides a poor guide if we want a more developed view of the ethical standards that ought to inform teaching. At best, it sets only a very minimal standard. That is perhaps what we should expect of the law. Legal standards tell us what we are willing to coerce. What we should hope for should be different. This is not, however, the most fundamental reason why the law is a poor guide to the ethical standards of the profession of teaching. Consider some additional reasons.

One reason is that the law does not specify ethical standards that are specific to the activity of teaching. For the most part, the legal issues would be what they are regardless of whether teaching was involved. Sexual molestation or aggression by adults against children should be proscribed regardless of whether the site is an educational institution or the parties teachers and students. The idea that conduct outside the workplace can be regulated by a public employer only if it negatively affects the employee's ability to do the job has little to do specifically with teaching. It would apply equally to the post office. Thus, for the most part, the fact that the law reviewed above deals with teaching is coincidental. The law does not inform us about any ethical standards that are specific to the professional activities of teachers.

However, there are ethical issues that are more closely associated with teaching. One such issue is indoctrination. Education is supposed to be a rational activity. Free people may be presumed to have a right to determine for themselves what they will believe. If so, then there are ethical grounds for preferring educational techniques that give students reasons, emphasize evidence, and help students develop a capacity for reasoned judgment. Likewise, there are ethical reasons why we should avoid teaching techniques that are coercive, manipulative, or merely rote. That teaching aims at understanding and rational belief is central to its character and is a significant factor in the ethics of pedagogy.

A second area of ethical concern that is closely associated with teaching is grading and evaluation. Teachers are expected to respond to student work with comments that are educationally informative and grades that are fair and accurate. If they are to do so, they must first of all be intellectually competent. One cannot respond competently to something of which one is ignorant. But grading, like any form of evaluation, has due-process requirements. Teachers must have reasons for the grades assigned, they should follow procedures that minimize bias (such as not attending to the names of students when reading papers or exams), and they must have a consistent standard from case to case and class to class.

A third area, one that raises significant problems if teaching is to become a profession, is potential conflicts between teacher autonomy and the tradition of democratic control over education. Perhaps the center of the idea of professionalization is a demand for control over professional activity by professionals that is rooted in expertise. "Those who know should rule." But what, then, of school boards, communities, parents, and children? What rights will they have in educational governance? How will teachers as professionals understand the rights of their clients?

These issues deal with ethical questions that are closely associated with the work that teachers do. They are, of course, only illustrative of a broad range of similar ethical issues. While they involve concepts, such as due process and democracy, that apply widely, the fact that these concepts are being applied to teaching is not merely coincidental to the discussion. An ethic for the profession of teaching would consist of detailed and codified answers to the kinds of questions raised above. The law on teacher morality has little bearing on such professional matters.

Another source of ethical principles for teachers is values that are internal to the subject matter. Teachers should be expected to teach their subjects in ways that respect the subjects' fundamental values. Consider, for example, that the values of health and justice are internal to the practice of medicine and law, respectively.[22] Doctors and lawyers who do not attempt to promote health and justice behave unethically. Likewise, there are values that are internal to various academic subject matters. Beauty and concern for the human condition are central to literature. A teacher who deals with poetry as though its sole function were to help students learn to write advertising jingles and to manipulate consumers perverts poetry's core values. A teacher who teaches with no concern for the internal values of his or her subject behaves unethically, just as does a doctor who practices medicine with no concern for health.

Thus, there are both ethical principles that are closely associated with the work of teaching and values that are internal to subject matter. These can be a source of ethical standards for teachers. However, the ethical principles that regulate the characteristic activities of teaching are more likely to be candidates for direct instruction in teacher education programs than those values that are internal to subject matter. The latter should be acquired in the process of mastery of subject matter.

An additional approach to the ethics of teaching that is not well represented in the law has to do with the connection between the character and behavior of teachers and the desired outcomes of education, especially ethical outcomes. Generally, the legal requirements for teachers fall under one of three requirements. First, teachers must not do bad things to students. They must not physically assault them or sexually exploit or abuse them. Second, teachers must not act in ways that are disruptive to the performance of their job or to the school's performance. They must not act so as to make themselves notorious or otherwise incapacitate themselves in dealing effectively with students, other teachers, or administrators. Finally, and most controversial from a legal point of view, teachers must provide desirable role models.

Just as the first two of these requirements have little to do per se with the fact that the activity they govern is teaching, they also have little to do with any special sense of what schools are for and with the connections between the teacher's character or behavior and such educational outcomes as may be desirable. The suggestion that teachers should be role models, however, does seem to suggest that the ethics of teaching should be connected directly with a set of desired educational outcomes. The assumption is that teacher character or behavior has some effect on student character or behavior. In the most simple case, students will model themselves after teachers. As the foregoing legal discussion has suggested, this approach is fraught with difficulties. The law is likely to make only the most obvious of assumptions (and even these will be controversial) and to reject only the most egregious behavior. More subtle connections between teacher character and behavior and student character and behavior will be matters for educational research and theory, not law. Consider what might be involved in connecting ethical issues to educational outcomes in a more detailed way. First, we would need to have some idea about what is desired. What should students be like or how should they behave? If the issue is character or ethical behavior, the problems here are obvious. How are we to have a common view of character or ethics in a pluralistic society? If we are to be able to answer this question, we must discover empirical connections between teacher characteristics and desired student characteristics.

I do not believe that the question of what ethical aims a liberal democratic society may have for students in its public schools is entirely unsolvable. Generally, there are three sorts of aims that schools can have without violating liberal neutrality and undermining pluralism. First, the very idea of a liberal democratic society assumes that human beings have or can have certain characteristics that allow us to view people as free human beings who are entitled to make choices for themselves and to participate in the governance of their own affairs—among which would seem to be autonomy and rationality. Let us call such characteristics "the capacities of self-governance."

Second, liberal societies are governed by views of justice and by institutions that are supposed to allow us to cooperate and live together while we pursue our own conception of our own good. People in liberal societies thus need to learn to respect justice and to function successfully within democratic institutions. The capacities required here may be called "the capacities of citizenship."

Third, while one of the characteristics of a liberal society is that it respects the value choices of individuals, individuals nevertheless need the capacity to wisely choose and develop their own conception of their own good. There are numerous requirements if such choices are to be made responsibly, among which are the capacity for reflective choice and the opportunity to explore various alternatives and participate in different communities organized by various values. Let us call these requirements "the capacities and conditions of reflective choice."

If we are to think about the ethics of teaching by reflecting on the characteristics students need in order to function in a liberal democratic society, we will have to flesh out what is required by the capacities of self-governance, citizenship, and reflective choice. We will then have to connect the development of these capacities to the character and behavior of teachers.

The discussion of this section leads to three important conclusions:

1. A serious dealing with the ethics of teaching requires a detailed discussion of the ethical standards that are to govern the characteristic activities of teachers.
2. A serious dealing with the ethics of teaching requires that teachers act in ways that respect the values and mores internal to subject matter.
3. A serious dealing with the ethics of teaching requires that we connect the characteristics and behavior of teachers with the moral purposes (and the overall purposes) of education.

The law of teacher immorality deals with none of these matters adequately. Its intent, rather, seems more to be to protect the student from the most serious forms of abuse that children might suffer at the hands of adults. Certainly this is an important function, but it is far from a sufficient guide to the ethics of teaching.

Teaching Ethics to Teachers

One of the things that characterize the work of teachers is that it is done in self-contained classrooms in comparative isolation from other teachers. Those aspects of their jobs that teachers perform in association with others are comparatively minor parts of their work. Despite this isolation, teachers also work in bureaucratically organized workplaces where they are responsible to an administrative hierarchy. It is fashionable to argue that their work is overly regulated and that they are denied significant responsibility for the basic decisions that govern their work.[23]

It is not clear which of these factors is the most significant when it comes to ethical decision making. Ethical responsibilities are not pre-packaged curricula. Teachers do not test their students for ethical conduct, and they are not responsible to administrators for their students' scores on ethical tests. Thus, the conventional accoutrements of bureaucratic responsibility are not there. On the other hand, teachers are called to account for alleged unethical conduct that comes to the attention of administrators.

Another factor concerning teachers' ethics is that they work with a particularly vulnerable clinetele. Children rarely know when they are being dealt with unethically. Even when they do, they are limited in their ability to characterize their complaints, and enforcement mechanisms are not available to them without the cooperation of parents and administrators.

A final characteristic of teachers' work is the lack of clear, predetermined, ethical guidelines. The National Education Association has a code of ethics, but it is brief and general and will not serve as a functional standard in cases of any ambiguity. Few school districts have codes of ethics. Generally, teachers must operate without specific guidance or collective wisdom as to what constitutes ethical conduct. Consequently, teachers are in the difficult position of having to make ethical decisions without much guidance. If they use or are accused of using poor judgment, they may find themselves called to account before an administrator who also has little guidance regarding an appropriate course of action.

These facts suggest that teachers need instruction in ethics. Since they rely on their own judgment as to what is ethical, they require the capacity to reflect successfully on ethical matters.

Teacher education programs thus should include instruction in basic ethical concepts. This should be distinguished from teaching abstract moral philosophy. Teachers must be taught how to apply ethical principles to concrete situations by learning to perceive a situation as involving an ethical issue and by reflecting on how principles are appropriately applied to the case. Since case studies provide a means of simulating the real world classroom, they are pedagogically useful.

The emphasis should be on teaching those ethical concepts that are central to the activities of teachers. Among the most important are intellectual liberty and intellectual honesty, respect for appropriate diversity, due process in such matters as discipline and grading, fairness in punishment, and equity in the distribution of educational resources such as the teachers' time.

And the emphasis should be on teaching substantive ethical concepts and developing ethical judgment—not on producing philosophers or improving character. I do not wish to devalue either, but courses on ethics that emphasize philosophical theories to the exclusion of basic ethical principles soon lose the interest of practitioners because their content lacks connection to practice.[24] It is, of course, earnestly to be desired that teachers be people of good character. I do not know how to reform the character of adult prospective teachers, and I am suspicious of those who believe they do. Getting people of good character should be treated as a problem of selection, not redemption, by those of us who teach teachers. It is, however, both possible and important to teach the content of basic ethical principles.[25]

We ought also to insist that administrators receive much the same kind of ethical instruction as teachers. As long as administrators must judge teachers, they must judge them by a set of shared standards.

Finally, considering the absence of agreed-upon and detailed ethical standards for the profession of teaching, we can expect teachers to exercise responsible and informed judgment about ethical matters. We cannot hold teachers to unknown and nonexistent ethical standards, but they must understand the basic ethical concepts that should inform their professional conduct and conscientiously apply them in their decision making. Our goal should be informed and responsible ethical decision making by teachers.[26]

In emphasizing informed and responsible decision making, I do not suggest that any decision that teachers make is acceptable as long as it is responsibly achieved. Nor is my view predicated on some form of ethical relativism. Ethical claims are capable of objective assessment in that moral reasons can be given for preferring one course of conduct to another. However, it does not follow that there is always one best response to any ethical choice. In complex cases, we may know that some courses of action are ethically unacceptable and that others seem preferable, but it is often difficult to discover which of these preferable possibilities is best. It is thus reasonable to hold teachers responsible for ethically wrong choices when it is clear that they are wrong. However, in the absence of a professional consensus about which among the ethically defensible choices is best, it is inappropriate to hold teachers to an exacting standard of professional conduct. Therefore, we can expect that teachers will not behave in ways that are patently unethical and that, in those more complex areas where what is best is not clear, they will choose reflectively and responsibly among the range of defensible options.

Alternative Views on Teaching Ethics to Teachers

While professional ethics is a relatively new topic of concern for educators, programs of moral education have been available for some time. It seems likely that one approach to teaching ethics to teachers will be to adopt such programs. I suggest that such an approach is undesirable—largely because none of the currently popular views has a suitable concept of what the subject matter of ethics for teachers should be. I argue this by reviewing several current views.

Values Clarification. Values clarification has been one of the most popular ways of dealing with values in education over the last several decades. The aim of values clarification is precisely what the name implies: It provides a variety of simple techniques to enable people to discover what their true values are. Values clarification's chief enemy is imposed values; almost any source of socialization is viewed as a kind of imposition. We might say that the central value of values clarification is authenticity. Values clarification assumes that what legitimates the holding of a given value is that it has been freely chosen and/or it represents the individual's true feelings about something. Its techniques often seem to suppose that in some way people "really know" what their values are but that they may be confused about them, perhaps because they have been indoctrinated by others into other, inauthentic values. Thus, if values are discovered, it seems that they are discovered within and not, say, as the result of action or experimentation or in literature or philosophical reflection.

Values clarification has several deficiencies that disqualify it as a viable approach to teaching teachers about ethics. Consider a distinction between two sorts of "values."[27] Philosophers often distinguish between the right and the good. Questions about the good have to do with the nature of worthwhile activities, objects, and, indeed, lives. Questions about the right have to do with the nature of our moral duties and obligations—with the kinds of actions that are right or wrong. "Canoeing is enjoyable," "Pleasure is the good," and "Bach is better than the Beatles" are claims about goods or the good. "Thou shalt not kill" and "We are obligated to treat others justly" are claims about the right.

One significant aspect of the distinction between the right and the good is that it seems far more reasonable to hold that people may freely choose their goods than it does to hold that they may freely choose their moral principles. If I value canoeing and you prefer hiking, there is no reason why I should insist that you change your mind. Other things being equal, I have no stake in your choice of your own goods, nor you in mine. Goods, therefore, may be freely chosen. But this is not the case for moral principles. It is desirable that people freely commit themselves to obey a set of reasonable moral principles. Nevertheless, moral principles differ from claims about the good in that the former are obligatory and enforceable. If my neighbor has not freely committed himself to the proposition that it is wrong to steal, it is nevertheless true that I have a right to expect that he not steal my property, and I have a right to have my property protected from him regardless of what his moral principles are.

Values clarification fails to distinguish between the right and the good. As a result, it often ends up treating moral principles as though they were goods and both as though they were a matter of taste or personal preference.

Consider the following conversation from a leading values clarification text between a student and a teacher:

> Ginger: Does that mean we can decide for ourselves whether we should be honest on tests here?
>
> *Teacher:*   No, that means that you can decide on the value. I personally value honesty; and although you may choose to be dishonest, I shall insist that we be honest on tests here. . . .
>
> *Ginger:*   But then how can we decide for ourselves? Aren't you telling us what to value? . . .
>
> *Teacher:*   Not exactly. I didn't mean to tell you what you should value. That's up to you. . . . All of you who choose dishonesty as a value may not practice it here, that's all I'm saying.[28]

Values clarification has left this teacher in an untenable position. He has insisted that values are up to the students. When faced with dissent about the value of honesty, he cannot consistently hold that there are reasons why Ginger should value honesty or that Ginger is morally obligated to be honest, however she feels. He must simply claim that honesty is his value and that, because he is in power, Ginger is compelled to comply. In short, he has moved in a few sentences from moral skepticism to moral fascism. Values clarification makes all moral principles into values and values into matters of personal preference. Its having done so, the enforcement of any value can only be an act of arbitrary will.[29]

It is evident that this cannot be the basis of a way of teaching ethics to teachers. Surely it is a disaster to have teachers face students with the conviction that teachers are entitled to their own personal values, whatever their content, and that they may enforce their values in their classrooms because they are in power there. Instead, teachers need to acquire a functional acquaintance with those ethical principles that have been found to be central to our common lives together, especially those that are central to the activities of teaching. They need to view these principles as obligatory because they are just and reasonable, not as matters of preference and taste.

Kohlberg. Lawrence Kohlberg has developed another view of moral education that has been widely used in schools. Kohlberg's views are rooted, on one hand, in a developmental psychology that owes much to Jean Piaget[30] and, on the other, in a view of ethics that owes much to Kant[31] and to the liberal philosopher John Rawls.[32] According to Kohlberg, growth in moral judgment is characterized by a progression through a sequence of moral stages. Each stage can be characterized as a particular set of criteria or standards according to which moral judgments are made. These stages are progressively more mature in their moral content. Higher is better.

People go through these stages in an invariant sequence. While there are developmental limits on how fast people may progress through these stages, it is by no means inevitable that people will progress through them at any particular rate or that they will ever reach the higher stages. Generally, Kohlberg holds that there are six stages but that most people do not get above the third or fourth. Some never get this high.

The task of moral education, then, is conceived as moving individuals to higher stages. One way this can be accomplished is by means of posing to students moral dilemmas. These are "hard cases" that cannot be adequately dealt with at the current stage of development. In Piagetian language, the student cannot assimilate the problem in his or her current moral schema. If the dilemma is to be resolved, he must move to a higher stage.

Kohlberg describes stage six, the highest of his moral stages, as follows:

> The universal ethical principle orientation: Right is
> defined by the decision of conscience in accord with

self-chosen ethical principles appealing to logical comprehensiveness, universality, and consistency. These principles are abstract and ethical (the Golden Rule, the categorical imperative); they are not concrete moral rules like the Ten Commandments. At heart, these are universal principles of justice, of the reciprocity and equality of human rights, and of respect for the dignity of human beings as individual persons.[33]

Even if these views are essentially correct, they do not provide an adequate basis for teaching teachers about ethics. The essential problem is that the emphasis is on the development of abstract principles of moral reasoning instead of instruction in the more concrete ethical principles that should inform the daily activities of the practicing teacher. It is no doubt desirable that teachers acquire sophisticated and abstract principles of moral reasoning in terms of which concrete principles that should guide their professional conduct seem reasonable. But a teacher who has a good grasp of abstract moral principles may nevertheless lack an adequate grasp of specific moral concepts, such as due process.[34] Moreover, teachers who have not achieved the highest levels of moral reasoning (which will be most of them) nevertheless must inform their conduct by reasonable moral rules.

The point may be put more generally. Growth in sophistication in abstract moral reasoning may be presumed to be a good thing, but it should not be assumed to be sufficient to promote the capacity for moral reflection. This requires, in addition, a store of more specific moral principles that deal more concretely with various kinds of human activities. Such principles do not come automatically with respect for persons or with the categorical imperative. They must be specifically acquired, and people must learn how to apply them to concrete situations. Kohlberg's views of moral education thus may be seen as contributing to a view of the education of professionals, but they are not sufficient. Nor should they be the central emphasis. Instead, the focus should be on teaching and developing sophistication in the application of those principles that inform the specific activities of professional conduct.

Caring. Recently, a rather different view of ethics has been developed by several feminist scholars,[35] partly in reaction to the views of Kohlberg but more broadly in reaction to what is seen as a predominantly male tradition in philosophical ethics. The central values of this feminine ethic are relationship and caring.

Nel Noddings characterizes the contrast as follows:

> Ethics, the philosophical study of morality, has concentrated for the most part on moral reasoning. Much current work, for example, focuses on the status of moral predicates and, in education, the dominant model [Kohlberg's] presents a hierarchical picture of moral reasoning. . . . One might say that ethics has been discussed largely in the language of the father: in principles and propositions, in terms such as justification, fairness, justice. The mother's voice has been silent. Human caring and the memory of caring and being cared for, which I shall argue form the foundation of ethical response, have not received attention except as outcomes of ethical behavior.[36]

Noddings goes on to characterize ethical caring:

> Ethical caring, the relation in which we do meet the other morally, will be described as arising out of natural caring—that relation in which we respond as one—caring out of love or natural inclination. The relation of natural caring will be identified as the human condition that we, consciously or unconsciously, perceive as "good."[37]

Noddings rejects an ethics of principle as ambiguous and unstable and as tending to separate us from each other. The notion that ethical judgment must be universalizable is similarly rejected. Instead, "Our efforts must be directed to the maintenance of conditions that will permit caring to flourish."[38]

This view of ethics has implications for the ethics of teaching. Education, according to Noddings, should be deprofessionalized.[39] This requires

> an attempt to eliminate the special language that separates us from other educators in the community (especially parents), a reduction in the narrow specialization that carries with it reduced contact with individual children, and an increase in the spirit of caring—that spirit that many refer to as the maternal attitude.[40]

But most centrally,

> The one-caring has one great aim: to preserve and enhance caring in herself and in those with whom she comes in contact. . . . Everything that is proposed as part of education is examined in its light. That which diminishes it is rejected . . . that which enhances it is embraced.[41]

The view of the ethics of teaching that I have developed above may be the sort of thing that Noddings wishes to reject. It is an ethic of principle. Its content is rules and obligations, rights, and duties. Caring does not form part of it. I need then to say a few words about how I see this view of ethics in relation to an ethic of caring.

It is impossible to be against caring. However one conceptualizes caring in a larger view of a satisfactory human life, caring is a central good and is at the root of many others. No coherent view of a desirable human life can simply reject it. Moreover, caring seems only one of many types of human relationships neglected by what Noddings calls an ethic of principle. Its concern for rules and duties seems to leave out such significant human relationships as love, charity, friendship, solidarity, collegiality, community, conviviality. Caring may or may not be at the root of many or all of these. But they represent a variety of types of relationships that human beings may have with each other that they can experience as valuable.

Nevertheless, an ethic of caring is an incomplete vision of ethics generally and is only a part of the ethics of teaching. Consider

that a fuller view of ethics should recognize the importance of the
following:

1. The *goods of relationship* are those that human beings expe-
    rience through their relationships with one another, such as
    caring, love, friendship, and community.
2. The *goods of accomplishment* are those experienced as a result
    of achieving skill or sophistication in those various human
    activities that human beings have found to be worthwhile, such
    as arts, sciences, crafts, and sports.
3. *Justice* specifies the duties and responsibilities that we owe to
    one another as people. It specifies the rules and institutions
    that regulate the common life of the members of society.

    In view of this, I have two criticisms of an ethic of caring.
First, it represents only an incomplete vision of the goods of relationship and is neglectful of the goods of accomplishment. Second,
it misrepresents the relationship between caring and justice.
    In part, the first point merely notes that an ethic of caring, as
Noddings develops it, leaves out a great deal that is valuable in
human life—or, at least, it does not work out the relationship between caring and other goods of relationship and of accomplishment. But there is something deeper to be noted. Noddings represents caring as a natural relationship and ethical caring as a development or elaboration of this natural relationship. However, the
goods of accomplishment are largely social in their character. That
is, they are achieved by virtue of the initiation of individuals into a
social repertoire of concepts, skills, customs, and practices. Moreover, many of the goods of relationship are highly dependent on the
goods of accomplishment for their realization. Friendships, for example, are commonly formed between those who share common
interests or who participate in common activities. We form our
bonds of friendship with those with whom we are engaged in the
pursuit of the goods of accomplishment. Much the same can be said
of the goods of community. Mature adults who have attained some
of the goods that constitute a valuable human life are more than
caring people. They are violinists, carpenters, citizens, physicists,
basketball fans, stamp collectors, Democrats, canoeists, and, of

course, teachers. These activities are not only the means for realizing the goods of accomplishment; they are also the context for friendship and community.[42]

It follows that an ethic in which caring is central is not only incomplete; it also provides a misleading model of education. Caring is a natural relationship. The extension of caring and the development of an ethic of caring build on this natural relationship. The realization of the goods of accomplishment and of relationship, however, depends on initiation into a cultural and social repertoire. Education as initiation is far more a process of socialization or enculturation than it is the elaboration of the natural. A view of the ethics of teaching that makes caring central may be inattentive to those values and moral principles that are internal to subject matter or to the characteristic activities of teaching.

Noddings's vision of an ethic of caring also has a misleading view of the relationships between caring and justice. Noddings appears to regard an ethic of caring as a competitor of justice (or an ethic of principle). I suggest that in fact they are not competitors. Instead, they deal with different contexts.

Noddings insists that caring, in her sense of the term, is a relationship between particular individuals. We may *care about* many things and many people, but we *care for* only specific people. This is, I believe, true of most human relationships. Not everyone can be the "one-cared-for." Not everyone can be a friend. Such relationships are inherently particularistic. If so, then, in addition to recommending the importance of caring and of relationship, we must also consider appropriate treatment of those for whom we do not care or with whom we have no relationship. This is the role of a view of justice. Justice tells us what duties we owe to people regardless of our relationship with them.

An ethic of principle has little to say about the goods of relationship or of accomplishment, because it does not see its task as stating the nature of a full and good human life. Instead, it seeks to lay down minimal conditions for human interaction. This view is often expressed in what has been called the conditions of justice.[43] Some philosophers have held that justice is appropriate to human relations when two conditions are present—competition and absence of benevolence. It may be a good thing for human relations to be dominated by such virtues as caring, friendship, or solidarity. When people care for one another, when they are motivated by one another's welfare, there is little need to think about justice. But justice is of concern in human relationships when people are in competition for resources and when benevolence cannot be taken for granted.

We need to remind ourselves that the relations in schools that are of concern are not only those between teacher and student. We must also consider relationships among students. When teachers are concerned about apportioning their time among students or grading fairly, it does not necessarily reflect a failure of care on their part. It may reflect the fact that students are in competition for scarce educational resources. Where there is scarcity, there is competition. However strongly we may wish to emphasize the goods of accomplishment or of relationship in schools, we cannot easily change the fact that knowledge and educational credentials function as commodities in our society and that, therefore, students will be in competition for educational resources and for educational benefits. No amount of concern about caring is likely to alter the fact that educators have responsibility for the distribution of scarce goods for which students are in competition. That being so, educators must have a concern for justice.

An ethic of caring thus has two deficiencies as a view of the ethics of teaching. First, it neglects those values that are internal either to the activities of teaching or to subject matter, because it is not sufficiently attentive to the goods of accomplishment. Second, it lacks a concern for justice. As a consequence, an ethic of caring is likely to be inattentive to such concepts as intellectual liberty, due process, and equity.

We should also ask whether caring can be taught in schools of education. Nothing I have said suggests that teachers should not care for their students, just as nothing I have said suggests that they should not be people of good character. Nevertheless, it is not obvious that it is possible for schools of education to transform future teachers into caring individuals, just as it is not clear that they can successfully reform those of bad character. Thus, while good character and caring are laudable traits for teachers, it is less clear that we should make character and caring into goals of teacher education programs.

These comments on a variety of views about moral education suggest at least two things. First, each of the three views discussed above has inadequacies as a view of moral education. For the most part, these inadequacies stem from an incomplete view of the nature of the ethical or moral life. Something is left out or distorted. Second, it is a mistake to think of teaching professional ethics to teachers as a form of moral education. I have argued above that the emphasis in professional ethics for teachers should be on teaching such concepts and principles as intellectual liberty, due process, and equity. This vision of professional ethics is rooted in a view of what teachers do, the circumstances under which they do it, and what it is possible to accomplish in an instructional program in schools of education. It is not primarily a vision of moral education. Theories of moral education are not reliable guides to the professional ethics of teachers. We need instead to emphasize the identification and transmission of those moral concepts and principles that regulate what teachers do.

Summary and Conclusions

What, then, do teachers need to know about ethics? I have argued that the law is a poor guide to the ethics of teaching. It is likely to forbid only the most flagrant abuses and has little to do with education or teaching per se. Instead, we will need a conception of ethics for teachers that takes more seriously the characteristic activities of teaching. This means that notions of intellectual freedom, equity, tolerance, and due process will be among concepts that teachers must possess. Since teachers tend to work alone, and since there is not currently a sufficiently detailed code of ethics to govern the teaching profession, the emphasis on teaching teachers about ethics must be on the development of the teacher's own ethical judgment. I have suggested that the analysis of cases provides a useful vehicle for this purpose. Finally, I have reviewed several views about ethics and moral education. While each of these views has its merits, I have suggested that each is deficient in not taking seriously the need to instruct teachers in those substantive ethical concepts that are central to the activities of teaching. This is a significant omission in the training of most teachers, one that desperately needs rectification.

Notes

1. *Pickering* v. *Board of Education,* 391 U.S. 563 (1968).
2. *Pickering* v. *Board of Education,* 391 U.S. at 571–573.
3. *Board of Regents of State Colleges* v. *Roth,* 408 U.S. 564 (1972); *Perry* v. *Sindermann,* 408 U.S. 593 (1972).
4. For details, see K. A. Strike and B. L. Bull, "Fairness and the Legal Context of Teacher Evaluation," in J. Millman (ed.), *Handbook of Teacher Evaluation* (Beverly Hills, Calif.: Sage, 1981), pp. 303–343.
5. *Application of Bay,* 233 Or. 601, 378 P.2d 558 (1963).
6. *Erb* v. *Iowa State Board of Public Instruction,* 216 N.W.2d at 339 (1974).
7. *Erb* v. *Iowa State Board of Public Instruction,* 216 N.W.2d at 344.
8. For discussion, see J. Gross, *Teachers on Trial* (Ithaca, N.Y.: ILR Press, 1988).
9. *Morrison* v. *State Board of Education,* 461 P.2d 375 (1969).
10. *Morrison* v. *State Board of Education,* 461 P.2d at 386.
11. *Sarac* v. *State Board of Education,* 57 Cal. Rptr. 69 (1967).
12. *Gaylord* v. *Tacoma School District No. 10,* 88 Wash. 2nd 286, 559 P.2d 1340 (1977).
13. *Gaylord* v. *Tacoma School District No. 10,* 559 P.2d at 1342.
14. *Gaylord* v. *Tacoma School District No. 10,* 559 P.2d at 1342.
15. *Gaylord* v. *Tacoma School District No. 10,* 559 P.2d at 1347.
16. For discussion, see L. Fischer, D. Schimmel, and C. Kelly, *Teachers and the Law,* 2nd ed. (White Plains, N.Y.: Longman, 1987), chap. 11, pp. 220–246.
17. It follows that what counts as immoral conduct may vary with time and place. As views on homosexuality become more tolerant, it is reasonable to expect that judicial tolerance of homosexual teachers will become more common. It is quite likely that some of the cases described above would be decided differently if they were brought up now.

18.   J. S. Mill, *On Liberty* (New York: Bobbs-Merrill, 1956), p. 13.
19.   B. A. Ackerman, *Social Justice in the Liberal State* (New Haven, Conn.: Yale University Press, 1980), p. 11.
20.   *Tinker* v. *Des Moines Community School District*, 393 U.S. 503 (1969).
21.   I have found that students often respond quite differently to these arguments depending on the example. The reader might test his or her own responses by applying them to both the homosexual and the Klan cases described above.
22.   See E. J. Haller and K. A. Strike, *An Introduction to Educational Administration: Social, Legal, and Ethical Perspectives* (New York: Longman, 1986), pp. 242–243.
23.   For discussion, see L. Darling-Hammond, "Valuing Teachers: The Making of a Profession." *Teachers College Record,* 1985, *87* (2), 205–218.
24.   Some attention to theories of moral justification is useful in teaching ethics to practitioners, for two reasons. First, sometimes these more abstract theories affect how we apply more concrete ethical principles. Second, one of the most significant difficulties in teaching ethics to practitioners is the degree to which moral relativism infects the student population. To be successful, one simply must deal with this.
25.   It is my impression that courses in ethics offered in many professional schools are less successful than they might be because they become bogged down in hard cases and abstract philosophy, or because people view them as some sort of attempt at character formation. The Ivan Boeskys of the world will not be enlightened or reformed by courses in ethics. However, it is possible to teach well-intentioned people the concepts required to transform good intentions into justifiable actions.
26.   Examples of materials developed to teach educational practitioners ethics that incorporate the features discussed in this section are K. A. Strike and J. F. Soltis, *The Ethics of Teaching* (New York: Teachers College Press, 1984); and K. A. Strike, E. J. Haller, and J. F. Soltis, *The Ethics of School Administration* (New York: Teachers College Press, 1988).
27.   Generally, I believe that the word *values* should be avoided in

discussions of ethics. As the following discussion will suggest,
the word can be the source of a great deal of confusion.

28. L. E. Raths, M. Harmin, and S. B. Simon, *Values and Teaching: Working with Values in the Classroom* (Westerville, Ohio: Merrill, 1966), pp. 114–115.

29. One should note that despite the fact that values clarification is often represented as a "liberal" view of values, in fact it undermines the liberal project. Liberals are committed to the view that we are entitled to choose and pursue our own conceptions of our own good but that our cooperation and interaction in the pursuit of our good must be regulated by a common view of justice. By treating views of justice as "values" and treating them as though they were also part of our sense of our own good and hence objects of free choice, values clarification makes the liberal position incoherent.

30. J. Piaget, *The Moral Judgment of the Child* (New York: Macmillan, 1965).

31. See I. Kant, *Critique of Practical Reason* (Indianapolis, Ind.: Bobbs-Merrill, 1956).

32. J. Rawls, *A Theory of Justice* (Cambridge, Mass: Harvard University Press, 1971).

33. L. A. Kohlberg, "From Is to Ought: How to Commit the Naturalistic Fallacy and Get Away with It in the Study of Moral Development," in T. Mischel (ed.), *Cognitive Development and Epistemology* (New York: Academic Press, 1971), p. 165.

34. It is simply not true that a grasp of some formal principle of reasoning is sufficient to understand all that follows from it. A grasp of the categorical imperative is no more sufficient to understand due process than a grasp of the laws of logic is sufficient to understand calculus.

35. See C. Gilligan, *In a Different Voice* (Cambridge, Mass.: Harvard University Press, 1982); N. Noddings, *Caring: A Feminine Approach to Ethics & Moral Education* (Berkeley: University of California Press, 1984).

36. Noddings, *Caring*, p. 1.

37. Noddings, *Caring*, p. 5.

38. Noddings, *Caring*, p. 5.

39. Noddings, *Caring*, p. 197.
40. Noddings, *Caring*, p. 197.
41. Noddings, *Caring*, p. 172.
42. As I noted in the first part of this chapter, many of the values that should govern the activities of teaching are internal to such practices. For discussion of the concept of a practice, see A. C. MacIntyre, *After Virtue* (Notre Dame, Ind.: University of Notre Dame Press, 1984).
43. For discussion, see Rawls, *A Theory of Justice*, pp. 126–130; D. Hume, *A Treatise of Human Nature* (Oxford, England: Oxford University Press, 1967), Book III, Part II, Section II; and M. J. Sandel, *Liberalism and the Limits of Justice* (Cambridge, England: Cambridge University Press, 1982), pp. 28–46.

7

Accountability, Trust, and Ethical Codes of Practice

Hugh Sockett

The "second wave" of American educational reform since 1983 is intended to bring improvement to the status and power of teachers and the "professionalization" of the occupation of teaching.[1] Over-regulated and restricted classroom functionaries of the "first wave" supposedly will give way to empowered and deregulated professional teachers entrusted with greater autonomy in school-based management. In the second wave the quality of teacher education will be improved through identification of the knowledge base of teaching and a stiffening of the arts and sciences base of preservice programs.[2] A national board for professional teaching standards will be the device to ensure the articulation of standards from the profession.[3] Ideally, competence "will be guaranteed in exchange for the privilege of professional control over work structure and standards of practice."[4] These goals are exciting prospects. Severe tensions remain, however, between the need for public control (exaggerated in the first wave) and professional autonomy (characterizing the second wave), and these must be resolved if reform is to succeed.

This second-wave project is incomplete without a clear understanding of professional accountability, which is at the core of the control issue. A practical model of professional accountability needs to be conceptualized. It must have three interlinked conditions for success: (1) the development of trust, (2) the establishment of a partnership between the public and professionals to dissolve the tension of competition for control, and (3) the teacher's role as a moral agent. The emerging professional teacher will be, in Goodlad's account, a "witting moral agent, with moral obligations derived from moral imperatives."[5] This is a claim to moral autonomy for a role, but that autonomy must fit with public demands and expectations. The difficulty is seeing precisely how a model of professional accountability can contain moral accountability.

Development of that model must start from scratch. Comparisons with other professions do not take us very far, because the character of the public interest in education differs from that for other occupations, because occupational histories are markedly different, and because the teaching profession, unlike law and medicine, is not in a strong bargaining position. The claims made for each of these conditions for professional accountability—trust, public and professional partnership, and the moral agency of the teacher—may be addressed through three questions: (1) What is professional accountability, and what is the significance of *trust* as a condition of its development? (2) Could a professional code of practice act as the vehicle for professional accountability, and what might the relationship then be to the public right to accountability? (3) How might new understandings of an individual professional's accountability be incorporated into teacher education?

These three questions form the structure of this chapter. In the first section, I suggest a formal accountability that is not at odds with moral agency, outline the four primary difficulties in placing moral agency within a substantive conception of accountability, and discuss the major features of a relationship of trust. The second section suggests that the profession needs to develop a reciprocal relationship between school-based codes of practice to enhance local trust and a profession-wide code developed from local experience. I conclude that only a coherent partnership between the public and professionals can support their accountability. In the third section, I suggest that these proposals demand a radical change in our conception of teacher education—that we need to educate *in* professionalism as a major part of teacher education programs.

Professional and Moral Accountability

Professionalization and Professionalism: A Prologue. In Chapter One, Goodlad points to three channels of discourse on professions. Each refers in different ways to two central issues in professions—the status of the occupation and the quality of its practice. Hoyle indicates that status and practice are captured in two terms used in describing professions: professionalization and professionalism.[6] *Professionalization* is a focus on the process by which an occupation becomes a profession and the changes in status that are implicit in that process. *Professionalism,* on the other hand, describes the quality of practice; it describes conduct within an occupation—how members integrate their obligations with their knowledge and skill in a context of collegiality and contractual and ethical relations with clients.[7]

Professionalization is about status; professionalism is about practice. This distinction enables us to ask logically, for example, whether a professional (in the status sense) is behaving as a professional should (in the sense of practice and its standards). We can comprehend how someone we call a "real pro" (expert in the practice sense) actually does not belong to a profession (in the status sense) but is a gigolo or an amateur. But even if the use of these terms, drawn from Hoyle, is considered stipulative, it remains crucial to grasp the distinction itself in debates on teaching as a profession. We must not confuse our discussions about status with our discussions about practice, our concerns for professionalization with our concerns for professionalism.

Viewed through the lens of professionalism, an accountability system must be compatible with three things: (1) existing best standards of practice, (2) the quest for improved quality of practice, and (3) a perception of the teacher as a moral agent. That focus will include not merely classroom conduct but also collegial relations and relations with parents and the community. The school as an institution and the teachers within them may be seen as accountable agents.

An accountability system for the professional teacher, therefore, is not to be constructed on the simple basis of status demands of the profession. Indeed, a teacher (or any other professional) is under a moral obligation to provide, to both the public in general and people in particular, an account of his or her endeavors and outcomes.[8] In the past, professions have had to be reined in by legislation to ensure effective modes of accountability. Since the task of education is a contribution to both the individual and the public welfare, the ethical demand that teachers be accountable cannot be gainsaid.

Indeed, it is not simply a matter of teachers being under an obligation. Professional teachers must *want* to find ways not merely to acquaint the public with educational actions but to explain achievements and failings. They must also *want* to build trust in the practices and the judgments they make as professionals, especially with the immediate constituencies of parents and students. This is both wise and virtuous. Put more politically, the profession must lead the drive to resolve the tension between public and professional control by examining forms of accountability that are publicly acceptable, rather than being dragged into a system complaining about threats to proper status.

The social context for such an endeavor is not encouraging. Present systems of accountability have been developed for two main reasons. First, the public began to distrust teachers, and *in loco parentis* gave way to due process. Second, interventive bureaucracies, facing an economic crisis in the early 1970s, needed to cap public expenditure, and political attacks on professional incompetence among teachers provided a rationale for tightened control. Although the second wave of school reform mentioned above engendered legislative enthusiasm, that may be short-lived. An observer of the 1988 meeting of the National Council of State Legislatures reported that "the debate on accountability suggested a more questioning mood among legislators after a period of enthusiastic spending on schools."[9] Sustaining the quest for professional accountability remains a central part of professionalism as an aspiration.

The Meaning of Accountability. There is an apparent incompatibility between the notion of accountability and that of moral agency, for whereas autonomous agency is central to morality, acting within prespecified limits and directions characterizes

individual role holders who become "liable to review and the application of sanctions if their actions fail to satisfy those with whom
they are in an accountability relationship."[10] Accountability implies money line management, or at best some form of stewardship,
rather than moral agency, wherein autonomy and perhaps self-realization would be implied.

There are two interpretations of accountability, the fundamental difference between them lying in the conception of the agent
and those to whom an account is delivered. First, accountability
may refer to an agent's responsibility to a provider, the provider being the beneficiary, and measured by the results produced through
the agent's skill in handling resources.[11] Notice two things about
this first formal account. While the agent may have customers or
clients and the provider may have access to the agent's skills, to
none but the provider is the agent accountable. (A manager of a
store has obligations to his or her customers but is not accountable
to them.) Second, both agent and provider could, in principle, be a
person, a group, or an institution. This basic model of accountability underpinning much of the first-wave conception of reform was
put in place in state systems in American education during the
1970s. The account was delivered to a single provider—the public
(as represented by local educational management)—rather than to
individual citizens with differing wants and expectations.

This interpretation leaves little room for the heterogeneity
and complexity of industrial, entrepreneurial, and professional activities. Any occupation *could* be forced to fit this conception, developed into a model; that may well have taken place in the 1970s.
Teaching, however, conceived as a profession with complex educational ends, does not fit. First, if the teacher is not to be limited to
trivial ends, the exercise of teaching will demand much greater autonomy than this conception would allow. As Langford puts it, the
teacher cannot simply be the agent of another but must act as principal as well.[12] Second, the teacher must not be limited to an accountability relationship with, say, the school board seen formally
as "the provider"; rather, there are many different constituencies of
accountability for the teacher—parents, colleagues, and students
among them. Third, many valued educational objectives cannot be
captured for measurement within the simplistic views of perfor-

mance contracting that found favor in the 1970s. A formal conception of accountability is needed that both fits the occupation, with the underpinning conception of moral agency, and has the teeth to bring about improvement and prove that that is being done to a public and to individuals with the right to know and to influence.

In this second interpretation, the accountability of the agents is not to the provider as beneficiary but to client beneficiaries and professional peers for results achieved and for the quality of standards maintained through occupational practice. The implications of this conception of accountability are profound. First, the agent has multiple constituencies to whom an account is due. This context implies a difference of demand. What the public interest may demand is not necessarily reflected in private wants. Second, attention is devoted to standards of practice. Provision must be made for standards to be maintained and promoted, and conditions of competence must be set out that enable a practitioner to meet them. Third, only the agent can have the responsibility for maintaining the standards of practice of the occupation.

This conception of accountability speaks more directly to the educational context and to the tensions that individual rights (of teacher or parent) and the public interest create. It thus accepts the rights of individuals (as parents, children, or colleagues) but does not posit unanimity. It addresses the complexity of teaching as an art by implying constantly changing standards. Some researchers have used different terms to bring out the significance of various constituencies by distinguishing among answerability to one's clients (moral accountability); responsibility to oneself and one's colleagues (professional accountability); and accountability to employers or political masters (contractual accountability).[13] Here, *accountability* will cover each and all of these, so there is no need to regard professional accountability as a contradiction in terms.

Accountability and Moral Accountability. Only the second interpretation of accountability (standards of accountability), or something like it, matches the notion of the teacher as moral agent, acting in his or her role with appropriate moral autonomy—as compared to a soldier who is "not to question why." Moral agency is nothing very fancy. It is simply that people consider the interests of others, do not make discriminations on irrelevent grounds, and have a clear set of principles or virtues in which they believe and on which they act.

Four distinct problems for teacher accountability arise from this conception. First, the problem of pluralism of moral ends and moral agency is reflected directly in the two interpretations of accountability. A major distinction in ethics is reflected in debates on accountability and in the two differing versions of it. This is the difference between a teleological and deontological ethic. Briefly, the former is interested in consequences or ends, the latter in principles. The former is interested in results, the latter in standards. Honesty is valued in the former insofar as it brings about desirable results, in the latter because it is valuable in itself. The imperatives of which Goodlad speaks in Chapter One could thus be very different. "Act always so that what you do brings about the greatest happiness of the greatest number" is rather different from "Act always as if you were a law-making member of the kingdom of ends," to use Kant's picturesque language. Very different practical policies could result from these imperatives. The emphasis on standards of practice, as opposed to achievements deriving from competence, provides a different *moral* basis for development of the second version of accountability. Yet the demand for *results* seems the very stuff of teacher accountability as practiced across the nation, certainly in the first wave.

Second, what moral accountability implies may well change with differing conceptions of morality. For example, a teacher may well regard God as the only proper one to whom an account should be delivered; if a person holds to a consequentialist utilitarian ethic, then it is the greatest happiness of the greatest number that would drive that individual's moral agency. Thus, to claim that the teacher is a moral agent is not to indicate that there is agreement among educators on ends or means. In policy terms, it is important to recognize teacher diversity but not thereby to suppose that there is nothing on which teachers might agree. For example, teachers might interpret quite differently the principle of being fair to children, even though there is agreement on its general significance. More controversial areas on which teachers would disagree, such as family-life education, directly influence teacher behavior.

Third, and of critical importance to a conception of the teacher's moral accountability, is that in any democratic polity there is conflict between private wants and public interest. In the United States, that conflict is very complex. This complexity is indicated in debates on legislation, but it is in the workaday circumstances of social life that the persistent power of the conflict is revealed. The typical parent of a schoolchild wants public education as a matter of the public interest, no doubt, but also because education gives the child economic superiority.[14] The steps that the parent takes to achieve private wants, particularly in a community of aggressive self-aggrandizement, may be in the public interest. Private pressure groups make efforts to convince others that their particular private wants are in the public interest—for instance family-life curricula.

Teachers in their working lives face the sirens of both private wants and the public interest. From students and parents the cry is for "better grades," while from crisis-happy government, it is that schools must deal with the problems of the day (drugs, AIDS, teen-age pregnancy), inviting the wrath of socio-political groups of various kinds; the former drip of mandates has become a flood from state legislatures. In that conflict between private interests and the public, the development of teachers as reflective professional practitioners is no easy task.

Fourth, and of greatest concern when we address the moral accountability of the teacher, is the apparent difficulty of even bringing moral considerations into public life and debate. If we are seriously seeking to construct a view of accountability that is congruent with the moral agency of the teacher, we are putting moral issues firmly where they belong—in the public forum. Yet some fundamentalist Christians, for example, feel bound not to observe the principles of tolerance and personal conscience familiar in more liberal points of view. Most ethnic groups have members who are followers of fundamentalism. If Bellah and his associates are correct, Americans have lost the vocabulary for ethical debate.[15] Allan Bloom portrays the young intellectual enmeshed in an individualist materialism in which there lies only a vestige of understanding of moral agency.[16] Teachers are not somehow above these social manifestations; this simply highlights the importance of teacher education.

Considering differing individual perceptions of morality, the deep-rooted conflict between results and standards as the core of judgment, and a pluralist society that may be losing its moral vocabulary, the task nonetheless remains the promotion of a comprehensive vision of the profession of teaching in which the individual professional teacher *is* a reflective moral agent. The tension must be resolved. An acceptable form of professional accountability consonant with public rights must be worked out. Such a development is utterly dependent on one particular condition among many—namely, trust.

The Significance of Trust. Trust is a relational condition between individuals. It has an *outside,* where formal systems and client individuals are linked through effective role holders, and an *inside,* in which professional relationships become personalized. Trust is established through stability and reliability of conduct according to particular virtues.

For the *outside* relational condition, Jennifer Nias has argued that trust demands two things: First, it implies being able to make accurate predictions about such things as "individual attitudes, reactions, and technical competence" and consistency in role behavior and in organizational procedures.[17] However, "people and routines become predictable only as one gains knowledge of them."[18] Second, perceived agreement over ends is also necessary; where there is disagreement about ends, so there will be greater need for formal procedures. These conditions are the basis of our sense that we trust the system.

The significance of trust in this outside sense is that it provides the opportunity for clients to trust a system, but it does not guarantee it. Where trust exists, individuals have confidence in both the system and the people operating it. Trust is created on the outside because the procedures are clear, public, and understood and because the officeholders want to promote their effective use and benefit participants. That outside is what is seen by the public at large as well as by the participants. Public satisfaction is not, however, the sum of private perspectives, nor do the judgments of realtors and politicians necessarily reflect the educational value of a particular school or the levels of trust enjoyed on the *inside.*

The establishment of trust thus demands a meaningful interplay of people and their roles visible outside but active inside. Schools, like other institutions, cannot establish trust if they are impersonal. Tellers at the bank might be extremely friendly and helpful, but the computer seems hostile. The family atmosphere of the small school where a nervous parent feels at home contrasts with the bureaucratic halls of the huge urban high school where that parent might fear to tread.

For the parent, as much as for the teacher, establishing trusting relationships is a matter of personal knowledge and, to some degree, an individual's idiosyncratic capacity for knowing more or fewer people. This is where the outside and the inside senses of trust meet—and it is a major part of the teacher's moral agency. He or she must contribute to creating trust in the system by working at trust inside the institution.

Trust is not simply the outside relational condition of persons and systems, mediated by role-holders. It is a relational condition of the inside life of a school, between individual teachers and children, among colleagues, between principal and staff, and so on.

Yet how can this condition be described? Only in terms, I think, of the virtues that constitute trust—namely, fidelity, veracity (honesty and an absence of deception), friendliness, and care. For a trusting relationship to exist, it is not enough that a school and its teachers be understood as "pro-kids." Teachers must be known by the parents and children as people they can trust.

The most important of these virtues is honesty, seen as the absence of deception. The need to shield young children from danger, to encourage them, to protect them from greedy and ambitious parents; the problems of being precise and accurate with information; and the general difficulties of that exquisite task that defines teaching (conveying understanding to someone who does not understand)—these create opportunities for deception, for lying to children. Sisella Bok's brilliant book *Lying: Moral Choice in Public and Private Life* clearly brings out the effects of deceit, in particular its impact on the deceived.[19] To be deceived is, at least, to be in the power of another person, to which no one wittingly surrenders and which must be anathema to the educational enterprise. The principle is veracity. "Trust in some degree of veracity functions as a *foundation* of relations among human beings: when this trust shatters or wears away, institutions collapse."[20] Moreover, she continues, veracity is the crucial underpinning for other central virtues of education—treating people fairly, looking after their interests, and not harming them. If a person's word cannot be trusted, why should anyone think that that person would be fair, concerned, and incapable of injuring? Why, in other words, should he or she be trusted?

Nel Noddings has written sensitively on the implications of the relational ethic of caring and its educational place.[21] Of particular interest is her discussion of dialogue, responsiveness, and response as part of the framework of trust. More complex in educational relationships is the place of friendship. The problem may be put like this: To create and develop the inside sense of trust, adults and children have to come into the kinds of close relations that mediate between them and the system. The closer the relationship, the more opportunity for it to turn into a friendship, as contrasted with friendly relationships. But friendship creates obligations that go beyond the rights and obligations of a role relationship, for friends have privileged access to each other. Thus, there are major problems in the development of friendships (as contrasted with friendly relations) between teachers and students and also between teachers and parents, and both these kinds of friendships influence the condition of trust on which a professional accountability relationship must be built. Not least because friendships have a measure of exclusivity about them, those outside the friendly relationship may see it as a threat to the roles they enjoy.

In an institution, fidelity is perhaps as important as veracity to achieve trust. From the child's or the parent's point of view, it is faith in the system, the individual teacher, or the principal. The teacher who sexually molests a student, the teacher who is attacked in a school because the institution is out of control, the counselor who talks in public about a student's private life, the principal whose special confidence is betrayed by a board member, the superintendent who ignores incompetence in a teacher who is a friend—each of these people commits a breach of faith or is a victim of one.

Fidelity is the virtue for which trust is the condition. A person may keep faith but not be trusted, for trust is a mutual condition

of a relationship. Each participant to the educational enterprise—
child, parent, teacher, and principal—is entitled to fidelity. Fidelity
is fragile. Together with veracity, care, and a sense of friendliness,
rather than friendship, it forms the core of the trust that is critical to
establishing professional accountability.

Trust incorporating these virtues is not easily built up, and it
is easily broken. Trust has to be earned. Trust makes partnership
possible. It provides the basis on which an accountability system,
while recognizing human weakness, assumes professional integrity,
rather than the other way round. It is only on the assumption of
professional integrity that a system of professional accountability
can be built. (We should also recognize that teaching, like any other
human activity, is full of political moral dilemmas, many of which
are versions of the claim that "in politics, the best is the enemy of
the good."[22])

Integrity does not describe the character of relations only
with clients but with other professionals as well. Critical to professional accountability is the notion of peer-group judgment, practiced widely in other professions. Teachers already judge each other
informally, usually not through direct observation but from the
comments of other teachers, children, and parents. Performance
evaluation schemes have created contexts for peer-group judgment.
The task for developing professional accountability is twofold: how
to create trust within the profession and how to convince a skeptical
public that teachers can be trusted.

Criteria for Professional Accountability. A system of professional accountability must be developed with trust incorporated as a
significant condition. That system must meet these criteria:

1. *A common moral basis:* It must embody a basis of agreed-upon
    principles, accepting that there will be validly held moral
    differences.
2. *Multifaceted judgment:* It must contain the potential for
    agents, professional peers, and constituents to deliver an ac-
    count—that is, make a judgment—according to standards re-
    garding the assessment of individual teachers' teaching skills,
    to student scores, and to teachers' veracity, fairness, and so on.

3. *Local accessibility:* It must have a local focus, answering primarily to the rights of students, colleagues, and parents and only secondarily to the public at large, and providing for redress of grievances.
4. *Teacher maintenance:* It must be constructed in such a way that professional teachers have a stake in maintaining its integrity and the public trust it develops.

A Professional Code of Practice

How can these criteria be given substantive form? The history of self-government in professionalism is mixed, usually involving legal status proposed by the particular profession. This is necessary for civil protection against professional misconduct, but it represents no aspirations. Rather, it is in the professional codes of ethics that such aspirations are to be found.

Codes of ethics have become a familiar part of the rhetoric of professional self-government and professional control. From the Hippocratic oath in medicine to the code of ethics of the National Automobile Dealers Association, a declaration of commitment to ideal behavior has provided one source of unity for members of an occupation. Yet the status and influence of such codes are uncertain. There is usually some ambiguity of purpose. Sanctions other than legal have to be used to stiffen the ethical resolve. Codes require policing, but they cannot solve major ethical dilemmas. For example, the Hippocratic oath can be used to support either side in the abortion debate.

Finally, generality of expression also contributes to the rhetorical character of codes of ethics, although they can also be quite specific. The automobile dealer's code runs from a general commitment to the "highest ethical standards" to the specific "never alter the odometer." The American Sociological Association has a detailed code of ethics that is meant to "sensitize all sociologists to the ethical issues that may arise in their work, to encourage [them] to educate themselves and their colleagues."[23] The more specific ethical guidelines for high school psychology teachers issued by the American Psychological Association are an equally precise code of practice for teachers.[24] Codes of ethics in teaching have been produced by unions, but it is unclear how they relate to practice in a non-self-governing occupation and how unions see the resolution of the public-professional tension. Could a code of some kind be the vehicle to meet the criteria for a system of professional accountability?

The task, it should be recalled, is to find some way, consonant with the moral and professional autonomy of the second-wave teacher, in which the tensions between public control and professional control may be resolved. A reinterpretation of the notion of a code of practice can contribute to that resolution. In the following discussion, I explore a proposal for the development of local codes of practice that could form the basis of a profession-wide code of ethics. The school must become the locus of accountability if the criteria I have described are to be met and if trust, in particular, is to be established. Each school has its particular milieu and modus operandi. The traditions, habits, and innovations of its teachers can be assessed, examined, and negotiated as the basis of a code of practice that can be made publicly accessible. There can be local partnership in both construction of the code and its implementation. (I have slipped out of the use of "code of ethics" and use "code of practice," which for the teacher who is a moral agent will be a code of practical ethics.)

Codes of Practice

Codes of practice can be examined under three headings: (1) form, which describes the shape that a code of practice in teaching might take, (2) content, which describes the substantive areas of the code, and (3) status, which describes how a code might be implemented.

Form. A code is a set of *rules* that establishes standards or norms in matters of individual or institutional conduct. The teacher as moral agent follows moral rules. A code of rules also offers guidance, particularly for the novice, the perplexed, or the wayward teacher. A code of rules can be constructed on the basis of a wide variety of sources—empirical observations, law, and convention—but its force is moral when it describes interpersonal relations. Like most sets of rules, a code will always require interpretation; new situations will demand new interpretations. A code also has to be administered and cared for. It requires an *authority* responsible for keeping it up to date and an authority responsible for the processing of grievances. Finally, a code must be *accessible* to the public, not merely as a document but substantively in terms of its construction and the facilities it offers for sanctions and redress. Sanctions and public accessibility raise significant problems pertinent to the issue of resolving the tension between the public and the professional. The connection between sanctions and public accessibility is this: It must be possible for a constituent client (parent, child, and so on) to hold a teacher or a school to account for fulfilling the public commitments made in the code.

It is a truism that a mode of accountability without sanctions is empty. If professional teachers want a system of accountability that will work, a code must provide not only for sanctions but, more particularly, for redress. That is, it is not enough for a principal to slap the wrist of a teacher for drinking too much in the presence of teenage students; it must be possible for a parent to seek redress by using the code.

It may be argued that in a community such as a school, in which collegiality is critical, the very presence of a code with sanctions will harm rather than promote professionalism. The problem is not just that there are unprofessional people in teaching, as there are in every occupation and profession. "Sanctions," writes H. L. A. Hart of legal systems in general, "are required not as the normal motive for obedience, but as a *guarantee* that those who would voluntarily obey shall not be sacrificed to those who would not. . . . What reason demands is voluntary cooperation within a *coercive* system."[25]

Sanctions thus provide a safeguard for those who suffer under the pressure of the informal system. They protect the weak. The willingness to put oneself under a sanctions system is, in part, to offer trust. We may wish we did not need the coercive framework to ensure our voluntary cooperation, but we cannot ignore the need to take human weakness into account.

At present, there are many areas of professional life that are left to convention—for example, relationships among colleagues, which are usually completely outside formal sanction. Sets of group habits, and not necessarily desirable habits, have grown up within the profession. Good habits can develop without legal pressure. But for the majority of us, the presence of the legal rule ensures that our habits change. We do come to wear a seat belt not because it is law but because we see the point of it. Similarly, the construction of a code with sanctions would not mean constant litigation. Its effect would be to turn desirable professional habits into regularly observed habits.

Ultimately, a code with sanctions provides the professional with two things: (1) pressure to adhere to the code as a guide to follow, not as a set of regulations to obey, and (2) confidence that competence, standards, and results can be measured because of the opportunity for the public to seek redress.

Traditionally, professional codes of ethics or of practice have been publicized but rarely displayed. You find diplomas across the walls of a doctor's office, but you never see the medical code of ethics displayed there (although you *can* find a code of ethics posted in some automobile dealers' offices). How could a professional code of practice in teaching, established at the local level, promote public access?

First, the composition of the code demands parental and public input. This is not a matter of public relations; rather, it is a matter of common experience (and common sense). The process of education looks different to the parent of the child from the way it looks to the teacher. It behooves the profession to attend to the perspectives of its clients.

Second, teachers, like other professionals, can be blinded by their role. The process of code composition by the professional should be based not on the question "Is this within my present competence?" but rather on the question "Would this satisfy me as a code for the teacher of my own children?" This test is not trivial sentiment. It is an expression of one of the deepest moral principles—moral equity. It obliges the teacher to take the public point of view.

Third, the code of practice has to be made publicly accessible for consultation and use. Many schools already publish documents of all kinds for parents and the public. There is no reason why a code should not be public. Mere publication, however, is not enough. The code of practice has to be used, and it should look inviting to parent-teacher conferences, PTA meetings, and public discussions. Constant reference to that code should be made to ensure that it becomes a living thing in the minds of the public.

In sum, the form of a code of practice, developed from many sources, is a set of rules and guidelines. It will require constant reinterpretation and maintenance under an authority that will also ensure an effective system of sanctions and public accessibility, particularly when it is being formulated. This is its *form*. For the purposes of this chapter, it is necessary to refer only briefly to matters of content.

Content. A code contains rules and guidelines governing action. Practice is the target. The content of a code describes what teacher-practitioners should do in their work

- In formal instructional settings and informal contexts with students
- In collegial relationships within schools
- In formal and informal relations with parents and other appropriate clients
- In management relations
- Within the discipline to which they have an allegiance, a discipline that is itself a living community of scholars with its own traditions[26]

It will be a code of best practice, one that includes wisdom and virtue.

The sources for the content of the code are numerous. It is important that the code address some of the stickier problems that teachers face and perhaps do not know how to face up to. Following are some examples of these types of problems:

1.   Under what sorts of circumstances should a teacher *not* inform a parent of facts about a student? At what age? In particular, should a teacher tell a fundamentalist parent that a child of nine spoke of his loss of faith? In general, what are the ways in

which a teacher should protect the child's right to privacy against his or her parents?

2. How can the rights of the child of parents who are conscientious objectors be protected in classroom discussions of war—or vegetarians in discussions of farming? (Is not the right to withdraw the child the most banal of managerial and professional responses to this type of situation?)

3. Should teachers respect without question the right of colleagues to be or to behave as they wish in classrooms? What is the line between collegiality and toleration of inefficiency or immorality?

4. Are there general "discipline-based" rules that teachers ought to observe in instruction, derived from the character of that discipline? Does it matter whether children guess answers in history or science, get the right answer by accident in math, or learn things that are false, even though commonly accepted as true?

5. What ought management do to respect the rights of teachers as citizens within schools? To what extent does management undermine a teacher's citizenship by restricting political discussion in classrooms?

To repeat, the context for this discussion of the content of a code of practice is a tension between public and professional control. In differing ways, each of these questions points to areas that will have much greater significance with greater teacher autonomy and professionalism. The alternative to professionals taking the initiative in working out a code that has been negotiated with relevant publics is for a school board to determine, on the basis of convenience, the actions that a teacher is to take and the limits of his or her freedom. On that basis, the teacher is neither autonomous nor a moral agent but is a purveyor of someone else's views. Whatever else the code must do, it must offer both guidance in points of difficulty and a public declaration of professional intent. Schools must be prepared to translate their professional habits and particular problems into early models of codes of practice.

Status. The aim of professional accountability must be, once again, to resolve that tension of public versus professional control.

There must be a form of public control. Professional aspiration
implies a measure of autonomy and thereby some professional control. The question is whether a code could satisfy both. The answer
is that it could, primarily through a partnership of the public and
the professional.

School-based professional codes of practice could be adopted
as part of the system of public control alongside more traditional
forms of accountability. Local codes of practice built by schools in
discussion with their constituencies would be viewed as recognizable, justifiable, and necessary elements of teacher and school accountability. These codes would satisfy the criteria outlined
previously. They would have a moral basis, refer to multifaceted
judgments, be locally accessible, and be maintained by teachers.
That is not a radical or a revolutionary suggestion, for school systems in many areas of the United States have developed codes of
practice. Many of these include the use of a model of instruction
throughout a school system; the development of annual or biennial
plans based on individual schools or communities; the development
of the use of mentor-teachers and teachers as evaluators of colleagues; and the movement toward school-based management with
much greater local responsibility. This is part and parcel of the
second wave as it washes through communities, bringing them into
much closer relations with the school.

The use of one model serves to focus on elements of classroom instructional behavior that act as a code of instructional practice for teachers. The development of annual or biennial plans provides the occasion for public declaration of the results to be achieved
and could also provide an admirable process for a statement of
standards of practice to be maintained and developed. School-based
decision making exemplifies the reliance of the institution on a
teacher's professional judgment outside the mere acts of instruction.
The use of mentor-teachers or teacher-evaluators is crucial in developing standards of practical professionalism, for here is peer-group
judgment at the cutting edge, focused on instructional practices.
The proper professionals do not simply put up with peer evaluation; they want it to improve their standards of practice.

The most significant of these different movements is the shift
to school-based management, because it recognizes professional re-

sponsibility and the delegation of that responsibility by school boards and central administrations to local and state regulations. It illustrates perfectly the local implications of the second wave and what it implies for the professional teacher. Central administration becomes not an extensive bureaucratic control mechanism responsive to the political will but a responsive support mechanism for the school in carrying out its social responsibilities.

This developing practice still contains the unresolved tension. There will be no professional accountability until the pattern is much more localized and professionals display the standards to which they are committed; until professionals, aware of their own problems but thoroughly confident of their competence, can invite the individual and the public to judge a teacher and call that teacher to account in terms of these standards; until there is a developed partnership between public and professional control. The public and individual citizens and parents need to see these and other developments as a move toward professionalism for teachers. They need to see the comprehensive unity it implies, and they need to be drawn into the discussions of institutional means that will resolve the conflict between public and professional control. However, it remains true that "professional status is most effectively guaranteed when professional codes are safeguarded by law but enforced by their own members."[27]

Codes of Ethics

The code of ethics for teachers, seen as the cumulative wisdom and virtue of local codes of practice, is something to hammer out as professionalism develops. "A Code of Ethics becomes necessary not only to assist the mechanical engineer in his conduct, but to acquaint the world with what it may expect from a professional man."[28] Both guidance and acquaintance have been suggested as significant features of a code of practice. They will be apparent in a code of ethics. As we discover what best practice is, such a profession-wide code can indeed incorporate best practice. But we must also expect a code of ethics to probe into details of classroom activity as the ethical guidelines for high school psychology teachers do.[29]

Yet is this not simply to replace the first-wave regulators with

a larger group? Maybe. However, there is an important and interesting problem for professionalism, seen as the development of
standards of practice, in all its present manifestations. What documentation may be expected from a national board for professional
teaching standards? What may we expect from the compilation of
the best wisdom-in-practice studies? Will these not have to be seen
as sources on the basis of which professionals make judgments?
Should they not become points of reference for professionals discussing particular dilemmas? Will they not be the basis of professionalism on which the novices in the profession are brought up?
We can anticipate comprehensive publications of some kind, of
which a local code would be one. A professional code of ethics
likewise will be regularly revised as new issues arise and are solved,
but it will have at its core fundamental principles of good practice.
The critical question is how teachers, in wanting to stand up and be
counted as professionals, will react to these implications of professionalism and what that does to the process of teacher education.

Professional Codes and Teacher Education

The task of professional education in teaching, then, becomes formidable but not impossible. The measure of an effective
teacher education program lies not in classroom competence but in
the development of a professional commitment within which such
competence is viewed. Educational administrators and teacher educators need to grasp the high significance of seeking to translate the
professional rhetoric into workable systems. There are five major
elements in this task:

1.   The motivation to teach, which the aspiring student and the
      novice manifest, must be developed to include the desire to de-
      liver an account to colleagues and clients.
2.   A sense of the importance of creating trust in one's own profes-
      sional behavior and an understanding of what that implies
      must be stimulated in preservice students.
3.   All teachers need to have training in negotiating skills with cli-
      ents, particularly parents, as part of the equipment of the car-
      ing, accountable professional.

4. There must be fostered a sense of openness to criticism of one's own performance and the stimulation of the central habits of reflective practice.
5. There must be fostered a sense of the significance of professional partnership across the profession and beyond it to its multiple constituencies.

This is not an original agenda, but since a public and professional partnership is seen as the key to the aspirations of professionalism at last emerging from the union of political and professional concerns, the possibilities can be cogently measured. The implications of each of these five tasks need to be worked out.

First, where do teacher education students get a professional moral education? Preservice students must be given consistent opportunities to face self-consciously their motivation for teaching. Too frequently, preservice students are judged on classroom performance only. Reaccreditation demands are, professionally speaking, somewhat exiguous. How can students examine themselves in terms of their openness to their own classes, their ability to discuss frankly the conduct and direction of their teaching, their style, a particular lesson, their wish to spend their professional lives in the company of young people? How can young teachers be helped to see their professional career as one demanding consistent advice, support, and critical appraisal from others and to want that critique because it matters? Without developing that sense, as compared to that competence, they will not acquire the initial professional motivation required.

But this is the motivational side of an ethical matter. The problem, as indicated by Lortie, is that "socialization into teaching is largely self-socialization: one's personal predispositions are not only relevant, but, in fact, stand at the core of becoming a teacher."[30] That idiosyncrasy needs to be opened up. The wisdom of an individual's choice of a profession, the fit between the demands of the job and personal temperament, personality, and competence require considered judgments of what individuals want, what they are capable of, and what is *worth* wanting. Without a framework of ethical understanding, it is difficult to see how choices and decisions can coherently be made. Where in their education do they get this opportunity and cognitive framework, as opposed to what they derive from the parade of thinkers in Ethics 101?

Second, teacher education needs contexts that show up the moral cast of the person beneath the speech-act. "A teacher develops standards of appropriate behavior and of teaching performance as a product of both innate moral propensities and through education and socialization which are external forms of influence."[31] How do teacher education programs provide us with knowledge of what a student will be like as a colleague, of those "innate moral propensities"? In the preparation of preservice students for teaching, how can they develop the sense of the importance not only of collegial support but also of being someone who can create a sense of trust? That sounds ineffable. Maybe a student creates a sense of trust simply through force of personality, but it is manifested in some behavioral traits, such as consistency in carrying out what is expressly said. A student *must* keep his or her word not simply where an express promise is made to a class but in the minutiae of commitments, for on that basis of classroom and professional habit the elements of fidelity, care, and friendliness may be built. But students also need to display themselves as colleagues—having them deliver reports of their own practice to mentors and student colleagues gives experience in sharing self-critique as an endeavor to create trust and fidelity and to show their moral cast.

Third, the dialogues that teachers have with their clients must be framed within an ethic of caring. Preservice education gives virtually no training in negotiating skills. Neither, I suspect, is this very common on in-service days. Communicating the problems of educating a child to his or her parents, however, is perhaps the most important facility with which a teacher can be equipped in respect of the problem of accountability—yet little is done in teacher education to ensure it. The danger is that negotiating skills are seen as akin to salesmanship, where trust is manipulated into existence and then infrequently sustained until it achieves a sensitive mutual awareness of wants and concerns. The necessary skills are valuable only as techniques within a wider moral purpose—helping parents or others reach an agreement with the school on what is best for the child. According to Noddings, these skills need to be framed as dialogue within the relational ethic of caring.[32] The central strength of her analysis is that it stresses the affective side of caring without sentiment, the professionalized concern and commitment enhancing knowledge and action. Yet professional teachers with these commitments can be assisted to make them more visible and prudentially executed.

Fourth, the reform of teacher education depends more radically on the attitudes and examples that teacher educators set than on the content they teach. The models presented to the preservice and the in-service student define professional conduct. The motivation to share through openness of practice is the initial condition of which reflective practice as a professional habit is the full flower. Openness and reflection, like other virtues, are taught mainly by example.[33] Just as there is some incongruity in giving an hour's lecture on "learning by discovery," so teacher educators and clinical faculty members must manifest in their own teaching those traits of openness and reflection to be inculcated in their students. That is a difficult task to accomplish with teachers whose perception of in-service programs is limited to either time serving for certification or practical tips of immediate utility.

Finally, the problem of professional partnership is the achievement of authenticity. One main burden of this chapter has been to express the significance of educational partnership as a way of attempting to dissolve the tension between public and professional control. It is possible, as in some marriages, for there to be a collaborative responsibility and mutual regard seen by both partners as a matter of convenience rather than conviction. The preservice student, for example, will easily be able to tell how authentic the partnership is between academic and clinical faculty members. A visitor to a school can soon establish the quality of the partnership between principal and staff, and so on. Like marriage, partnership has to be worked at. It can be defeated by the weight of externally imposed bureaucratic rules as much as by a person who breaks faith. Professionals get caught in role conflicts of all kinds; they may feel unable to develop partnerships because they sense hierarchical disapproval. The stance must be one in which we seek to remedy the inadequacies of educational partnership, to provide contexts in which animosities or misunderstandings can be revealed, rather than to assume that authentic partnership looks after itself.

The complexity of that task is daunting, for the profession of teaching is split among research, administration, and practice, and professional subcultures have grown to match each of the three. There is not much mutual trust across these divides. We need to look for new model institutions to dissolve our interprofessional tensions.[34]

Conclusion

The idea of teaching as a profession is a worthy aspiration, but it is undermined by its limitation to the restricted rather than the generic conception of a teacher. That aspiration includes higher levels of competence at career outset with a framework of a professional moral commitment to deliver increasingly better service to the public, parents, and children. Professionalization will not be complete without two things: first, the dominance of practice on the research agenda, with researchers rather than bureaucracies serving the schools and the teachers, and, second, the determination of the occupation to find effective ways of being accountable for offering trust and being trusted.

This chapter has suggested that the process of accountability must begin with individual institutions, that a code of practice provides a familiar conception within which the problems of accountability may be addressed, and that a code could meet the major criteria of making a system effective. Of course, these suggestions present a formidable challenge, primarily because they become the vehicle of a much richer partnership of trust between schools and parents. The problem of how the teacher as a professional moral agent makes him- or herself accountable must be recovered from its status as an audit. A localized code of practice seems the only cogent way to realize the aspiration of a profession for teaching.

Notes

1. L. Darling-Hammond and B. Berry, *The Evolution of Teacher Policy* (Washington D.C.: Rand Corporation, 1989).

2. L. Shulman, "Knowledge and Teaching: Foundations of the New Reform," *Harvard Educational Review*, 1987, *57* (1), 1–22; Holmes Group, *Tomorrow's Teachers* (East Lansing, Mich.: Holmes Group, 1986).
3. Shulman, "Knowledge and Teaching."
4. L. Darling-Hammond, "Policy and Professionalism," in A. Lieberman (ed.), *Building a Professional Culture in Schools* (New York: Teachers College Press, 1988), p. 59.
5. J. I. Goodlad, "Studying the Education of Educators: Values-Driven Inquiry," *Phi Delta Kappan*, Oct. 1988, *70*, 109.
6. E. Hoyle, "Professionalization and Deprofessionalization in Education," in E. Hoyle and J. Megarry (eds.), *The Professional Development of Teachers*, World Yearbook of Education (London: Kogan Page, 1980), pp. 42–57.
7. H. T. Sockett, "Research, Practice, and Professional Aspiration," *Journal of Curriculum Studies*, 1989, *21*, 2.
8. Sockett, "Research, Practice, and Professional Aspiration," p. 2.
9. N. Mathis, "State Law Makers Focus on Accountability," *Education Week*, Aug. 3, 1988, p. 23.
10. M. Kogan, *Educational Accountability: An Overview* (London: Hutchinson, 1986), p. 12.
11. H. T. Sockett, "Teacher Accountability," *Proceedings of the Philosophy of Education Society of Great Britain*, 1976, *10*, 5–22.
12. G. Langford, *Teaching as a Profession* (Manchester, England: Manchester University Press, 1978).
13. R. Becher, M. J. Eraut, and J. Knight, *Policies for Educational Accountability* (London: Heinemann, 1981).
14. F. Hirsch, *The Social Limits to Growth* (London: Routledge & Kegan Paul, 1977); M. Hollis, "Education as a Positional Good," *Journal of Philosophy of Education*, 1982, *16* (2), 235–244.
15. R. N. Bellah and others, *Habits of the Heart* (New York: Harper & Row, 1985).
16. A. Bloom, *The Closing of the American Mind* (New York: Simon & Schuster, 1987).
17. J. Nias, "The Nature of Trust," in J. Elliott and others (eds.),

School Accountability (London: Grant McIntyre, 1981), pp. 211–224.

18. Nias, "The Nature of Trust," p. 211.
19. S. Bok, *Lying: Moral Choice in Public and Private Life* (New York: Vintage Books, 1978).
20. Bok, *Lying*, p. 33.
21. N. Noddings, "An Ethic of Caring and Its Implications for Instructional Arrangements," *American Journal of Education*, 1988, *96* (2), 215–231.
22. M. Hollis, "Dirty Hands," *British Journal of Political Science*, 1983, *12*, 385–398.
23. American Sociological Association, *Code of Ethics* (Washington, D.C.: American Sociological Association, 1984), p. 3.
24. American Psychological Association, *Ethical Guidelines for the Teaching of Psychology in the Secondary School* (Washington, D.C.: American Psychological Association, 1983).
25. H. L. A. Hart, *The Concept of Law* (Oxford, England: Oxford University Press, 1961), p. 193.
26. American Psychological Association, *Ethical Guidelines*.
27. R. G. Corwin, "Teachers as Professional Employees: Role Conflicts in the Public Schools," in R. G. Corwin (ed.), *A Sociology of Education* (New York: Appleton-Century-Crofts, 1965), pp. 217–264.
28. C. W. Price, "Ethics of the Mechanical Engineer," *Annals of the American Association of Political and Social Science*, 1922, *101* (190), 73.
29. American Psychological Association, *Ethical Guidelines*.
30. D. Lortie, *Schoolteacher* (Chicago: University of Chicago Press, 1975), p. 79.
31. Kogan, *Educational Accountability*, p. 31.
32. Noddings, "An Ethic of Caring."
33. G. Ryle, "Can Virtue Be Taught?" in R. F. Dearden, P. H. Hirst, and R. S. Peters (eds.), *Education and the Development of Reason* (London: Routledge & Kegan Paul, 1972), pp. 434–447.
34. H. T. Sockett, "Practical Professionalism," in W. Carr (ed.), *New Directions in Theory and Practice* (London: Falmer, forthcoming).

8

The Teacher and the Taught: Moral Transactions in the Classroom

Christopher M. Clark

For nine months of each year, teachers are among the most influential adults in the lives of their students. Teachers are with their students for as many waking hours as parents typically are. Teachers and students interact in close, complex social systems behind closed doors. School is mandatory for children under sixteen, and teachers exercise considerable power over their students by law, by circumstance, and by tradition. As Philip Jackson observed two decades ago:

> School is . . . a place in which the division between the weak and the powerful is clearly drawn. This may sound like a harsh way to describe the separation between teachers and students but it serves to emphasize a fact that is often overlooked, or touched upon gingerly at best. Teachers are indeed more powerful than students, in the sense of having greater responsibility for giving shape to classroom events, and this sharp difference in authority is another feature of school life with which students must learn to deal.[1]

A teacher's authority is not absolute, however, although it may seem so at times. Teachers are held responsible for their actions and decisions by law, by tradition, and by moral code. To educate is to lead responsibly—to influence students' knowledge, skills, and

251

dispositions in ways that will serve them and their society well and to do so in morally defensible ways.

Novice teachers are typically earnest young people who have given much more attention to the subject matters that they will teach and to techniques and methods of teaching than to the moral dimensions of teaching. When moral issues are addressed, prospective teachers can feel left at loose ends. It seems that the only criterion for moral decisions is the teacher's personal preference; one must simply look at the situation and make up one's own mind. In the moral domain, however, one opinion is *not* as good as any other. Overarching principles have been agreed on in our society and within the teaching profession—principles dealing with honesty, fairness, protection of the weak, and respect for all people. The real work of teaching, morally speaking, is carried out when a teacher rigorously struggles to decide how best to act in relation to these general principles. Just as teacher decision making in intellectual and pedagogical matters has been shown to be at the heart of professional teaching,[2] so too is decision making central in the moral domain.

What follows will not make moral decision making easy and automatic for teachers. These case descriptions are intended to illuminate how decisions and actions that have serious moral implications look and feel in context and to illustrate the power and value of thoughtful teachers who take the time and invest the energy to do the right thing. Teaching is a moral craft as much as it is a technical and procedural endeavor.[3] This chapter offers food for thought about the moral relationship between the teacher and the taught.

Case 1: Honesty

Honesty is an essential virtue for the survival and operation of any human organization. Most laws have to do with honesty. Dishonesty and deceptiveness are despised among the powerless and the powerful alike. The school could not operate without substantial honesty; the guiding ideal of the university is the pursuit of truth, which is the fundamental referent of honesty.

What is this virtue called honesty? The positive side of the definition concerns telling the truth and acting in ways that are wholly consistent with what you know or believe to be true. The negative side of the definition involves refraining from cheating, lying, representing the work of another as your own, stealing, and other dishonest deeds. The temptation to dishonesty is almost always laced with self-interest, making honesty a particularly difficult virtue to practice for the young and the immature of any age.

Much of the teacher's concern with encouraging honesty among students has to do with telling the truth and preventing or correcting cheating. Consider this example from a teacher's textbook more than one hundred years old:

> At Harrow, two boys brought me [Canon Farrar] exercises marked by the same grotesque mistakes. It seemed certain that those exercises could not have been done independently. Both boys assured me that there had been no copying. One whom I had considered a boy of high morale assured me of this again and again with passionate earnestness. I said to him, "If I were to send up those two exercises to any jury in England, they would say that these resemblances could not be accidental, except by something almost like a miracle. But you both tell me that you have not copied. I cannot believe you would lie to me. I must suppose that there has been some extraordinary accident. I shall say no more." Years after, that boy, then a monitor, said to me: "Sir, do you remember that exercise in the fourth form?" "Yes," I said. "Well, sir, I told you a lie. It was copied. You believed me, and the remembrance of that lie has remained with me and pained me ever since." "I am inclined to think," says Canon Farrar, "that boy was more effectually taught and more effectually punished than if I had refused to accept his protests."[4]

Except for the dated language, this example might be used in the contemporary preparation of teachers. But look again. Canon Farrar resorted to dishonesty himself in the apparent belief that this would be the most effective and humane way to inculcate honesty in the two boys. Can we believe that the boys did not know at the time that he was lying, toying with them, laying a trap and levying a corrosive burden of guilt on them? Canon Farrar fails us (and the Harrow boys) as a model of honest and courageous confrontation of cheating and lying. Dishonesty by the teacher, however well motivated, inspires cynicism, guilt, and resentment at hypocrisy, but not necessarily honesty. Morally flawed means promote morally damaging ends.

A contemporary case of a teacher's response to plagiarism gives us a more constructive model: Dr. Stevens wished that this were not happening to him. One of his undergraduates in a course on instructional design, a varsity football player but not a varsity scholar, had just turned in a written assignment that was manifestly not his own work. The topic of William's paper was appropriate for the assignment but was not one that he knew much about. The task analysis and instructional design were sophisticated and complete; the language was clearer and more forceful than any that William had ever demonstrated. Most damning of all, Dr. Stevens recognized this paper—it had been written the previous year by another of his students.

As Dr. Stevens looked into the matter further, it became more involved. George, the original author of the paper, had received a "deferred" grade for the course. The final revision of the paper had never reached the professor. It had been deposited in Dr. Stevens's mailbox but must have been stolen. Dr. Stevens remembered reading and providing feedback on an earlier draft of this paper, and George still had a copy of the draft, which he delivered to Dr. Stevens. As in Canon Farrar's case, any jury would see that the resemblance between William's and George's papers could not be accidental.

What to do, what to do? Dr. Stevens called William and the academic adviser for the athletic department, told each what he had discovered, and arranged for a meeting of the three. William confessed to having had help but said that everyone he knew did this kind of thing and that, after all, he had changed some of the wording of George's original text. The academic adviser said, "Flunk

him"— a tempting and unequivocal way for the professor to termi-
nate the problem.

Instead, Dr. Stevens proposed that the athletic department
hire one of his own graduate students to work with William on the
assignment in question during the next four weeks. William would
be expected to select a new topic, analyze how he would teach this
topic to another person, and design and write a detailed plan and
program of instruction. With this help, William did complete the
assignment and passed the course. Today he is a professional football player.

What did William learn from this painful episode? In Dr.
Stevens's view, he learned that (1) cheating does not work; (2) there
are legitimate ways to get help with challenging assignments; (3)
with help, William had what it takes to do the work and learn the
content of the course; and (4) honest work takes about the same
amount of effort as dishonest work, and it does not make one feel
guilty afterward. At a more fundamental level, William learned
about respect and forgiveness. Dr. Stevens expressed his moral responsibility to respect each of his students by taking the substantial
time and trouble to treat William as a responsible human being, to
connect him with the tutorial help that he needed, and to provide
detailed feedback on William's written work. Respect and forgiveness combined in Dr. Stevens's clear refusal either to join the lie
(that the first paper was substantially William's work) or to act on
the "one mistake and you're dead" principle implicit in the athletic
department adviser's advice to fail William. For Dr. Stevens, and for
teachers generally, honesty, respect, compassion, and forgiveness
mean more work, not less. Morally responsible teaching requires
that we go beyond (sometimes far beyond) the letter of the law of
technically effective teaching.

A final point about this confrontation of dishonesty with
honesty: Dr. Stevens solved his problem by reframing it in the form
"How can I help William to do and learn the skills that are at the
heart of this course?" Dr. Stevens stayed with his morally grounded
assumption that all students *can* learn. By turning the moral, interpersonal, legal mess into a pedogogical problem that he thought he

could solve, Dr. Stevens both taught effectively and lived up to his
moral responsibility.

Case 2: Responsibility

One of the most difficult professional decisions that can confront a teacher educator is to fail a practice-teaching student, which
could mean that the student will never be certified as a teacher.
Because it is the penultimate stage in most teacher education programs, the bad news comes after months or years of more or less
successful performance, stopped just short of the prize. Failing a
student teacher also declares a failure of the faculty and the cooperating teacher to teach the student to become an adequate beginning
teacher. There is plenty of pain to be shared in this situation.

Nancy was the field supervisor on whom one of these decisions fell. She had been a university field supervisor of students for
eleven years; during the last six years, she supervised pre-student-
teaching and student-teaching field experiences in a selective, sixty-
student elementary-teacher preparation program. This teacher-edu-
cation program was one of five in a large college of education from
which approximately seven hundred teachers graduate each year.

How did Nancy make the decision to fail her student, and
how does she remember and explain these events? What was difficult and painful about this situation, and what role did moral delib-
eration play?

The story of Nancy and Jenine extends over more than a year.
Jenine came to Nancy's attention as a student who was having problems in course work by the middle of the first year of her program.
Jenine's attendance and attitude problems were severe enough during the spring of her first year that she was given an incomplete
grade for the spring course. From Nancy's point of view, each bit of
progress by Jenine in one area was offset by new problems. By the
fall term of Jenine's senior year, when she was in a pre-student-
teaching field placement, it became more and more clear to Nancy
that Jenine could not handle even routine elementary classroom
demands.

The program goal of having Jenine take responsibility for
the elementary classroom four mornings per week by the end of the

fall term was never achieved. It was then that Nancy decided that Jenine was not ready for full student teaching. The cooperating teacher declared that she could no longer work with Jenine; she had tried her best, and it had not worked. Nancy arranged for Jenine to repeat the pre-student-teaching experience with another cooperating teacher during the winter term. The pattern of disappointment of the fall was repeated in the winter, and at the end of this term, Nancy assigned a no-pass grade to Jenine's field experience, terminating her status as a prospective teacher.,

Was this a difficult decision for Nancy? "Yes," she said, "extremely difficult," for two reasons: First, Nancy defined her own teacher education role as helping students reach their goal to become teachers. Jenine never did let go of that goal, and Nancy felt that she had failed in her responsibility to Jenine. Second, this was a difficult decision for Nancy in that the criteria for judging success or failure in a student teacher's field experience are not clear, clean, and easy to judge. Especially troublesome was the question of when to say, "Stop, you've tried long enough."

This decision was painful because Nancy and Jenine had developed an intense personal relationship around helping Jenine to succeed—to learn from experience, to get it all together—and Nancy had to declare that Jenine had failed to meet expectations and that trying again would be futile. (Nancy reported that this decision process became a bit easier when Jenine became hostile and threatening, thus breaking the intimacy of their relationship.)

How did Nancy make sense of this difficult decision? What did she tell herself about this situation, and how does her understanding of the process inform us about the nature of teaching? Nancy's recounting of this story had four organizing themes—used by other teachers and by all of us when making sense of difficult and painful decisions: (1) I did what I could; (2) I was right in my perception of the situation; (3) My action prevented harm to others; (4) My action did some good.

I Did What I Could. Nancy supported her claim of having done what she could to help Jenine succeed by describing the extra efforts that she and others had made on Jenine's behalf. These efforts began as soon as problems were noticed, and they far exceeded the level of individual attention that other students in the program received. Nancy also supported her claim of helping Jenine by noting that she had given her extra chances to make up for failure (the second pre-student-teaching placement) and had changed the criteria for judging adequate progress. Nancy had redefined the goal of Jenine's final field placement from helping this student achieve all of the special and particular ideals of a selective teacher education program to helping the student reach minimal acceptable standards in five generic domains of professional performance (instructional design, management, content knowledge, methods of teaching, and professional attitude). In the end, Nancy rephrased this theme by saying, "I did everything I knew how to do, but it didn't work."

I Was Right in My Perception of the Situation. It was important to Nancy to be sure that her assessment of Jenine was accurate and fair and was not the result of bias, selective perception, anxiety while under observation, or artifacts of an inappropriate field placement. Nancy did trust the testimony of her own observations and conversations with Jenine. She also determined, through conversations with the cooperating teachers involved, that her observations were representative of Jenine's performance. Beyond confirming her own observations, Nancy saw these conversations as important for keeping both Jenine and the cooperating teachers aware of the fact that things were not going well and that remediation was called for. Nancy also had conversations with the director of the teacher education program in which she sought and received support and counsel as the long decision-making process proceeded. Finally, Nancy cited specific examples of Jenine's behavior and responses to feedback as evidence that this was indeed a case of a student consistently failing to meet minimum expectations for successful teaching.

In sum, Nancy pursued three avenues to validity: the collection of direct evidence (well documented), reaching consensus of opinion with other observers, and validation through appeal to authority (the authority of the program director). The last two avenues suggest an additional professional norm: that one should consult other professionals in difficult, nonroutine cases. As Nancy said, "I wouldn't want to make a decision like this on my own."

My Action Prevented Harm to Children. Teacher educators who evaluate the performance of student teachers are the last gatekeepers for the profession. As such, they have a moral responsibility to the generation of schoolchildren whose lives will be affected by teacher graduates. Nancy saw this responsibility as a fundamental, almost taken-for-granted moral imperative in her work, and she felt this responsibility when she explained that failing Jenine was the right thing to do and the only moral thing to do, because it protected countless children from a teacher who would teach badly or not at all.

In Jenine's case, Nancy was faced with a true dilemma in which a teacher educator's responsibility to respect, teach, advise, and support a prospective teacher was at odds with the moral imperative to ensure (insofar as one can) that no harm will come to helpless schoolchildren.[5]

To resolve the dilemma, Nancy drew on her observations of Jenine in two elementary school classrooms. Jenine behaved selfishly toward the children. She was more concerned with meeting her own needs (for example, doing college course homework in the back of the classroom) than with learning about responding to the needs of second-graders. Jenine tended to blame others (including children) for problems that she herself had created or exacerbated. Jenine was physically absent from the classroom often and emotionally absent always. Providing feedback and a second chance proved insufficient to remedy these fundamental problems. Envisioning Jenine as the sole adult authority over twenty-five eight-year-olds was terrifying to Nancy.

My Action Did Some Good. Nancy asserted that, for all the pain and disappointment her decision brought about, it was a good learning experience for Jenine. Nancy came to realize that this was the first time Jenine had been forced to make a significant personal decision for herself and by herself—the decision about what to do with her life now that a career as an elementary teacher was foreclosed. Nancy values autonomous personal decision making and believes that a college senior should at least begin exercising those faculties. In Nancy's reconstruction of the case, it seemed good for

Jenine to learn this lesson, which she felt would probably serve Jenine well throughout her life.

It is important to highlight the fact that when Nancy failed to pass Jenine, she did not know or have reason to hope that it would be good for Jenine developmentally. On the contrary, Jenine seemed ready to fall apart completely. But after the no-pass decision was final, Nancy continued to counsel and support Jenine, staying with her moral obligation to this devastated young woman long after she was technically obligated to do so. During this time, Nancy learned that Jenine had been driven to choose and stay firm in her intent to become a teacher by parental pressure. Jenine had been living out her parents' script, not her own. Jenine's failure provided her with an opportunity to begin to live life autonomously.

A second good result of this difficult situation was the creation of a seminar and support group within the teacher preparation program to provide for early identification and possible remediation of problems like those that plagued Jenine. Nancy was moved to work with a colleague in supervision to create a more clear and objective set of performance criteria for judging pre-student-teaching performance. What began as a clinical teaching and evaluation process for one student became a formative evaluation and developmental process for an entire teacher education program.

Case 3: Respect

A Hispanic student speaks of his high school experience:

> I may look like a student who doesn't like his classwork, who just messes off in class, but I'm not. Teachers just look at me and they say, "Oh, another mess off." I'm not dumb. They didn't care what was the result of my tests. I know I got a perfect score! It is like prejudice, but it's not prejudice. . . . I just ignored it. I had this problem before. I had U.S. History, but somehow my teacher didn't like me. I don't know why. He told me I did not belong in that class. And I did good on the tests. History is my best subject. I felt like hitting him! He said I did not have what it takes to be a

student there. I went to my counselor and told her.
Same thing. But you see, that made me feel mad![6]

As with other aspects of schooling, the moral relationship
between teacher and student is most conspicuous when it breaks
down. In the quotation above, one can see the unraveling threads of
a relationship between adult and adolescent; between Anglo and
Hispanic; between authority and compliance, inclusion and exclusion; between learning and alienation.

A fundamental responsibility of teachers is to create and sustain conditions that will promote learning for each and all of their
students. They must assume that every student is capable of learning. This is both a pedagogical and a moral imperative. To meet
this responsibility, teachers plan, decide, create, and reflect on conditions for learning. The basic learning conditions include motivation and encouragement, knowledge of subject matter, opportunity
to learn, time, space, appropriate curricular materials, clear instruction, and methods of measuring student learning progress. If any
one of these conditions for learning is absent or inadequate in some
way, the whole learning system can come to a grinding halt. Seven
of these eight conditions may be in place and operating at optimal
levels, but when an eighth is missing or weak or selectively violated
for some students, learning is compromised, and the teacher is not
fulfilling his or her moral responsibility to students.

The neo-Vygotskian perspective on cognitive development
offers a useful frame of reference for understanding the social, psychological, and moral dynamics of school learning.[7] Three central
ideas of this theoretical position are that (1) learning is a socially
and culturally mediated process (as distinguished from a private
and individual process), (2) the role of teacher consists of creating
conditions that enable a gradual shift of the locus of learning activity from the teacher to the collective of learners, and (3) teacher,
learners, learning activities, and materials must interact with the
learners' "zone of proximal development" for effective learning to
take place.

Let us now use these neo-Vygotskian ideas to examine the
case of the young man quoted above. What went wrong here, mor-

ally and pedagogically? What does it tell us about the moral relationships involved?

First, it seems clear that this student felt excluded from the learning group and the U.S. history class and that he blamed his exclusion on the teacher ("He told me I did not belong in that class"). We do not know what the teacher intended by that statement, but the student took it as a teacher's judgment that he did not have what it takes, intellectually speaking, to succeed or even to try to succeed in the class. The judgment came early, was harsh, and was at odds with the student's estimate of his own ability ("I'm not dumb. . . . History is my best subject"). Furthermore, the teacher's delivery of his harsh judgment was gratuitous, since the student did stay that semester in that class.

What did the teacher accomplish by his act? From a classroom management point of view, the teacher reduced the heterogeneity and effective size of his U.S. history class. While not succeeding at physically removing this "different" student from class, he effectively removed him from complicating participation patterns by putting him in his place early on. This tactic of classroom management by selective discouragment can be inflicted in much more subtle ways than we see here. To be ignored, to be ridiculed (only once), to be singled out for a "special" pull-out program, to be nailed with a low grade for the first assignment or test, to be segregated in the "slow group" in the first grade—these commonplace occurrences can indeed simplify some of the work of teachers, but at great expense to the learning and lives of some students.

To create and sustain conditions that will promote learning for every student in a class, a morally responsible and pedagogically effective teacher must pursue a commitment to *inclusion* as opposed to selective *exclusion*. Teachers should ask questions such as: Who is being left out? How can I organize learning activities so that all feel included and are learning? What can I do to begin a reversal of the chain of failure experiences that some of my students have had? How can I accommodate my teaching to the full range of individual differences in aptitudes, learning history, culture, and dispositions that describe my students? How can we help one another to learn and change together? What do I have to learn from each of my students?

These difficult questions cannot be answered once and for all. This set of questions reframes the teacher's definitions of the problem space and shifts the tone of teacher-student relationships from adversarial-technical to collaborative-supportive. A policy of inclusion, as reflected in sincere pursuit of answers to these questions, presupposes an attitude of respect for and genuine interest in each student and in the class as a social organism—a learning community. As well, it requires that the teacher act with both the authority of a knowledgeable adult and the eager humility of a learner and member of a learning group. Respect for and interest in students, in turn, are related to the moral maturity and degree of ego development of the teacher. Adults do not ask such questions lightly, risk failure eagerly, or share power, authority, and voice without trepidation. Inclusive teaching is risky business, but the risks are worth the cost.

In neo-Vygotskian theory, the aim of good teaching is to give the game away to the learners. Through "scaffolding"—the gradual transfer of responsibility and control to the group of students—the adult teacher moves away from center stage to become a coparticipant or even an outsider in the learning community. The course may be about algebra or art or history or English, but in this framework, schooling is also about collectively initiating, creating, and sustaining an inclusive learning community. In the long run, this community-building feature of inclusive teaching may be of as much social, developmental, and educational value as are the learning and remembering of academic content.

Discussion

What have we learned of the moral relationship between the teacher and the taught by reflecting on these few cases? First, it seems clear that moral issues are intrinsic to and ubiquitous in teaching. The American political principle of separation of church and state does *not* mean that what goes on between teachers and students is morally neutral. What educators and parents fear most about bad teaching and celebrate most about good teaching are manifestations of fundamental moral virtues. Really bad teaching is "bad" in a moral sense; really good teaching is "good" in a moral sense. No amount of technical virtuosity in instruction can compensate for or excuse morally flawed, irresponsible behavior.

Second, morally responsible teaching is difficult, complex, and sometimes painful and thankless work. Teaching is a fundamentally moral enterprise in which adults ask and require children to change in directions chosen by the adults. Understanding teaching in this light confronts a teacher with potentially unsettling questions: By what authority do I push for changes in the lives of these children? At what costs to their freedom and autonomy? Where does my responsibility for these young lives begin and end? How should I deal with true moral dilemmas in which it is simply not possible to realize two goods or avoid two evils? How much pain and discomfort am I willing to endure on behalf of my students? How are my own character flaws affecting the lives of others?

These questions are quite different from the questions and topics used to organize teacher education curricula and professional development programs for experienced teachers. Perhaps the time has come to rethink what we do in the name of teacher preparation and professional development in light of a heightened sense of the moral challenge and complexities of teaching.

Third, reflecting on these cases can give us some insight into some of the temptations to moral failure frequently encountered in the relationship between the teacher and the taught. Dishonesty is a common and dangerous failure for both teachers and children, taking many forms and justified by motives both lofty and mendacious. Disrespect for persons or categories of persons, no matter how subtly expressed, leads to moral terrorism. Selfishness and egocentrism in adult teachers hurt both the teachers and the students. The temptation to employ morally unjustifiable means (for example, humiliation, segregation, violence) to achieve desired ends (for example, order, obedience, compliance) is an institutionalized commonality of schooling.

No one essay or set of exhortations and object lessons can make the moral complexities of teaching simple, straightforward, and unerringly good. My hope is to raise questions in the minds of educators about honesty, respect, selflessness, and moral scrutiny of means and ends. How do these moral virtues (or their violations) help explain life in classrooms? How can we design programs and teach more responsibly in light of these principles? How can we better serve our present society, as well as generations to follow, by taking the moral dimension of teaching as seriously as we do test scores and transcripts? At its core, teaching is a matter of human relationships. Human relationships, whatever else they may be, are moral in character and consequence. After that between parent and child, the most profoundly moral relationship our children experience is that between the teacher and the taught.

Notes

1. P. Jackson, *Life in Classrooms* (New York: Holt, Rinehart & Winston, 1968), p. 10.
2. C. M. Clark and P. L. Peterson, "Teachers' Thought Processes," in M. C. Wittrock (ed.), *Third Handbook of Research on Teaching* (New York: Macmillan, 1986), pp. 255–296.
3. A. Tom, *Teaching as a Moral Craft* (New York: Longman, 1984).
4. J. Allen, *Mind Studies for Young Teachers* (New York: Kellogg, 1887), p. 120.
5. M. Lampert, "How Do Teachers Manage to Teach? Perspectives on Problems in Practice," *Harvard Educational Review*, 1985, *55*, 178.
6. H. T. Trueba, "Peer Socialization Among Minority Students: A High School Dropout Prevention Program," in H. T. Trueba and C. Delgado-Gaitan (eds.), *School and Society: Learning Content Through Culture* (New York: Praeger, 1988), p. 206.
7. M. Cole and S. Scribner, *Culture and Thought: A Psychological Introduction* (New York: Basic Books, 1974); J. Wertsch, *Vygotsky and the Social Formation of the Mind* (Cambridge, Mass.: Harvard University Press, 1985).

9

The School as a Moral Learning Community

Bruce R. Thomas

This chapter examines the moral universe of teaching through four case studies. Three are current; the fourth is a half century old.[1] The older case is included because without the past we cannot clearly see the present. Common to each case is the confrontation with a moral decision or dilemma. In the first three cases, drawn from the experience of teachers at work today in our nation's classrooms, the confrontation is individual; the teacher as an isolated moral agent must initiate action to achieve resolution. In the fourth, action is collaborative.

My purpose—to advance the fact that teaching is an inherently moral enterprise—is aided by the use of a simple vocabulary to describe teaching:

- Parents entrust their children to school. Trust obliges teachers to be careful. Teachers are to proceed carefully with the work of empowering students.
- Empowerment is remarkable. One human being sets out to make others strong and able. That one human being is not to exploit, coerce, or manipulate the others. What *is* required of such a human being? What kind of person must he or she be? At the outset, we can at least say that the empowering teacher must be powerful, for impotence does not call forth potency.
- Parents entrust their children to teachers. School is mandatory, and that mandate settles on the shoulders of the teacher. The

266

teacher, then, is obliged to care for children and be responsible for their empowerment.

Such simplicity of description restores clarity to an enterprise whose moral character is otherwise obscured by legal or technical vocabularies. *Trust, care, obligation,* and *responsibility* are words that carry the burdens of morality. Teaching is a moral enterprise because it is a social enterprise. Schools are densely peopled. Children arrive in groups to be taught in groups, and groups of adults are in charge of schools.

How is the behavior of people, young and old, to be regulated? There are rules, of course, but ground rules serve more to facilitate than to regulate. The important decisions are made by the individual moral agent—the teacher or the student. Rules move students along corridors so that they arrive on time in classrooms to sit in assigned seats where they perform assigned tasks. But the moment the door closes and class begins, choices must be made and made continually. The student chooses to pay attention. The teacher chooses whether to slow down instruction to accommodate the needs of students with slower paces of understanding. How are such decisions made? If instant and reflexive, they are but the consequence of earlier decisions. These choices embed themselves in and arise out of individual moral agency grappling with obligation to others. Morality is the necessity born of humanity's "fantastic interindividuality."[2]

Schools loom large in a culture's morality. They are at once sources of moral instruction and sites of moral struggle. At the center of both source and site is the teacher, who, alone in the school's adult populace, is for long hours each day in the company of children and youths whose presence compels the making of moral choices.

Isobel

Isobel teaches third grade in a public school located in a poor neighborhood of a large city. Her initial college training was in business, and her first job was with the telephone company, but a dormant itch to explore the world of teaching finally demanded scratching. She began taking courses at a teacher-training center staffed by educators trailing deep roots into progressive education and with long trans-Atlantic links to British infant school traditions. She acquired credentials.

The third-grade position is her first job. As she comes to know her students and colleagues, fundamental differences with her colleagues emerge. They are grounded in attitudes toward the children and ambitions about the future. The two are related. Isobel's colleagues are either members of the middle class or aspirants to it. Their notions of school embrace a vision of happy, orderly, well-dressed children compliant with adult authority—obedient to the explicit and inexplicit regularities of schooling. The children do not conform to this vision. Their disorderliness can take either passive or aggressive form. Some seek invisibility within the classroom, others boisterously disrupt, but all manifest a sense of school as an adversarial encounter they have little chance of winning.

Winning has meaning for the teachers as well, and the children threaten teachers' prospects of victory. Their achievement scores will not reflect what leads to desired promotions and transfers. So teachers have distanced themselves from the children and, in some measure, dismissed them as unteachable, or so conversation in the teachers' lounge would suggest. But in the crucible of daily practice, the instinct toward human connection and the motive to empower surface. The teachers find promise in several children and invest themselves in them. This investment in individual children coexists with the hostile, dismissive attitude toward the children as a group. Isobel recognizes the paradox, and it tempers her feelings about her colleagues.

The attitudes of the administrators of the school are consistent with those of the teachers. The principal has an implicit agreement with his faculty: "Keep the lid on; preserve the appearance of an orderly, effective school; we will fiddle with testing as necessary and safe; I will handle the extremes of behavior."

For Isobel, William represents one such extreme. His needs are imperial; undealt with, they rule the class, but dealing with them also converts the class into a room with one student, for then Isobel has little time and attention to give to other students. Through reading files and contact with William's family, Isobel has compiled in her mind a history of William's life—a steady rain of abuse and neglect that goes far to explain his reign of terror in the classroom. Isobel's grasp of his history deepens her compassion for William. It does not solve her problem, however. What is she to do with him? He is the worst of four whose disruptive emotional necessities regulate the class and fundamentally impair the enterprise of teaching.

The available answer is to dispatch him to the principal's office. Isobel tries this a few times. It provides relief, not solution. Moreover, Isobel comes to learn that the principal's response is either to beat William or to keep him in isolation.

What, then, is Isobel to do?

"I decided to just shut the damn door and find a way of living with these kids" is Isobel's solution. To her students, she says wordlessly: "You and I are stuck here. We are going to have to work out a way of living and working together."

She cannot do it alone. She does not try. She needs help and begins with William's aunt. The culture of the school tends to dismiss families as resources. Isobel tests that generalization by going in off-hours to see the aunt, who has become William's guardian. Conversation with William's aunt uncovers a mutual commitment and concern. Individually at wit's end, the two initiate collaboration. The aunt finds a male relative willing and able to spend time with William and to invest attention in him. Isobel focuses on assembling the resources, conceptual and material, for transforming the class into a culture capable of absorbing William.

She uses connections established at her teacher-training center to get help in ideas and materials. Activity centers emerge in a classroom becoming alive with varieties of animal life. A library of paperback books grows. Children acquire and do daily tasks of maintenance and record keeping. Through her gradually expanding network, she tracks down a skilled child therapist, who agrees to meet several times with William and speak periodically with herself. Over time, she gets a steadily firmer grasp on William's odd behavior and a surer sense of how to respond. Apace with her developing skill with William, she gets a firmer grasp on the workable groupings by which she can break the twenty-eight children into smaller units able to sustain work around one of the activity centers.

All this takes time—weeks extending into months—but the process is also the product, for the ends inhere in the means. The children become citizens of the polity of the classroom, the growth slow at first but then rapid. Isobel recollects the moment the week before Halloween when one child asks to stay in the room after the dismissal bell at the end of the day. The example infects; others begin to linger as well.

The price Isobel pays for this solution is isolation within the culture of the school. Her success in accomplishing both "control" and acceptable levels of tested performance ensures tenure, but she has little time for teachers' lounge conversation and must arrive early and depart late. She violates regularities of teacher behavior frozen into place through union contract. That proves threatening. Competence is her guarantor within the school; outside it, her community is the network she has woven in support of her transformation of the class.

Fred

Fred teaches English in a public high school located in the outer ring of an urban area. The students are a kaleidoscopic mix of race and ethnicity. A sociologist would likely classify them as predominantly working- to lower-middle-class. Most are cautiously ambitious and acknowledge the necessity of a high school diploma as a wedge to opportunity. The authoritarian atmosphere in the school is consistent with parental experiences, coincident with their beliefs, and comfortable to district administrators.

Fred has taught for fifteen years—his entire career—at this one high school. Although the abrasions of experience have worn away much of the idealism that fueled his choice of career, he finds its intrinsic rewards sufficiently frequent to warrant staying in the classroom. In the daily battle to win over and retain student interest in English, he is a victor sufficiently often to keep his spirits up.

His disposition toward students helps. He likes them, sympathizes with their struggles, and construes the enemy to be a national culture that has become increasingly indifferent, if not hostile, to the written word. He has developed and honed a variety of skills targeted at the induction of students into active engagement in learning. His reading list combines curricular prescriptions with student suggestions. His planning before the beginning of each term leaves room for the play of student interest and opinion. His reputation among students as an adult genuinely interested in them helps in his efforts to move beyond the ritual gamesmanship of the classroom.

Responsible for running a school of 3,500 students, the school's administrators negotiate the middle way between a central bureaucracy located miles away and the living presence of students in the school. Throughout Fred's fifteen years in the school, principals have come and gone. His memory of them is a collective blur save in the rare cases of extreme competence or incompetence. The most recent principal has so far warranted no notice.

Fred begins to observe trouble in one of his students—a fifteen-year-old boy. Papers usually on time and well done are late and show haste in composition. Changes in the boy's behavior prompt Fred to suggest a meeting with a school social worker. The social worker says that the boy is troubled but will not say why, although he has agreed to continue talking.

Fred hears nothing for several weeks and then receives a call from the social worker. The boy has begun to talk, and the evolving story is that the principal is regularly coercing students into sexual acts in his office. The social worker tells Fred that she was initially skeptical but has become convinced that the students are telling the truth. Fred, too, is skeptical and asks the social worker whether she thinks the boy will talk to him. Under the right circumstances, she says, he will. She agrees to ask him and sets up a meeting out of school hours and off school grounds. As a result, Fred is convinced that the story is true. Fred and the social worker are then left with the question of what to do. The principal is a veteran of the school system; he has a powerful set of connections throughout its many levels. He is known to be skilled in the pursuit of power and occasionally ruthless in its exercise. It is clear that the reaction of the system is as likely to be self-protection as it is protection of the students.

What is Fred to do?

The answers do not come easily or quickly. They emerge through time and after episodes of a nightmarish quality. He explores the reactions of other faculty members and finds a three-way division. Some reject outright the story of sexual abuse and will fully support the principal against any charges. Others accept the possibility, even probability, of the charges being true but decline to participate in any overt action. A third small group is willing to act. With its help, Fred gains further documentation of the sexual abuse to build a case, but presentation of the case to authorities within the system brings no results. A combination of delay through process and denial augurs a policy of attrition on the part of the system's administrators.

In the end, Fred and those willing to fight with him bypass the school system entirely and contact public legal authority. After months of effort, the principal is brought to trial and convicted. Later, Fred recalls the comment of one colleague who joined in the struggle. "The moral of this story," says the colleague, "is not that nobody knew; it is that only nobodies knew."

Hal

Hal, in his mid-thirties and married with two young children, has taught in both public and private schools. He is now teaching in a parochial high school located in a pleasant suburb of a major urban area. His first love in teaching is history; he has at times taught other subjects, including communication and drama.

He is a perceptive, thoughtful critic of what prevails in American education. He says:

> What I find most frustrating are the limitations on my own sensitivity and energy. There's so much that I could be doing that I can't do. You cannot work in our schools and not see where changes have to be made. It doesn't make a lot of difference whether the school is private or public. I've worked in both. Our high schools are highly standardized across the line that separates public and private. There are variations, but the basic model is the same. And you know what? That model does not correspond to the ways people learn. It is not designed to impart a real education.

Let's look at high school kids. Here you have a group of people at their peak of physical energy. So what do we do? We make them sit in uncomfortable chairs for six or seven hours a day—that's supposed to be efficient. I see a basic conflict between efficiency and effectiveness. If we want our schools to be effective, then we're going to have to set aside a lot of the structures and practices that got set into place when people were concerned about efficiency. How can an ineffective school be efficient? It's those supposed efficiencies of yesterday that are shackling our effectiveness today.

I have a son in second grade, and he's enthralled with learning. He loves school! I compare him in my mind with some of the kids I work with every day at high school, and I see no sign of that enthrallment. What happens? Something happens in the passage between those early years and later.

When I was at another school, I found a couple of other teachers who felt much the same way I did, and we started putting stuff down on paper. Then we decided to put in for a grant to do what we wanted to do.We designed a self-contained school where there's continual interaction between the teachers and the students, where out of that interaction we'd keep getting a better and better idea of their interests and motivations and react accordingly.

Ours was a school where a teacher could spend an entire day on one subject, or where you could just take one topic and see how it might cut across virtually every discipline. We really got excited about it. But then I had to leave that school because of budget cuts, so we never brought it to completion.

One of the best teaching experiences I've had recently was in a communications class. What made it work was an openness to the feelings and emotions that kids have. I remember one day a girl came in who was clearly upset. She was in no shape to participate in the class. I told her best girl friend just to take her out of the class and into the girls' room and talk. Out of that came one of the best discussions we ever had.

I am continually impressed by the needs that high school kids have to find adults they can talk to; who they can trust with the issues that are immediate and live to them, with the situations they get into. I talk with kids about suicide—fourteen-, fifteen-, sixteen-year-olds—they often have suicidal thoughts. And enough kids act upon the thought to make it real. I have kids who get pregnant. They need adults they can talk to. It seems to me that the possibilities of being a good adviser, a good counselor, those possibilities are born in the classroom. We're the ones who are with the kids all the time. I've been in schools where I spend more time in one day with a kid than that kid spent with a counselor the entire year.

As Isobel had an itch toward teaching, Hal has an itch toward action in the interest of school transformation. His daily interactions with students underscore in his mind the need for change and outline the direction that change must take.

How can he exercise that obligation in an arena wider than the dimensions of his classroom?

Action and chance bring an answer. In his own teaching, Hal continues to create ways to induct students actively into the work of learning. His skill is noted and appreciated. He is chosen as one of a select group of teachers honored each year for achievement in the classroom. Selection brings immediate benefits in terms of some time off from teaching and access to resources that would otherwise be unavailable. The longer-term benefit is membership in a steadily expanding company of teachers committed to strengthening the profession.

This company of teachers, however—each from a different school—takes its place among and competes for scarce resources with a host of other entities that exist at the periphery of the central and abiding institutions of schooling: the school system, the teachers' union, and the key regulatory bodies. His voice, joined with that of others in the company, is louder, but it still must take but one place in a rowdy chorus of voices claiming authority in the search for change.

The Eight-Year Study

Background. In the early spring of 1930, some two hundred teachers, principals, and parents assembled in the nation's capital to seek answers to one question: How can high schools better serve· America's youth? Many proposals were made; none survived the fact of the obstacles and problems each brought to the surface:

> The meeting was about to end in a sense of futility and frustration. However, someone with courage and vi-sion proposed . . . to establish a Commission on the Relation of School and College to explore possibilities of better coordination of school and college work and to seek an agreement which would provide freedom for secondary schools to attempt fundamental recon-struction.[3]

The commission idea was accepted. Today, it might well provoke a yawn, but it proved to be an unusual commission. Its twenty-eight members were practicing educators. It took as its first task an assessment of American secondary education.

The commission found that schools had an overreaching purpose; that students failed to grasp their heritage as citizens and were not prepared for the responsibilities of community life; that schools neither knew their students well nor guided wisely; that the curriculum and the real concerns of students were widely separated; and that all too few graduates could write English competently.[4]

That was not all. The commission found that schools were failing to "create conditions necessary for effective learning" and to release and develop student creativity. The high school curriculum revealed neither unity nor coherence, and its subjects "had lost much of their vitality and significance."[5]

The commission did not, however, issue a report and exhort others to action. It assumed responsibility for action. Change was

imperative; to change, schools required a measure of freedom, secured by winning an agreement on the part of three hundred colleges and universities to waive their traditional subject and unit
entrance requirements for the graduates of selected experimental
schools.[6]

The commission then recruited thirty schools to join in the
experiment. They varied in auspice, size, gender of students, and
location. Some were public, some private; some were purely senior
highs, while others combined junior and senior highs. They were
located in every region of the country except the South.[7] The Thirty
Schools began the work of "fundamental reconstruction" in the fall
of 1933. Each was free to pursue reconstruction on its own terms and
in its own ways, but representatives of the schools met regularly to
develop guidelines and share experiences. As a group, they evolved
two guidelines for reconstruction. First, school life and teaching
method "should conform to what is now known about the ways in
which human beings learn and grow." Second, the American high
school "should re-discover its chief reason for existence."[8]

The paths to reconstruction were various but commonly exciting, frustrating, and frightening. At the first meeting of school
principals:

> Everyone had a strong sense of sharing in a great ad-
> venture; few anticipated the hard work, the problems,
> the discouragements, and the eventual satisfactions
> which were to come. No one present at that first con-
> ference will ever forget the honest confession of one
> principal when she said, "My teachers and I do not
> know what to do with this freedom. It challenges and
> frightens us. I fear that we have come to *love our
> chains.*"[9]

The search for the rediscovery of purpose proved particularly troublesome. Many dismissed it as a feckless exercise in academic
philosophizing:

> Even as late as 1935 there was still reluctance on the
> part of many representatives of the schools to devote

any considerable portion of the annual meeting of school Heads and the Commission to consideration of fundamental principles of American education. At the conclusion of a session devoted to search for the meaning of democracy, several principals said, "This has been very interesting, but let's give no more time to philosophy. What we need is discussion of the practical job of curriculum revision." But two years later, everyone recognized the need of a sound philosophy for reconstruction of American secondary education.

They found what they sought in the democratic ideal, in the American way of life. "The high school in the United States," they said, "should be a demonstration, in all phases of its activity, of the kind of life in which we as a people believe."[10]

Such belief, wedded to the purpose of meeting the needs and interests of students, formed the foundation of purpose on which the reconstructed high schools arose. By 1936, the results were ready for a test. To assay the mettle of the reconstructed high schools, 1,500 of their graduates were tracked in college, beginning with the graduates in 1936 and continuing through the class of 1939. Each graduate was matched with another student in the same college.

Overall, the Thirty Schools' graduates did "a somewhat better job than the comparison group whether success is judged by college standards, by the students' contemporaries, by the individual students."[11] Students from the experimental schools did as well as their counterparts from the control schools on traditional tests but exceeded them in areas requiring problem-solving skills, creativity, and other abilities stated as central to the purposes of the experimental group. Moreover, the more experimental the school— the more radical the reconstruction—the more pronounced the differences in favor of the experimental group. When the graduates of the two most experimental schools were assessed, their superiority "was greater than any previous differences reported" in earlier studies.[12]

The experiment came to be called the Eight-Year Study. It was the most sustained effort of educational reform ever undertaken

in this country—and the most extensively and carefully documented. Five volumes, published in 1942 and 1943, record what was
done, how, by whom, and with what results.[13] Those volumes found
few readers. They were released while the nation was embroiled in
World War II and have disappeared into the archives. For all that
the Eight-Year Study has been referred to occasionally in contemporary reform, it might just as well never have happened.

Meaning of the Eight-Year Study. The Eight-Year Study did,
in fact, happen. Its disappearance from memory is revealing. Its
recovery provides an invaluable asset to the examination of American education as a moral enterprise and helps us better understand
the situations of Isobel, Fred, and Hal. Those who gave birth to,
shaped, and conducted the Eight-Year Study confronted and acted
from a moral challenge: "How can the high school improve its
service to American Youth?"[14] Groups of Americans acted *together*
from the outset. Each needed others to accomplish a goal and found
it necessary to fashion or join a group.

By contrast, Isobel, Fred, and Hal all began alone.[15] In two of
the cases, the group dissolves over time because it takes no institutional form. In the third case, Hal's, the group is institutional but
located on the margin of the educational universe.

In the Eight-Year Study, established educational institutions
are the locus of action. The commission served as an ad hoc en-
abling device. Its work completed, it dissolved. It dissolved because
thirty schools had been reborn in varying degrees and in varying
ways. The rebirth grew out of the quest to rediscover purpose—a
central, powerful, and organizing purpose that gave zest and meaning to method, as well as substance to evaluation. Those in the
Eight-Year Study recognized and acted on a problem that Herbert
Thelen (himself a participant in the Eight-Year Study) accurately
described several decades later:

> We have made hard and fast divisions between think-
> ing and doing, creating and applying, planning and
> acting, preparing and fulfilling. . . .[T]hese divisions
> have made modern life purposeless. For as long as we
> maintain the division, we shall never have to find an

organizing principle to integrate the parts. The organizing principle we have thus succeeded in avoiding is
purpose. Thus, by one of those odd paradoxes that
frequently represent the highest wisdom, the hidden
purpose of modern society is to avoid the necessity for
purposes. Since the practical importance of purpose is
to enable us to see how to recognize and choose among
alternatives, the practical consequence of avoiding
purposes is avoidance of the necessity for choosing,
and with this, of course, the flight from freedom, for
freedom without choice is impossible.[16]

The Eight-Year Study confronted the issue of purpose. The
effort was not painless, but the practice of inquiry convinced the
skeptics. That practice ensured a revealing consistency of means and
ends, for, in the embrace of democracy as the purposeful mission of
schooling, the schools concluded that secondary-education "should
be a demonstration, in all phases of its activity, of the kind of life in
which we as a people believe."[17] In short, living democratically in
school was the best way of learning democracy.

The realization of purpose required freedom. The commission secured a grant of freedom through its agreement with the three
hundred colleges and universities to waive existing entrance requirements. Freedom *from* was used as freedom *to:* freedom to accept and meet reclarified responsibility.

The course of responsibility in the Eight Year Study is illuminating. The commission took responsibility for the results of its
assessment of secondary education and acted to create the conditions
under which change could take place. Responsibility then shifted to
the individual schools, and the commission's role became supportive. Within the schools, reconstruction unfolded as a schoolwide
enterprise. When it did not—when responsibility remained largely
in the hands of the principal or a small group of faculty members—
then reconstruction faltered.[18]

This logic of democratic participation proved inexorable in
its procedural encirclement. It encircled students. Schools learned
the ways of engaging students in decision making. They did so not
from romantic posturings but from an experienced appreciation of

the obstacles to be overcome. Their realism rested on a fundamental recognition: "Each pupil, of course, makes the decision as to what will be learned."[19]

> The experience of teachers using teacher-pupil planning with classes over a period of years indicates that students can and will plan very intelligently. Their contribution at first will be meager and often insincere because they are attempting to guess what the teacher wants. It takes time and skillful teaching to convince students that their honest thinking will be respected. They are conditioned to docility and the playing of the age-old games of bluff and out-guessing the teacher.[20]

In each of the first three case studies presented in this chapter, we find the same instincts regarding student engagement. Isobel, Fred, and Hal act on the necessity of inducting students into a measure of responsibility for their own learning. Each must, of course, also heed the requirements of curricula imposed from above. So each performs a feat of reconciliation. Those feats are accomplished individually—each teacher is an isolated moral agent. In the Eight-Year Study, schools became fellowships of reconciliation. In groups, supporting each other in trials and tests of effort, teachers explored the ways to active engagement. Students had to have a role in deciding what would be learned, how, and in what sequence. They make such decisions anyway. What is the alternative to ignoring their moral agency?

Student engagement was not purely an issue of method. It answered a question of content as well. Purpose for the Thirty Schools was twofold: first, teaching democracy as a way of life and, second, meeting the needs of adolescents. The schools concluded that students need to learn how to make decisions and how to work in groups. "How can such training better be given than by group consideration of such matters of vital concern to them as what they will study and how they will study it?"[21]

The twofold definition of purpose adopted by the Thirty Schools reflects the conflict that schools must always resolve. One purpose is social, the other individual. How and where are the two reconciled? There is only a limited number of ways to accomplish reconciliation. One is to ignore the conflict, an option much favored by educational reformers in recent years. Excellence will be regulated into existence. It never works, of course, except with those students for whom it has always worked—students who can both accept and meet the societal expectations loaded into schools. A second way is that exemplified by the Eight-Year Study: to honestly and perserveringly grapple with and define purposes and then openly search for the means of reconciling the conflicts. When that approach is not adopted, teachers confront difficult choices alone. The teacher must act individually to either reconcile or perpetuate the fiction of a paper curriculum. If the latter, then *Othello* appears on the eleventh-grade reading list. Papers based on it and rendered at performance levels ranging from fourth grade on up are accepted.

The Eight-Year Study helps us to see more vividly the isolation of teachers such as Isobel, Fred, and Hal. It was a richly and pervasively collaborative effort from its inception. What educators did in groups teachers most often do alone. The Eight-Year Study also illuminates in other ways the debasement of teaching. The comment of Fred's colleague at the end of the prolonged struggle to remove the abusive principal, that "it is not that nobody knew: it is that only nobodies knew," underscores the moral bankruptcy latent in systems whose neatly scaled hierarchies underwrite a competition for place and power in which advance in place and gain in power are commensurate with distance from the classroom.

The sordid history of such systemic incoherence begins with the disempowerment of the teacher. Disempowered teachers cannot revise school practice to meet either new social or student needs. The fit between school and the needs of those it putatively serves becomes increasingly awkward. Exit becomes the solution of preference: students drop out, teachers move on. Those who remain become nobodies.

In the universe of schooling evoked by the Eight-Year Study, there was no place for a nobody. The teacher was understood to be central; the purpose of the schools was as much to nurture the development of teachers as it was to nurture students, for without the one there could not be the other.

The case of Isobel forces us to see the perverse effects today of an active moral autonomy—moral action isolated rather than embedded her in the school context. When school is not the coherent, moral, learning universe that the Eight-Year Study intended it to be, and when incoherence creates a de facto work-to-rule culture, then the competence born of care, commitment, imagination, and sheer hard work affronts the dominant culture. The assertion of individuality in a context shaped by its counterfeits becomes threatening and must be dealt with, usually in abrasive ways.

In the case of Hal, the Eight-Year Study forces us to see more clearly the vast inefficiencies of modern educational reform. In the study, high schools were the primary institutions, colleges the second; their collaboration was required to secure the freedom for change. Thereafter, the school was the focus. The study never mistook for a moment the central figure in the school—it was the teacher. The landscape of change was sparse; it included the school, the community served by the school, the college, and an interim commission that disappeared once its mission had been accomplished.

Today, the landscape of change is thick with a profusion of institutional actors. Each has its rationale; viewed in isolation each rationale cannot easily be gainsaid. But viewed in the aggregate, the profusion bespeaks an inability to deal directly with the central institutions of schooling. The Eight-Year Study did so deal; that was the major source of its efficiency.

Two other significant sources of that efficiency were clearheadedness and tough-mindedness. In making the case, for example, that schools launched upon reconstruction must view it as continual, the study set out the intellectual prerequisite for self-assessment. "Open-minded analysis of assumptions," Wilford Aikin wrote in *The Story of the Eight-Year Study*, "is a strong stimulus to vigorous, constructive thinking."

> Constructive thinking requires the capacity to break one's customary patterns of thought and to create new ones. This is especially necessary in those who would see education afresh. Usually education is thought of in patterns of school buildings, classrooms, classes, textbooks, courses, grades, credits, diplomas. It is only

when these paraphernalia of education can be pushed into the background of one's thinking that realistic thinking becomes possible. Only then is the teacher able to see the student as a young human being growing up in a very complex and difficult world. And only then can the teacher begin to see clearly and constructively what the school should be and do.[22]

As for the time required for teachers to break through the custom of educational thought and begin acting upon fresh vision, the study was very clear. The authors of *Exploring the Curriculum* observed that

The preparation of teachers, parents and students for a change in procedure has occupied most of the years of the experiment. Because that is true . . . impatient pioneers and critics of educational radicalism will both be compelled to revise their notions regarding the speed with which real and substantially thought-out change in education can take place.[23]

To summarily review the meaning of the Eight-Year Study, we need to allude to the twin tenets of the democratic idea. One is the moral autonomy of the individual; the other is the political sovereignty of the people. If the individual is to act in morally meaningful ways, the little sovereignties we call institutions must constitute a context that nurtures and rewards such action.

The schools in the Eight-Year Study worked themselves through to unwavering clarity on this point. The promotion and refinement of democracy as a way of life set the purpose: Central to democracy was the primacy of the individual. Therefore, a member of one school faculty said, "The test of every social and political organization is the effect which it has upon the individuals who are touched by it."[24]

If little sovereignties such as schools and school systems are to nurture and reward democratic individuality, they must themselves be disciplined by democratic ideals and the methods that flow from them. When they stray from that discipline, citizens must fash-

ion the freedom to recover and restore purpose and discipline. That
is what happened in the Eight-Year Study. Moral individuality was
secured through collective provision and action. The moral agent
most centrally responsible for the shaping of those apprenticeships
was the teacher.

The Teacher as Resource. Over the last several months, I
have had a number of conversations about the Eight-Year Study
that have confirmed its disappearance from cultural memory and
also proved revealing in the matter of resources. Time and time
again I have been asked, "Who funded it?" The important answer—
which tends to provoke disbelief—is *no one.* The Commission on
the Relation of School and College, which sponsored the study, met
for two years at the expense of its individual members. The Carnegie Foundation provided funds to the commission in 1932 and later
helped underwrite its evaluation and curriculum consultant staff.
The work of reconstruction at the Thirty Schools, however, received
no funding. The critical grant was one of freedom, secured through
the release of the schools from the bondage of college entrance requirements. Freedom released the resources of the teachers—their
energy, enthusiasm, and creativity—and of many others as well. To
read all five volumes of the Eight-Year Study is to be profoundly
impressed by the number of people involved, none of whom was
dominant. What took place over the eight years was a long, horizon-
tal bubbling of activity, individually played out on a democratically
level stage.

Voluntarism suffused the enterprise. The Thirty Schools
chose to participate; for much of the project, commission members
contributed their time. Once reconstruction was under way, the
staffs created by the commission—one for evaluation, one for curriculum—had to win the spurs of acceptance by the schools. Government, at any level, was conspicuous by its absence.

The artifact of thousands of men and women, most of them
teachers, the study was, in many ways, a prolonged essay in professional development. That the teacher was seen as the core of the
curriculum is revealed in the placement of the discussion of teacher
growth: in the second volume, entitled *Exploring the Curriculum.*

The central problem posed by teacher growth was "how to

bring all the capacities of each teacher into fullest use."[25] The first prerequisite was self-confidence, defined largely as the absence of fear:

> Constant fear of failure, fear of fellow-workers, fear of the administration, fear of the community, fear of not imitating the successful example of someone else who is promoted, fear of change, fear of loss of work, fear of failing to follow the edicts of state departments or colleges of education—such daily fears are almost purely negative in effect. They result in thinking about how to be safe rather than how to be effective. In place of fear, self-confidence will come to the teacher whose fellow-workers and administrative superiors understand and cooperate to work out clearer concepts and new means of achieving them. With every advance will come a corresponding increase in the sense of freedom and release—freedom to think and do; release of all one's energies and capacities.[26]

The second prerequisite was freedom—more accurately, the feeling of freedom. "In some schools studied, it took several years for faculty members to arrive at the feeling that they could actually take the colleges at their word and alter the traditional patterns of college-entrance requirements."[27] Freedom required authority commensurate with the responsibility newly devolved upon teachers. It also required a security whose prime corrosive was fear.

The third prerequisite was faith. "With the conviction that 'I can do well' must come the conviction that the job is *worth* doing well. In other words, faith."[28]

The fourth prerequisite was broad experience, particularly forms of experience that give birth to a "range of understandings and feelings."[29]

The final prerequisite was a habit—that of analysis and synthesis: the "coordination of study and doing. . . or . . . a working combination of the habit of thought and action—which we call scientific—and another combination which we call art."[30]

Assume that these prerequisites are met. What, then, actually triggers and sustains growth? *Exploring the Curriculum* argues that it begins with a challenge. The challenge may come from any of a variety of sources: the impulse to combine two separate subjects, the revelation of a school's grievous misjudgment of a student, or visits to students' homes.[31] Following on the challenge is a discovery: "some kind of revelation." The provenance of discovery is often the induction of students into a share of curricular governance: "When the fullest understanding and abilities of students are drawn upon, release of energy and enthusiasm is often prodigious."[32]

Threaded through the pages of *Exploring the Curriculum* is a premise its authors found so self-evident that they never made it explicit: Teacher growth must parallel student growth. The growth of teacher individuality is the ultimate guarantor of student individuality. The best way to teach moral autonomy is to embody it in teacher practice.

If we were able to realize the fantasies of a *Star Trek* world and beam Isobel, Fred, and Hal back through time and into one of the Thirty Schools, they would clearly have flourished, furthering the flourishing of other teachers and students. Each has the individual power necessary for the work of empowering others; each acts as an independent moral agent. The three remind us that the fundamental unit of democracy—the morally autonomous individual—is still with us. For a time.

The duration of that time is contingent on the vitality of our democratic sovereignties as moral communities, for the moral autonomy of the individual requires a moral context. Moral autonomy is inseparably wedded to the practice of responsibility. The practice of responsibility takes place in a social context. Meaningful social contexts are moral contexts—they are moral communities.

Moral Learning Community

As Wilford Aiken moved toward closure of *The Story of the Eight-Year Study,* he wrote these words:

> The purposes of the school cannot be determined apart from the purposes of the society which maintains the school. The purposes of any society are deter-

mined by the life values which the people prize. As a nation we have been striving always for those values which constitute the American way of life. . . . It follows, therefore, that the chief purpose of education in the United States should be to preserve, promote and refine the way of life in which we as a people believe.

This, then, is the conclusion which grew out of the continuing search for guiding objectives in the Thirty Schools. This great, central purpose gave direction. What part of the school's curriculum should be retained? That part which promotes the kind of life we seek. What changes in young people are desired? Those which lead us in the direction of democratic living.

But what is the American way? What are the principles of democracy? These are the questions which individual teachers and school faculties sought to answer. . . .

Therefore, if our youth are to know and prize the American way of life, their studies should take them back to its origins and on to the great issues before us in a world in which we cannot live apart.[33]

To fully grasp the import of these words, we must recall the circumstances under which they were written. The Depression had idled one-quarter of the nation's labor force; the specter of war was on the horizon. By the time the Eight Year Study was being written up, the war against fascism was under way. It would be hard to imagine a time when our nation was more anxious at home and more threatened from abroad. And yet, under those circumstances, thousands of men and women committed to the practice of educating America's youth reacted with neither panic nor competitive defensiveness. Rather, they simply and calmly reaffirmed our most basic civic value—belief in democracy as a way of life—as the surest guide to both the means and ends of reconstructing a school. The exercise of democratic sovereignty ensured its continuation.

The crisis of American education in the 1980s has evoked

response of a different caliber. How are we to understand these voices of a half century back? What is this language?

We are helped in the search for answers by a book, published in 1985, entitled *Habits of the Heart,* which traces the history of an American individualism whose moral content has shriveled down to the contingencies of self-interest amid the interplay of personality, in a context decisively shaped by economic imperatives. The interdependencies and dependencies of life hide behind the veil of a radical individualism. The authors write that

> Much of the thinking about the self of educated Americans, thinking that has become almost hegemonic in our universities and much of the middle class, is based on inadequate social science, impoverished philosophy and vacuous theology. There are truths we do not see when we adopt the language of radical individualism.[34]

What are those truths? One answer, in words strikingly similar to those used in *Habits of the Heart,* comes in a paragraph from *Exploring the Curriculum:*

> In the excitement of the intellectual, emotional, and physical adventure which we call human development or education, there seems to be a paradox: at one and the same time, growth is highly individual and highly social—it springs from within the person, yet it receives its most precious value from the sense of belonging to a social group. Yet the paradox may not be so difficult to understand after all, since it is this very sense of shared ideals or values which gives each human being the greatest feeling of inner and individual rightness and security.[35]

We find here, then, a conversation going on through generations. In fact, *Habits of the Heart* sets out the notion of culture as "dramatic conversations about things that matter to their participants."[36] In the ongoing American conversation, the book identifies

three dominant strands: biblical, republican, and modern individualist. The first two are in tension with the third:

> From its early days, some Americans have seen the
> purpose and goal of the nation as the effort to realize
> the ancient biblical hope of a just and compassionate
> society. Others have struggled to shape the spirit of
> their lives and the laws of a nation in accord with the
> ideals of republican citizenship and participation.[37]

The biblical and republican strands were powerfully in the
minds of the men and women who shaped and conducted the Eight-
Year Study. Schools for them should and could embody the cultural
practices that animated democracy's morality. Ultimately, any culture is a morality, what Weston La Barre termed "a moral geometry—a system *not* inalternatively embedded in the physical world,
but a contingent means of triangulating one's course through
reality."[38]

Our decisive contingent means are embedded in institutions.
Modern humanity has ever more steadily thickened life with institutions. What can we say about our institutions generally and about
educational institutions in particular? To achieve clarity, we need
to use what *Habits of the Heart* calls the second language of American culture. The first is that of radical individualism; the second
enables moral discourse. It is a language of "tradition and commitment in communities of memory."[39]

The Eight-Year Study is couched in this second language. Its
language is simple, hence democratically accessible. Writing for the
committee that edited the contributions from each of the participating schools that made up the final volume of the study, Paul Diederich notes that the editors eliminated "as much educational jargon
as possible."[40] The language is also honest. The study did not com-
pile a record of unblemished success; its five volumes narrate the
history of a struggle. Much that was attempted did not, in the end,
work. Diederich characterizes the reports from the individual
schools as "temperate in their estimates of success and candid about
mistakes and failures."[41] The study's achievement was to demonstrate the reality of continuing self-assessment and self-renewal in

schools free to be democratically responsible. The vision of schools in the study is reflected years later in Herbert Thelen's notion of "education guided by unattainable values."[42] Finally, the language is morally grounded. In the third volume, which reports on how the schools met the challenge of alternatively assessing and recording student progress, the term *evaluation* is at the outset defined as "the process by which the values of an enterprise are ascertained."[43]

With similar attention to pristine meaning, we can further develop a portrait of our educational institutions. We often hear, for example, that teachers are demoralized. In everyday discourse, the word *demoralized* means having lost morale, but literally it means "shorn of values." Are we to conclude that teachers are amoral or immoral? The cases of Isobel, Fred, and Hal tell us otherwise. Do these three represent a majority of teachers? How can we know?

What we can know is that for decades, teachers by the thousands have abided the vicissitudes of policy, the vagaries of reform, the stultification of bureaucracy, and the ineptitudes of administration and ever more intricate thickets of regulation, while continuing to enact those individual feats of reconciliation that express both moral obligation and moral agency.

What we can also know is that the institutions of education are demoralized, which is to say that they are debased. They are cut loose from the basics, as the Eight-Year Study would have understood the term. The basics center around purpose. Without clear purpose, institutions are vulnerable to debasement. Just how vulnerable is illustrated in the horror confronted by Fred when institutional obligation to youth had become utterly superseded by the institution's need to mask its moral incoherence.

Our schools depend ultimately on the moral agency of the individual teacher. No matter how closely regulated, teaching requires continual choice, and the hardest choices are moral in nature. We have depended on that individual moral agency, even when denying its reality. Such denial is of a piece with the mentality that, in reducing individualism to little more than sanctioned indifference, produces its counterfeit. The forgery is revealed in the hostility to action born of authentic moral autonomy. As Tocqueville foresaw a century and a half ago, individualism unwedded to moral tradition and commitment is ever pregnant with the illicit child of conformity.

Summary

At the outset of this chapter, I premised that teaching is a moral enterprise. The decisive, moral factuality of teaching has long been obscured, because, as a culture, we could assume it. Such an assumption is consistent with a broader range of assumptions about the moral basis of our social institutions, including the economic. In public discourse, we have long shunted morality to separate higher spheres, such as religion; in fact, the separation has always been unreal. Fred Hirsch, in *Social Limits to Growth,* illuminated with singular insight both the moral predicates of a market economy and their depletable nature.[44]

To appreciate Hirsch's argument, we need only pause and reflect on the events of everyday life to recognize our implicit dependence on the moral actions of others for our safety and well-being. Just as modern transportation is unthinkable without brakes, so modern society is unthinkable without the morality that people practice, for the most part, most of the time. The exceptions prove the rule. The poisoning of pain-relief capsules focuses attention on the usually high quality of drugs and forces us to recognize the morality of the overwhelming number of the people who produce not just drugs but all of the substances that we regularly take into our bodies.

Morality is not a private practice, although we have long believed it to be so. Such belief is a cultural luxury we can no longer afford. If individuality, understood as autonomy, is to flourish, institutions must be morally disciplined. So talk of institutions as moral communities, while it hints of the exhortative, is plainly factual.

If institutions thrive on loyalty paid as the price of security provided, and if the loyalty is to an ethic of concealment and deception, then individual moral autonomy is hazardous, its practice the province of nobodies. Many of our nation's institutions today so thrive. That legislation has been proposed to protect whistle-blowers—those who expose the practices of deception and concealment—is far more a revelation of the depth of the problem than the source of a solution.

Elementary and secondary schools, because they figure so prominently in the tapestry of democratic ideals and possibilities that we have woven as a nation, have a compelling obligation to understand themselves as moral learning communities. A half century ago, a large number of American educators acted from that understanding. They found the American high school demoralized. Their remedial action was to remoralize. Schools first had to rediscover purpose. Choice of purpose is a moral act. Clarity of purpose led to consistency of means and ends; to effectively teach democracy, schools had to be reconstructed by democratic means into democratic polities. To accomplish remoralization, educators had to work together; collective action and provision were required to ensure individual autonomy.

The narrative of their action has come down to us as a story—the story of the Eight-Year Study. It has almost completely disappeared from cultural memory. *Habits of the Heart* helps us to recognize the importance of its recovery to memory:

> Communities, in the sense in which we are using the term, have a history—in an important sense they are constituted by their past—and for this reason we can speak of a real community as a "community of memory," one that does not forget its past. In order not to forget that past, a community is involved in retelling its story, its constitutive narrative, and in so doing, it offers examples of the men and women who have embodied and exemplified the meaning of the community. These stories of collective history and exemplary individuals are an important part of the tradition that is so central to a community of memory.[45]

The story of the study tells of Americans who took seriously the nature of democracy as a form of *social* organization and who grasped the meanings of that form for individuality rooted in moral autonomy. They were comfortable in the paradox of human growth as both highly individual and highly social. They spoke simply and sincerely. We might today see their simplicity and sincerity as naive. Such a reaction, however, tells us more about ourselves and our situation than it does about the narrators of the story, for there is in the story profound wisdom—wisdom tested, wisdom won. Without that wisdom, we cannot today adequately explain to ourselves why and how our educational institutions have become debased, nor can we know how to act responsibly to restore their character as moral communities.

Notes

1. The first three cases studied use pseudonyms and omit or alter details in order to preserve confidentiality.
2. W. La Barre, *The Human Animal* (Chicago: University of Chicago Press, 1954), p. 237.
3. W. M. Aikin, *The Story of the Eight-Year Study* (New York: Harper & Row, 1942), p. 2.
4. Aikin, *The Story of the Eight-Year Study,* pp. 4–8.
5. Aikin, *The Story of the Eight-Year Study,* pp. 5–7.
6. No complete list of the cooperating colleges and universities is to be found in the five volumes of the Eight-Year Study. However, the fourth volume, *Did They Succeed in College,* lists the twenty-five colleges selected for intensive tracking of the graduates of the Thirty Schools.
7. For convenience, these schools came to be known as the Thirty Schools. In fact, there were twenty-nine; one dropped out in 1936. The arbitrariness of the number thirty is compounded by the fact that some of the schools were, in fact, school systems. One, for example, included five senior high schools and fifteen junior high schools as part of the study.
8. Aikin, *The Story of the Eight-Year Study,* pp. 17–18.
9. Aikin, *The Story of the Eight-Year Study,* p. 16. Italics are in the original.
10. Aikin, *The Story of the Eight-Year Study,* pp. 30–31.
11. D. Chamberlin, E. S. Chamberlin, E. Drought, and W. E. Scott, *Did They Succeed in College? The Follow-Up Study of the Graduates of the Thirty Schools* (New York: Harper & Row, 1942), p. 208.

12.   Chamberlin, Chamberlin, Drought, and Scott, *Did They Succeed in College?* p. 209.

13.   The Eight-Year Study reports constitute a series titled *Adventures in American Education:* W. M. Aikin, *The Story of the Eight-Year Study* (1942); H. H. Giles, S. P. McCutchen, and A. N. Zechiel, *Exploring the Curriculum: The Work of the Thirty Schools from the Viewpoint of Curriculum Consultants* (1942); E. R. Smith, R. W. Tyler, and the Evaluation Staff, *Appraising and Recording Student Progress: Evaluation, Records and Reports in the Thirty Schools* (1942); D. Chamberlin, E. S. Chamberlin, N. E. Drought, and W. E. Scott, *Did They Succeed in College? The Follow-Up Study of the Graduates of the Thirty Schools* (1942); and *Thirty Schools Tell Their Story: Each School Writes of Its Participation in the Eight-Year Study* (1943).

14.   Aikin, *The Story of the Eight-Year Study*, p. 1.

15.   Recent films about teachers invariably reenact this drama of the isolate loner: *The Marva Collins Story, Teachers, The Principal, Sylvia,* and *Stand and Deliver.*

16.   H. A. Thelen, *Education and the Human Quest: Four Designs for Education* (Chicago: University of Chicago Press, Phoenix Books, 1972), p. 215.

17.   Aikin, *The Story of the Eight-Year Study*, p. 31.

18.   Aikin, *The Story of the Eight-Year Study*, pp. 33–36, 127–128.

19.   H. H. Giles, S. P. McCutchen, and A. N. Zechiel, *Exploring the Curriculum: The Work of the Thirty Schools from the Viewpoint of Curriculum Consultants* (New York: Harper & Row, 1942), p. 77.

20.   Giles, McCutchen, and Zechiel, *Exploring the Curriculum,* p. 55.

21.   Giles, McCutchen, and Zechiel, *Exploring the Curriculum,* p. 73.

22.   Aikin, *The Story of the Eight-Year Study*, p. 130.

23.   Giles, McCutchen, and Zechiel, *Exploring the Curriculum,* p. 302.

24.   Aikin, *The Story of the Eight-Year Study*, p. 31.

25.   Giles, McCutchen, and Zechiel, *Exploring the Curriculum,* p. 210.

26.   Giles, McCutchen, and Zechiel, *Exploring the Curriculum,*
       p. 215.
27.   Giles, McCutchen, and Zechiel, *Exploring the Curriculum,*
       p. 215.
28.   Giles, McCutchen, and Zechiel, *Exploring the Curriculum,*
       p. 217.
29.   Giles, McCutchen, and Zechiel, *Exploring the Curriculum,*
       p. 217.
30.   Giles, McCutchen, and Zechiel, *Exploring the Curriculum,*
       p. 218.
31.   Giles, McCutchen, and Zechiel, *Exploring the Curriculum,*
       p. 212.
32.   Giles, McCutchen, and Zechiel, *Exploring the Curriculum,*
       p. 213.
33.   Aikin, *The Story of the Eight-Year Study,* pp. 132–133.
34.   R. N. Bellah and others, *Habits of the Heart: Individualism
       and Commitment in American Life* (New York: Harper &
       Row, 1985), p. 84.
35.   Giles, McCutchen, and Zechiel, *Exploring the Curriculum,*
       p. 290.
36.   Bellah and others, *Habits of the Heart,* p. 27.
37.   Bellah and others, *Habits of the Heart,* pp. 27–28.
38.   La Barre, *The Human Animal,* p. 221. Italics are in the
       original.
39.   Bellah and others, *Habits of the Heart,* p. 154.
40.   *Thirty Schools Tell Their Story: Each School Writes of Its
       Participation in the Eight-Year Study* (New York: Harper &
       Row, 1943), p. xxi.
41.   *Thirty Schools Tell Their Story,* p. xxi.
42.   Thelen, *Education and the Human Quest,* p. 10.
43.   E. R. Smith, R. W. Tyler, and the Evaluation Staff, *Appraising and Recording Student Progress: Evaluation, Records and
       Reports in the Thirty Schools* (New York: McGraw-Hill,
       1942), p. 5.
44.   F. Hirsch, *Social Limits to Growth* (Cambridge, Mass.: Harvard University Press, 1976).
45.   Bellah and others, *Habits of the Heart,* p. 153.

10

Society, Schooling, Teaching, and Preparing to Teach

Kenneth A. Sirotnik

What a grandiose title! Its immodesty is warranted only because I have the preceding nine authors (and their chapters) to rely on, each of whom has worked through to considerable depth what may be the most problematic issue of our time and of all time—that of simultaneously preserving the interests of individuals and those of society by grounding their interactions in fundamental, moral principles.

The issue addressed by the authors may seem simpler than this, since, by the nature of the book, their analyses are limited to K–12 public education and schooling in the context of American society. I would suggest, however, that the issue cuts to the deepest layers of what it means to be human, what it means to be with other humans, and what rights and responsibilities would seem to follow.

Certainly, in the specific sense that Goodlad argues in Chapter One for teaching as a special case among the professions, our topic can be reasonably circumscribed. Yet it may well be that the chapters in this book are but special cases of more fundamental matters. It seems intuitively plausible that the foregoing arguments could be extended to education beyond grade twelve, to public institutions more generally, and, indeed, to educational and noneducational institutions in the private sphere of society.[1]

I have some degree of confidence in this assertion in view of the growing body of convergent thinking that is turning inquiry in social, psychological, political, and economic realms back to its normative root—back to considerations of fundamental values, beliefs, and human interests.[2] Much support, I think, can be taken from this movement for our commitments in this book to the moral and ethical grounding of the purposes of public schooling, the role of educators in schools, and, by implication, the imperatives for educating educators for our schools. For this larger body of work suggests not only that we have taken morally defensible positions but that essentially the same positions ground the normative context within which public education must succeed.[3]

My tasks here are to synthesize what appear to be the basic arguments put forth in this book with whatever fresh insights I might bring to the task and to draw out implications for teacher education. In the former instance, I will appeal to fundamental assumptions, first principles, and moral imperatives that I think are implicit in each of the preceding chapters. This synthesis will be sketchy at best and, if it were to stand alone, would require a great deal more substantiation. If my interpretation is at all reasonable, however, the required substantiation can be found in the pages of this book and the cited references. Packaging it all together in more depth, to the extent useful, will have to be a project for another time.

The latter task has already been started for me by many contributors who have begun to note some implications for teacher education. I will gladly make use of their work as well as of the experiences we have accumulated during the Study of the Education of Educators referred to in Chapter One.[4]

Society and the Human Condition

At the end of Chapter Two, Soder challenges us to wrest the stick from the Zen master—to argue from definition, from what might be called first principles, in seeking to establish the ethical roots and hence the moral praiseworthiness of teaching as a profession. There are definite risks in taking up this challenge. One had better do something powerful with the stick lest it be taken back and perhaps used even more ferociously than originally planned. Nonetheless, compelled by the rhetorical grounding of his argument, I have no choice but to proceed as directed. I can only hope that the impending beating will be worth the clarity that might be achieved as I write my way through thickets of thorny issues.

Soder suggests that the basis for arguing from definition can be found in the nature of the relationship between those who teach and those who are taught. Indeed, aspects of this relationship have been germane to the discussions in all the chapters of this volume. As I wrestled with this relationship in search of first principles, however, the roles of teacher and student became less and less important. Escalating in importance was their common condition—what it means to be human and to be with humans.

To be sure, the lack of parity in power, knowledge, and volition that characterizes the teacher-student relationship is crucial and intensifies the imperative nature of moral responsibility. But the ethical roots go deeper, into the human condition itself. I will outline five; there may be more, or a different categorical arrangement, but these seem sufficient to synthesize our work here.

Inquiry. The commitment to rational thought—to nurturing and exercising the capability of human inquiry—is an implicit assumption underlying each of the contributions to this volume.[5] This is not to suggest that the contributors deny the irrational nature of man. To do so would be clearly foolish. The best of our rational arguments and intentions are often ignored in the irrationality of action. We worry about getting on airplanes but never think twice about getting into our cars. The relationship between educational policymaking and what we know and care about in the theory and practice of schooling is often difficult to discern, at best. Several authors in this volume note (or imply) that there are obviously no guarantees that their well-reasoned arguments will necessarily lead to consistent action by people, even those proclaiming sympathies with the expressed moral points of view.

Yet, as a species, we struggle to be rational, both in our relationships with people and with ideas. In the prologue to a seminal work, Hannah Arendt tells us that "the highest and perhaps purest activity of which men are capable [is] the activity of thinking."[6] Nowhere in our book can I detect a championing of the irrational, an advocacy of thoughtlessness, whether in terms of human relationships (as between teachers and the taught), the principles of professionalism, or the ways in which knowledge can be organized and experienced.

A moral commitment to inquiry, then, is a first principle, an ethical root, that sustains the project undertaken in this book. Some readers may find it curious that one needs to express moral commitment to what appears to be a gift of life—rational thought. However, that Descartes did not formulate his well-known aphorism as "I am, therefore I think" is noteworthy. A matter of increasing concern to many observers of the human condition is what appears to be a decline in thoughtfulness, in reflective habit, in the value placed on inquiry itself—an "eclipse of reason," as Horkheimer has put it.[7]

Arendt ends her book on the same note on which she began it, the supremacy of thought, by quoting Cato's observation on the human being: "Never is he more active than when he does nothing, never is he less alone than when he is by himself."[8] How unfamiliar this implied habit of thought is when set up against a culture that may be "amusing itself to death."[9] Too often we have heard educators say something to the effect, "Well, that's interesting, but it's just philosophical; let's get back to what we can do in the real world." "Thinking" appears to have become increasingly alienated from "doing," in stark contrast to the connection envisioned long ago by Dewey: "When philosophy shall have co-operated with the course of events and made clear and coherent the meaning of the daily detail, science and emotion will interpenetrate, practice and imagination will embrace."[10]

It seems imperative that we acknowledge explicitly our moral commitment to inquiry. I have couched this imperative in ontological and deontological terms; that is, I have argued for the commitment from considerations of the nature of being human and from considerations of duty and obligation to exercise nature's gift. Although I will not pursue them, teleological arguments are relevant too; the consequences of not being thoughtful, of succumbing, as a society, to an "eclipse of reason," could be devastating to our way of life in a political democracy.

Knowledge. Inquiry without knowledge is fraudulent. Knowledge without inquiry is impossible. The implied circularity is essential and welcomed. Whether knowledge is passed on through verbal utterances, cave paintings, written language, or the like, our species has found its generation and preservation to be essential. This commitment to knowledge has at least three sources: our desire for immortality, an obligation to record our thinking for ourselves and future generations, and a prudential consideration of the benefits to be accrued through funded knowledge.

The contributors to this book have all acknowledged, implicitly or explicitly, a fundamental commitment to knowledge. But to what kind of knowledge are these commitments directed? Is it to a "banking" concept of knowledge (and hence education)?[11] Is knowledge being conceived as bits and pieces of information that can be deposited and withdrawn—as a series of facts that can be compiled in directories and sampled as test items to examine people's memories? The answer is a resounding no—unless I have grossly misinterpreted the preceding nine chapters.

It seems clear that the expressed commitment of the contributors is to a concept of knowledge far more encompassing and dynamic than a corpus of accumulated information. Feinberg's critique in Chapter Five of Hirsch's notion of "cultural literacy" is illustrative.[12] As important as the "facts" are, taken separately or together they do not constitute knowledge. Knowledge is what we make of the facts; knowledge is what we learn through explanation, interpretation, and understanding. In short, knowledge is what we gain through inquiry; moreover, inquiry is stimulated and sustained by what we know. This is not accomplished solely through memorization and trivial pursuit. It is accomplished through active and intellectual engagement with information in the context of being human. It is accomplished through associative, analytical, synthetic, and evaluative processes grounded in historical, contemporary, and future accounts of funded knowledge. A commitment to knowledge at a lesser level would be an affront to the human condition and would render pedagogy but a science of information retrieval.

Competence. "Things worth doing are worth doing well" is a common aphorism, though less commonly heeded. Signs of incompetence are all around us and seem to be growing by leaps and bounds. The reasons for this are many in an increasingly complex society; certainly, the lack of training and the lack of commitment are among them. There is much evidence to suggest, in fact, not only that we have to protect ourselves from incompetence but that social organizations will protect the incompetent.[13] Incompetence, moreover, can be deliberate in ways other than just plain maliciousness. For example, social pressures associated with "rate busting" in organizations can lead to purposely lowered performance among workers.

Notwithstanding these problems, competence—not incompetence—is the more natural aspiration for human beings. We aim to reward success, not failure; excellence, not mediocrity. What goes on display in those places that record and collect the fruits of human labor is usually the best—not the worst—of our work. The fact that the words *competence* and *competition* have the same Latin roots is noteworthy: We compete to achieve excellence, not failure. Competing and being competent are particularly close in meaning when one is in competition with oneself—that is, when one is trying to do better what one has already tried to do. This could also be called *learning*.

Once again, therefore, it would seem that we must make a commitment to what appears to be a natural predisposition. Moreover, it is a commitment that appears to be prudent; an incompetent society is not likely to be one that survives. An "ethic of competence" or a moral commitment to doing, and learning to do, things well seems to me to be presupposed by each of the contributors to this book. The discussions of professionalism and professionalization in earlier chapters are all concerned, in one way or another, with rooting out malpractice and promoting quality practice. Those discussions that focus on justice and human interrelationships do so under the assumption that people will serve each other well, not poorly.

Caring. We are not alone. As individuals, we cannot help but be in relationship with each other, whether we like it or not. And I will argue here that, basically, we do like it. Mother-child relationships; parent-children (immediate family) relationships; extended family relationships; neighborhood, community, region, state, na-

tional, and international relationships—all are clearly evident.
Arendt tells us that "No human life, not even the life of a hermit in
nature's wilderness, is possible without a world which directly or
indirectly testifies to the presence of other human beings."[14] The
idea of a society and the implied relationships between people is
basic to the human condition.

Nel Noddings, in her important essay on the ethic of caring,
begins her analysis with a comment that I will rephrase as a question: Why is it that we often hear the complaint "Nobody cares!"?[15]
The expressed sentiment, of course, suggests the more fundamental
predisposition. That "nobody cares" is good news indeed; it suggests that we *care* about caring, naturally, as well as out of obligation, in being human and being with humans.

By "caring," I am not referring to just raw, emotional sentiment or to declarations of affect of the type that might be found on
Hallmark greeting cards. Following Noddings, *caring* is taken here
to refer to a deep relationship between people based on mutuality,
respect, relatedness, receptivity, and trust. "Caring" is an abiding,
empathic relationship that resembles an affective version of the
Golden Rule. In Noddings's words:

> Apprehending the other's reality, feeling what he feels
> as nearly as possible, is the essential part of caring
> from the view of the one-caring. For if I take on the
> other's reality as possibility and begin to feel its real-
> ity, I feel, also, that I must act accordingly; that is, I
> am impelled to act as though in my own behalf, but in
> behalf of the other.[16]

Clearly, there are both ontological and deontological components in this analysis, and they are intertwined. Noddings puts it
thus:

> Recognizing that ethical caring requires an effort that
> is not needed in natural caring does not commit us to
> a position that elevates ethical caring over natural car-
> ing. Kant has identified the ethical with that which is
> done out of duty and not out of love, and that distinc-

tion in itself seems right. But an ethic built on caring strives to maintain the caring attitude and is thus dependent upon and not superior to, natural caring. The source of ethical behavior is, then, in twin sentiments—one that feels directly for the other and one that feels for and with that best self, who may accept and sustain the initial feeling rather than reject it.[17]

It was not happenstance, I would argue, that Bellah and his associates (following the lead of Tocqueville) were led to the heart to find ways of stemming the tide of radical individualism, nor that Etzioni was led to extensions of Buber's I-Thou concept for reconciling self and community interests in an alternative theory of economic transactions.[18] That "Nobody cares!" is not an indication that nobody cares; it is an indication that, as somebodies, we have to work at caring, and we are not always successful. Some of us may have even given up on caring in the sense that I noted above in regard to the declining habit of inquiry. Some of us are unable to care at all; but we do not label this *natural*—we label it *pathological*.

This brings us to the crux of the controversy between those, such as Noddings, who eschew moral principles based on a logic of social justice free of sentiment and those, such as Rawls, who eschew sentiment in favor of morally binding contractual arrangements between people that preserve (at least in theory) their freedom and their well-being. Which position is correct? Both, I would argue. In this book, for example, the moral imperatives of social justice play heavily in some chapters, whereas in others the moral imperatives characterizing human relationship are emphasized.

Humans are not perfect. Caring comes in degrees. Pathology is not rare. Because we care about ourselves and each other, we need to *watch out* for each other. But that does not mean that it is possible to care for everyone in the sense that everyone is *cared for*. Although I may be adding a teleological component to Noddings's argument that she would not endorse, caring, I would argue, must be prudent and wise. I agree, therefore, with Strike's position in Chapter Six that a liberal conception of justice is required precisely because we cannot guarantee care for everyone. Yet, as Sockett sug-

gests in Chapter Seven, this does not render an ethic of caring any
the less fundamental.

Freedom, Well-Being, and Social Justice. Arendt, again, on
human inquiry: "Thought, finally . . . is still possible, and no
doubt actual, wherever men live under the conditions of political
freedom."[19] This, of course, may be an overstatement, since rational
thought is clearly possible in an authoritarian state as long as it is
consistent with ideological canons or kept private. Arendt, however,
had a public concept of shared inquiry in mind: "Men, in so far as
they live and move and act in this world, can experience meaning-
fulness only because they can talk with and make sense to each other
and to themselves."[20]

And so we come to the heart of the matter, a series of age-old
dualities: freedom versus control, individual versus the state, anarchy versus totalitarianism, and the like. As is usually the case with
fundamental dichotomies that have been with us ever since there
have been philosophers, their resolution is not accomplished by
taking sides. Rather, clarity is achieved by recognizing the inherent
dialectic as fundamental to the human condition, as a source of
human behavior, and, consequently, as content for normative
inquiry.

This is precisely the tack taken by our forefathers in devising
a remarkable guideline for our political democracy. The philosophical underpinnings of the liberal state have been developed and
debated at length in the literature, and several authors in this volume (Bull, Feinberg, and Strike) have illuminated our understanding of the requisite concepts. As in the ethical positions above,
ontological, deontological, and teleological arguments are evident
in making the case for social justice: Freedom and well-being are
essential features of the human condition, we are duty-bound to
preserve and protect these features, and, as James Madison astute-
ly observed, "If men were angels, no government would be
necessary."[21]

To put it briefly and personally: I value my freedom and
well-being and would resist, mightily, efforts to take it away. Yet I
am aware that I am not alone. And although I care about others and
expect others to care about me, I am wise enough to recognize that

we humans are the most dangerous animals on earth.[22] I value my well-being as much as my freedom. How do I get both—that is, enough of both—in a democratic society?

The answer, of course, is in a logic of restricted freedoms for everyone that is pretty much equivalent to an ethic at least as old as the Bible: Do unto others as you would have them do unto you (and do not do unto others as you would not have them do unto you). The argument, of course, is much more complicated than the Golden Rule might suggest. In this book, Strike (in Chapter Six) has outlined some of it in his discussion of the liberal construction of the law, and more of the details have been presented by Bull (in Chapter Three) in his discussion of self-defeating and risk-laden freedoms and Dworkin's principle of liberal integrity.[23]

Rawls's theory of justice-as-fairness, of course, is seminal in this regard, as is, in my view, Alan Gewirth's *Reason and Morality*.[24] In the latter treatise, Gewirth manages to reason in a convincing way from "is" to "ought" by first deriving a Golden Rule-like principle from generic claims arising out of human action—claims to freedom and well-being. Second, once the principle is acknowledged as a social good, it becomes categorically and morally imperative for all actors on "pain of self-contradiction."[25] In his own words:

> Every agent logically must acknowledge certain generic obligations. Negatively, he ought to refrain from coercing and from harming his recipients; positively, he ought to assist them to have freedom and well-being whenever they cannot otherwise have these necessary goods and he can help them at no comparable cost to himself. The general principle of these obligations and rights may be expressed as the following precept addressed to every agent: Act in accord with the generic rights of your recipients as well as of yourself.[26]
>
> The agent is logically compelled to make [the] transition from a prudential to a moral judgment, because if he did not he would be in the position of denying what he had previously had to affirm,

namely, that being a prospective purposive agent is a
sufficient justifying condition for having rights to
freedom and well-being.[27]

The bottom line of these arguments is a conception of justice
that preserves, protects, and defends the interests of all individuals
and, therefore, of the community (writ large). This is a conception
of *social* justice. This conception does not view freedom and well-
being as a utility function to be maximized, as a cost-benefit equation where some win and some lose as long as the overall gain is as
great as possible. On the contrary, social justice is conceived in the
Rawlsian sense of justice as fairness. Giving advantages to selected
individuals or groups is fair only to the extent that the least advantaged are so advantaged. Quality and equality, therefore, are constructs considered as achievable simultaneously rather than as in-
commensurable and achievable only in terms of one at the expense
of the other.

Arguments such as Gewirth's and those of others such as
Rawls and Dworkin are ostensibly deontological in nature insofar
as they ultimately appeal to fundamental values and moral obligations reasoned not from considerations of ends but from considerations of what is right. Their claims for universality generate intellectual discomfort among a number of other moral and political
philosophers and are a main source of controversy in the literature.
Of course, this discomfort, whether rational or irrational, is part
and parcel of the same basic duality: relativist versus absolutist in-
terpretrations of individual and community rights. Writers such as
MacIntyre, Sandel, Sullivan, and Walzer have criticized the liberal
philosophers for ignoring the impact of social and cultural contexts, of the ideal of civic virtue and republican responsibilities, and
of the potentially changing nature of social realms and values from
one period of history to the next.[28]

Frankly, I take a dim view of these relativistic arguments, yet
I endorse strongly the importance of community. Relativists have a
penchant for appealing to our democratic tradition of keeping an
open mind while, at the same time, using arguments that appear to
be based on fundamental assumptions. In a cogent critique of this
literature, Phillips points out a number of these inconsistencies.[29]

For example, he notes this quotation from Walzer: "When people disagree about the meaning of social goods, when understandings are controversial, then justice requires that the society be faithful to the disagreements, providing institutional channels for their expression, adjudicative mechanisms, and alternative distributions."[30] The circularity and equivocation regarding first principles are painfully obvious in the "justice requires" phrase. "What conception of justice imposes such a requirement? If justice is . . . a matter of following shared understandings, then what if there is no shared understanding about the meaning of social justice? In the absence of consensus about what justice *is,* there is obviously no way of establishing what 'justice requires.'"[31]

Some contributors to this book show a bit of discomfort with non-relativist positions, even though, I would argue, establishing a set of first principles is exactly what this book is all about.[32] I would suggest that none of the authors of Chapters One through Nine, nor the critics of universal principles of social justice referred to above, would endorse or even negotiate a new conception of "justice" based on racial determinism, hedonism, nihilism, or no ethical stance whatsoever. As Kohlberg pointed out to his critics, "No philosopher ever has seriously attempted to demonstrate that an alternative substantive principle to justice could function in a universal prescriptive fashion in a satisfactory way."[33]

But if universalism is still a troublesome concept, then I would urge readers to at least ponder the rationale that unites the states of America. To be sure, America is a collection of multiple communities defined by different interests, races, ethnicities, regions, economic stratifications, religions, and so forth. Celebrating these differences is part of what makes this nation great. But there is a community—a moral community—that transcends the special interests of individuals, families, groups, that stands for what this nation is all about: liberty *and justice* for all. This "community," of course, is an abstraction. It is a "moral ecology" held together by a political democracy and the fundamental values embedded in the system.[34] Without the stipulation of these values, the contributors to this book would have no basis for argument. Within this moral community, then, the arguments for social justice cited above and contained in this volume become particularly convincing. Within

the subcontexts of public institutions and particularly those requiring compulsory attendence, the arguments are all the more
compelling.

I therefore see little conflict of practical import between arguments for social justice from first principles, on the one hand, and
the concept of a moral community, on the other. Etzioni makes this
point by using the metaphor of "the human arch" (bricks are individuals, and the arch is the social realm): "The debate among social
philosophers points to a *moral* position . . . supported by [the human arch]: both individuals and the community have a basic moral
claim, and any position that omits one of these two intertwined
foundations leads to positions that even their respective advocates
find hard to defend. Hence the [contemporary liberal philosophers']
scramble to determine a place for communal obligation, and the
efforts to establish a *principled* basis for individual rights and a
critical stance within the communitarian camp."[35]

Schooling

What could be more central to education generally and public schooling particularly than moral commitments to inquiry,
knowledge, competence, caring, and social justice? It seems to me
that the moral imperatives for schooling (and teaching and preparing to teach) suggested by these ethical roots are obvious and have
been implied with differing emphases throughout Chapters One
through Nine. I will summarize them at the schooling level in this
section and then discuss them further in relation to teaching and
teacher education in the subsequent sections.

We have argued in this book for a set of moral commitments
that transcend the special interests of individuals or groups. These
are moral commitments that meet the interests of all individuals
and, therefore, are in the public interest. We have attempted to construct the kind of normative vision that Sarason calls for in a triadic
connection between individual, collective, and moral responsibilities; that is, "a guiding vision that reinforces a bond between the
sense of I and the sense of we, a kind of meeting ground where the
nature of the vision is under constant scrutiny and discussion and
informs proposals for action."[36]

A guiding vision does not come automatically with birth and with family or other group membership. It comes with membership to *the public* and, therefore, requires public initiation into the vision. By "public initiation," of course, I am referring to the aim of public education, to what others in this book have referred to as the socialization or enculturation function of education, or to what Oakeshott refers to as initiation into the human conversation.[37] As Phillips argues in relation to moral principles of social justice, "the question arises as to how individuals are to come to learn and accept these principles. This involves a concern with the mechanism of *socialization*."[38]

The intended meaning of our terminology is crucial here. Enculturation or socialization into what? Initiation into whose conversation? Clearly, in view of the context of this discussion, we are not talking about a relativistic conception of society or a culturally reproductive function of education. We are talking, instead, about socialization not necessarily into all the ways things are but into the way things *ought* to be. We are talking not so much about internalizing "society's values" as about internalizing the values of a *just* society. This is what I would call the process of *critical* socialization (following Goodlad's terminology in Chapter One), which I take to mean a deliberately educative experience grounded in ethics of inquiry, knowledge, competence, caring, and social justice.

So where does critical socialization take place? In households? Churches? Clubhouses? Scout meetings? Businesses? Other places? Perhaps some of it does, or at least the potential is there for critical socialization to take place in these informal and nonformal educational settings. But formal education (public or private) is our only available point of deliberate intervention between individual and societal interests. It is through this means that the public has the moral responsibility for critically socializing its young during their formative years. Space does not permit developing this argument for private education. That the proposition is valid for public education and schooling would seem to follow virtually by definition.

What schools *should* be for follows directly from the critical socialization function and the ethical roots underlying that function. Not coincidentally, the broad educational aims (for example,

intellectual, social, and personal development) typically endorsed
by our society are embedded in the moral commitments to inquiry,
knowledge, competence, caring, and social justice. The connections
to inquiry, knowledge, and competence should be obvious and have
been spelled out by Goodlad and others in this book. The connection to caring, although perhaps less obvious, is none the less compelling and is particularly evident in the chapters by Fenstermacher,
Clark, and Thomas. Ask students what the most important characteristic is of a good teacher. Chances are their first response will be
something like "A good teacher cares about you, respects you as a
person, is someone you can trust." Their second response might be
something like "A good teacher is someone who knows his or her
subject" or "someone who can keep control of the class."[39]

Finally, the connection of social justice to schooling is as
fundamental as it is controversial. The kind of social justice argued
for in this book demands that schools provide equal access to and
equal receipt of a quality education for *all* students. Any structures
or practices that interfere with the simultaneous goals of equity and
excellence, that perpetuate preexisting social and economic inequities, are subject to critique and elimination. Schools and those responsible for them are compelled, therefore, to get beyond the
trendy rhetoric of "equity" and "excellence" and really do something about what is implied by the concepts. At a minimum, this
requires making explicit the normative assumptions involved, challenging constructively the prevailing and counterproductive conventional wisdom guiding current practices, and developing sensible, long-term accountability systems that appraise the health of
schools, keeping the twin aims of equity and excellence at the core.[40]
In this way, schools not only serve the best interests of all students;
they provide a valuable educational lesson by modeling the just
society—a case of the institution behaving in a moral manner analogous to the expectation for teacher behavior vis-á-vis students discussed by Fenstermacher in Chapter Four.

Tying it all up rather neatly, Kerr concludes her analysis of
the purpose and function of schooling thus:

> In sum, this cultural conception of education is fun-
> damental to [social] justice, to cultural continuity, to

democracy, and to our ability to interpret what we
see—to structure experience. It is this broad and basic
conception of education that justifies the institution
of schooling generally and universal public schooling
in particular. . . . [T]he central task of schooling [is]
education as an initiation into the ways of understanding and inquiring. Education so conceived cannot be improved by courses in critical thinking, for it
is itself an initiation into the disciplines of critical
thinking. It cannot be passed over in favor of "basic
education," for there is no education that is more
basic.[41]

Teaching

If the moral commitments to inquiry, knowledge, competence, caring, and social justice and the moral imperatives that derive therefrom for schooling are taken seriously, the burden of
ethical responsibilities on educators who work in schools and educators who prepare those who work in schools is enormous and
appropriate. The web of moral commitment and ethical responsibility, of course, is societal in scope and includes the executive, legislative and judicial branches of federal, state, and local
government; school boards; teacher's unions; parents and other
community advocacy groups; the staffs of local educational agencies; and so forth. Without intending to deny the importance of this
moral ecology, I will focus on the school level in the spirit of arguments developed elsewhere.[42]

Ethics of inquiry, knowledge, competence, and caring place
as many demands on the behavior of teachers and the school organization as they do on the curriculum for students. A nonintellectual
and/or nonreflective classroom environment is hardly conducive to
a thoughtful engagement with information and knowledge beyond
rote learning. Teachers who lack competence in their disciplines
and/or who teach outside their areas of competence, as well as those
who conspire in such practices, disgrace the very concept of pedagogy and are engaged in clearly unethical activities. For children
and youths in the care of adults upward of six hours a day for
approximately 180 days a year, the very idea of an uncaring, disre-

spectful, distrusting relationship between these adults and students is a contradiction in terms.

The bottom line is an ethic of social justice. Signs of social injustice pervade the schoolhouse, and it is not difficult to find enduring patterns of inequity: one group of students, typically white, wealthier, and college-bound, receives an intellectually challenging, knowledge-rich curriculum delivered in a competent and caring manner; another group, typically minority, poorer, and non-college-bound, receives an attenuated educational experience in a low-affect classroom environment.[43] Tracking practices such as these at the secondary levels of schooling have their antecedents in the primary levels, where children are sorted and stratified into static learning groups that create self-fulfilling prophecies for the rest of their academic lives. Worse yet, decisions continue to be made about children on the basis of unidimensional conceptions and tests of "intelligence" that are not only racist in their origin but faulty in their theoretical grounding.[44] The freedom and well-being of people—as children, adolescents and adults—are placed at serious risk by such educational practices. To endorse, support, or engage in such practices is unethical and a serious breach of moral commitment to social justice.

But the implications of moral commitments to inquiry, knowledge, competence, caring, and social justice go farther than the curriculum and classroom experiences. They go to the very heart of the moral ecology of the organization itself. This can be readily seen in the extent to which these commitments are reflected in the work environment of educators outside of classroom teaching per se. To what extent does the organizational culture encourage and support educators as inquirers into what they do and how they might do it better? To what extent do educators consume, critique, and produce knowledge? To what extent do they engage competently in discourse and action to improve the conditions, activities, and outcomes of schooling? To what extent do educators care about themselves and each other in the same way they care (or ought to care) about students? To what extent are educators empowered to participate authentically in pedagogical matters of fundamental importance—what schools should be for and how teaching and learning can be aligned with this vision? That the second or third "waves" in our most recent cycle of reform are now pointing to these concerns suggests that the answer to these "to-what-extent" questions is "Not much."[45] This is not a new set of concerns, but rather a seasonal blooming of perennial issues:

> The formulation of school policy should be a coopera-
> tive process capitalizing on the intellectual resources
> of the whole school staff. This participation in the
> development of educational policy should not be
> thought of as a favor granted by the administration
> but rather as a right and obligation. . . . This proce-
> dure promotes efficiency through individual under-
> standing of policies and through the acceptance of
> joint responsibility for carrying them into effect. What
> is far more important, it provides a democratic process
> through which growth in service is promoted and the
> school service itself profits from the application of
> heightened morale and of group thinking to school
> problems. It makes the school in reality a unit of de-
> mocracy in its task of preparing citizens for our demo-
> cratic society.[46]

The five ethical roots put forward in this chapter merge together in what I have argued elsewhere to be a process of *critical
inquiry*—a process that brings dignity and moral praiseworthiness
to the work of educators and, if we must use them, to the terms
profession, professional, and *professionalism*.[47] To *professionalize*
teaching, in my view, would be to create and sustain cultures of
critical inquiry from classrooms, to school buildings (and the offices supporting them), to halls and classrooms of higher education
and schools of education particularly.

Critical inquiry is not a complicated idea; it is just difficult
to carry out in environments where people are isolated, communication is a lost art, time is bought and structured for different purposes, and beliefs and human interests are considered off limits for
discussion. To inquire is to be thoughtful, reflective, and informed;
to seek and use information; to describe, explain, interpret, and
evaluate new and existing knowledge; and to be sensible in all this,

be it quantitatively or qualitatively, inductively, deductively, or dialectically. To be critical is to question and question constructively; to appraise knowledge in the context of practice; to challenge existing knowledge and practice with an eye toward improvement; to situate knowledge and practice in historical, current, and future perspective; to recognize the reflexivity of human inquiry, of knowing and acting; to consider and reconsider fundamental values and human interests in knowing and acting; and to ethically ground the actions that people take that affect the lives of others. Critical inquiry, obviously, is dependent on competent communication; that is, rigorous and sustained discourse marked by (1) a climate of trust, respect, receptivity, and responsiveness (caring), (2) rules of fair play (equal rights to begin, enter, question, or refute discourse), (3) legitimate claims for knowledge, and (4) a willingness to contend with the content and process of moral argument.[48]

Critical inquiry, therefore, is a moral activity. It is what educators ought to be modeling in their classrooms and what they ought to be engaged in as individually reflective practitioners and as reflective collectives of practitioners. As I sift through the visions of teachers and teaching offered by the authors of the preceding nine chapters, the features of critical inquiry are latent, if not manifest, in their contributions—teachers bearing the burden of moral judgment (Goodlad); the moral praiseworthiness of teaching (Soder); teaching as the exercise of liberal integrity (Bull); teaching as human action undertaken in regard to other humans (Fenstermacher); responsibility of teachers in the collective critique of the public-forming process (Feinberg); informed and responsible ethical decision making (Strike); moral accountability and a code of ethics in teaching (Sockett); teaching as principled in honesty, fairness, respect, and protection of the weak (Clark); and teacher as moral agent, moral agency as public practice (Thomas).

Preparing to Teach

If we are at all correct in our arguments for teaching as a profoundly moral activity, then not just anyone can be a teacher, nor is teaching just for anyone. As the authors of this book have strongly suggested, there is substantial content implied in the moral commitments to inquiry, knowledge, competence, caring, and social justice. If teaching is, as I have interpreted it, a process of critical inquiry-in-action, the idea of *pedagogy* cannot be an empty concept.

Common sense and the uncommon virtue of using it well suggest that pedagogy is content-laden. Despite aphorisms such as "Those who can, do; those who can't, teach," portrayals of educators as bumbling fools by the entertainment media, beliefs that anyone can teach if they know more about the subject than their students, and conceptions of teacher education as nothing more than apprenticeship, those of us who have been there know otherwise. Despite having seen, as students, the job modeled for us for twelve years or more, *being* the teacher is a brand-new experience. Those of us who teach for a living, who have just tried to teach our own children, who have witnessed someone clearly expert in his or her field fumble around miserably in the classroom, or who have watched a highly experienced teacher do very well what should not be done to kids know that teaching is not just a matter of taking on the role. Whether it is preparing to be a plumber, politician, podiatrist, priest, or pedagogue, there is, indeed, preparation to be done.

In each of Chapters One through Nine, implications for teacher education have been suggested. Goodlad has stressed the *foundations*—that is, the need to understand and internalize the role of public education in a democratic society and the moral imperatives of excellence and equity; knowledge and the ways of knowing by which we interpret and improve the human condition; competence in the special knowledge and skills of teaching; and experience in exercising the burden of judgment. Soder's "rhetorical shift" to grounding the profession of teaching in its moral praiseworthiness leads, in his analysis, to the importance of new and increased emphasis on selection and evaluation of students in preservice teacher education, on continuing education for those already called teachers, and on careful consideration of the ends as well as the means for teaching and learning. Bull argues for a critical understanding of the principles of the liberal state, of the autonomy and moral responsibility that fall to teachers by virtue of their exercising risk-laden freedoms, and, therefore, of the importance of negative evaluation and licensing (that is, screening out incompetence).

The foundational themes accumulate with each successive chapter. Although he recognizes that pedagogical content, advanced knowledge, and technical skills are important, Fenstermacher argues that they are insufficient without clear visions of and commitments to educative intentions, moral purpose, and the teacher-student relationship. By implication of Feinberg's analysis, those becoming teachers must have a critical understanding of the history of public education, the importance of a public larger than special interests, and the role of educators in preparing students to participate in the public conversation. Strike argues that the bottom line for competent teaching is competent ethical reasoning and decision making; those who aspire to be educators will need deliberate instruction in what it means to reflect on ethical matters, in how to apply ethical principles, and in the dilemmas and concerns around moral relativism.

These themes begin to suggest that teacher education is more a process of building moral character than a process of building a knowledge base, skills, and expertise (not that the latter are unimportant). Indeed, Sockett suggests that educators-to-be acquire a sense of personal and collegial accountability, a desire for creating climates of caring and trust, a habit of reflective practice, and a sense of community. The virtues of honesty, responsibility, and respect, argues Clark, must be ingrained in the beginning teachers lest they resort to the temptations of nonmoral behavior in the heat of pedagogical struggle under difficult and complex conditions. Finally, Thomas reminds us that moral character and responsibility must be recognized in a moral ecology—a moral learning community, as he calls it—and that teachers must be prepared to break through the culture of isolation and act on a moral obligation to collaborate.

Clearly, the moral and ethical foundations of public education in a democratic society and the requisite character of educators have received the most emphasis in this book. Ironically, in our view, they have received the least emphasis in today's programs for educating educators. The foundations, the history, philosophy, and sociology of education—the areas where issues raised in this book are most likely to be raised—have been substantially eroded, not only under the houses of education generally but under teacher education (and educational administration) specifically. Of the

twenty-nine schools, colleges, or departments of education we visited during the 1987–88 academic year, only one had an intact
foundations area.[49] In most of the others, what used to be a foundations area had since been merged into educational psychology, curriculum and instruction, educational administration, measurement
and statistics, or some combination of these.

More important than the organizational structure, however,
is the curriculum delivered. We found no instances where it could
be argued that the moral dimensions put forward in this book, the
purposes and functions of schools in a democratic society, and the
ethical responsibilities of public education and educators served as
organizing elements or themes to integrate the education curriculum. Foundations usually took the form of an introductory course
composed of a potpourri of mostly contemporary issues—sex education, multicultural education, school prayer, home education,
mainstreaming, vouchers, how to get a teaching job, and so forth.
When interviewed during their student-teaching year and asked
questions regarding underlying philosophies of education and
teaching, students articulated classical positions of moral relativism—"To each his own." When asked to recall the most important
issue they dealt with in "Intro Ed," many had trouble remembering
any, and, for those who could, among the more popular recollections was "AIDS."

Without belaboring the issue, these interviews with students
reflected our interviews with the members of many teacher education faculties. Notwithstanding the fact that there were individual
faculty members in every institution who appeared to care about the
moral issues being raised in this book, there was no evidence of
curricular imperative based on these cares. Instead, the curricula of
teacher education looked remarkably the same from place to place,
reminiscent of Counts's description some fifty-five years ago: "as
like as peas in a pod."[50] The lockstep of teacher training was evident
in the typical course sequences of "Intro Ed," "Ed Psych," "Methods," and "Student Teaching."

To be sure, there were some variations in places, and, in rare
instances, courses were blocked into more integrated curriculum
units toward connecting theory and practice. Nonetheless, most
programs resembled training in the sense of skill acquisition, rather

than education in the sense of initiation into the fundamental knowledge and experiences suggested as essential by the contributors to this book. The vision of teachers as critical inquirers, of schools as centers of reflective practice, of educators as moral agents, and of schools as places for both equitable and excellent education for all students was not manifest in the programs we visited. Perhaps there are programs organized more in accord with this vision. Our concern, however, is that what we found may be the rule, not the exception. We need to make the exceptional the rule.[51]

Moral commitments to inquiry, knowledge, competence, caring, and social justice require character and character building. The question arises as to how much character people acquire naturally over the course of their life experiences and how much can be deliberately socialized in a preparation program for educators. The answer is to worry less about the question and to worry more about doing both: Teacher educators must give far more attention than is currently being given to screening, selection, and evaluation of students and beginning teachers.

It was our experience in visiting teacher education programs that selecting in and screening out students from the programs were among the most sensitive and troubling issues for faculty. Understandably, negative evaluations, no matter how gently or constructively fashioned, are not pleasant undertakings. Negative educational experiences for children, however, are also unpleasant. Ethics of competence and caring imply honest and rigorous judgment as to who gets into and who gets out of teacher education programs.

Getting into teacher education programs seems to be mostly a matter of meeting modest grade point average criteria that shift with the shifts of supply and demand. Getting through the programs seems to be mostly a matter of getting by. Generally, students would have to do something outrageous in student teaching before they would be dismissed from the program. Policies such as these, of course, parallel the difficulties of dealing with incompetence and unethical practice once the credential is in hand.

The combined arguments presented in this volume strongly suggest that not just anyone *should* be a teacher, and not just anyone *can* be a teacher. Those responsible for preparation programs for educators must take this proposition extremely seriously.

They must enter into the hard work of developing and sticking to better selection, screening, and evaluation procedures. For example, in-depth interviews, written philosophy statements, close and continual monitoring, supervision and observation, daily logs and journals, and so on, are crucial sources of knowledge for making more informed judgments not only about the competence of potential teachers but also about their character.

Goodlad's notion of the "burden of judgment," therefore, applies to both educators in schools and educators in universities and colleges. By design, attention in the present volume has focused more on the former than on the latter. Yet the accumulated arguments in this book for teaching as a moral activity immediately suggest the argument for teaching teachers as an equally moral activity. To explore this implication adequately requires another book. I will merely suggest here that moral commitments to inquiry, knowledge, competence, caring, and social justice transfer directly to people in institutions of higher education that are in leadership and instructional roles related to the education of educators.

In a general sense, this refers to everyone in the university or college; more specifically, the focus of responsibility, commitment, and leadership is on the central office, faculties in schools, colleges, and departments of education, and affiliated faculty in the arts and sciences. The track record here is not good. Previous and current work suggests that the major research universities tend to pay little attention to their schools of education or to the problems of public schooling; worse yet, the "ed schools" within these multiversities, ironically, focus less on their mission as a professional school in preparing educators and more on the emulation of the disciplines in research and publication.[52] In our visits to the twenty-nine institutions, we found that this pattern, with varying intensity, was evident in all types of higher education institutions, public and private, major and regional, comprehensive and four-year liberal arts.

The moral responsibility that educators have in universities and colleges, in schools of education, and in educator preparation programs is enormous. In my view, they are ethically bound to act on that responsibility. Presidents and provosts must be visibly supportive, in spirit and resources, of their schools of education. Liberal arts faculty members must recognize and communicate the praiseworthiness of teaching as a career. Faculties in schools of education must support the centrality of educating educators and must sustain a responsible core of participation in the development and operation of programs. Promotion and tenure criteria must reflect the appropriate aims and functions of a school of education.

Schools of education cannot continue to emulate inappropriate models or have their functions determined by others. A *professional* school within an institution of higher education that allows criteria of scholarship, service, and teaching to be invented for it is not worthy of the title.

Conclusion

It is not easy to talk of "moral imperatives" in today's society. In swimming counter to the tides of moral relativism, one has to be prepared for an occasional dunking by accusations of demagoguery, sophistry, and the like. We have taken the plunge, in this book, precisely because of our commitments to society and its future and, therefore, to young people, to teaching, to the preparation of educators, and to compelling arguments that teaching is a moral activity.

An antirelativist position, however, does not automatically resolve fundamental questions, dilemmas, and issues. Inquiring critically is not like reasoning in Euclidian geometry; initial assumptions (axioms) are not connected tautologically to sets of truths (theorems). Moral commitments to inquiry, knowledge, competence, caring, and social justice provide an ethical framework for engaging in the dialectics of praxis; they do not automatically dictate the outcomes. It might be said that in this book we have helped to locate the moral and technical dimensions of a Pandora's box of educational concerns. We have helped to supply what Peters calls "a form for the moral consciousness [for] what is relevant when we think about what is right and wrong."[53] In this way, I hope, we have moved, in Bernstein's words, "beyond objectivism and relativism" and "to the practical task of furthering the type of solidarity, participation, and mutual recognition that is founded in dialogical communities."[54]

Some may take us to task, using the old "so what?" criticism:

"Obviously, teaching is a moral activity; who can disagree, at least in principle, with the basic positions outlined; but so what?" If the moral dimensions of teaching are obvious, I can only report that this was not the case for hundreds of students and faculty members interviewed during our study of teacher education programs. Moreover, educational practices in schools and universities do not appear to be all that consistent with the moral commitments outlined here.

Another line of criticism is likely to emerge from our American predilection for "getting on with it": "What about the pragmatics of existing circumstances, about the estimated need for a million teachers over the next five years, about the realities of practice in today's schools and teacher education programs?" It is my view that there is nothing practical about many current practices in education. Practice too often reinforces a vicious circle of amorality and mediocrity in education and the education of educators. The myopia of merely focusing on the immediate guarantees even bigger problems for the future.

As an increasingly technological society, we are apt to really believe that science will provide all the answers, that all we have to do to improve schools is just develop the technical skills of those we label teachers. We are apt to reject the importance of a moral ecology and the delicate balance of moral relationships between society, schooling, teaching, and preparing to teach. We are apt to reject the importance of community in favor of ourselves and the importance of ethical foundations in favor of radical individualism. This will be a series of serious mistakes, the consequences of which were suggested some time ago by Bateson:

> If you . . . see yourself as outside and against the things around you [and if] you arrogate all mind to yourself, you will see the world around you as mindless and therefore not entitled to moral or ethical consideration. The environment will seem to be yours to exploit. Your survival unit will be you and your folks or conspecifics against the environment of other social units. . . . If this is your estimate of your relation to nature *and you have an advanced technology,* your likelihood of survival will be that of a snowball in

hell. You will die either of the toxic by-products of
your own hate, or, simply, of over-population and
overgrazing. The raw materials of the world are
finite.[55]

Mistake not the context of Bateson's remarks. The moral
ecology of society-schooling-teaching-teacher education is no less
susceptible to the same fate as the snowball's. Although he may be
referring in this quotation to the physical environment, Bateson
intends the "ecology of mind" to have far broader implications.
"Toxic by-products" run not only in our rivers but in our minds
and actions. It would be an error to consider our human resources as
infinite and therefore expendable. What we do with our children
now will affect profoundly the physical *and* moral ecology of the
future.

Notes

1. See, for example, A. Etzioni, *The Moral Dimension: Toward
    A New Economics* (New York: Free Press, 1988).
2. Selected examples are R. J. Bernstein, *The Restructuring of
    Social and Political Theory* (Philidelphia: University of
    Pennsylvania Press, 1978); E. Bredo and W. Feinberg, *Knowl-
    edge and Values in Social and Educational Research* (Phila-
    delphia: Temple University Press, 1982); F. R. Dallmayr and
    T. A. McCarthy (eds.), *Understanding and Social Inquiry* (No-
    tre Dame, Ind.: University of Notre Dame Press, 1977); A.
    Giddens, *New Rules of Sociological Method* (New York: Basic
    Books, 1976); J. Habermas, *Knowledge and Human Interests*
    (Boston: Beacon Press, 1971); J. S. Nelson, A. Megill, and D.
    N. McCloskey (eds.), *The Rhetoric of the Human Sciences:
    Language and Argument in Scholarship and Public Affairs*
    (Madison: University of Wisconsin Press, 1987); P. Reason
    and J. Rowan (eds.), *Human Inquiry: A Sourcebook of New
    Paradigm Research* (New York: Wiley, 1981).
3. I am thinking of a broad array of work here, samples of which
    are P. G. Altbach, G. P. Kelly, and L. Weis (eds.), *Excellence*

in Education: Perspectives on Policy and Practice (New York: Prometheus Books, 1985); M. W. Apple and L. Weis (eds.) *Ideology and Practice in Schooling* (Philadelphia: Temple University Press, 1983); A. Berlak and H. Berlak, *Dilemmas of Schooling: Teaching and Social Change* (London: Methuen, 1981); R. V. Bullough, Jr., S. L. Goldstein, and L. Holt, *Human Interests in the Curriculum* (New York: Teachers College Press, 1984); P. Freire, *Education for Critical Consciousness* (New York: Continuum, 1981); H. A. Giroux, *Schooling and the Struggle for Public Life* (Minneapolis: University of Minnesota Press, 1988); A. Gutmann, *Democratic Education* (Princeton; N. J.: Princeton University Press, 1987); D. Hawkins, *The Science and Ethics of Equality* (New York: Basic Books, 1977); D. Sloan (ed.), *Toward the Recovery of Wholeness: Knowledge, Education, and Human Values* (New York: Teachers College Press, 1981); K. A. Strike, *Educational Policy and the Just Society* (Chicago: University of Illinois Press, 1982); A. R. Tom, *Teaching as a Moral Craft* (New York: Longman, 1984). These are all contemporary examples; for the sake of historical continuity, it would be well to include J. Dewey, *Democracy and Education* (New York: Macmillan, 1961; originally published 1916).

4. Overviews of this study can be found in J. I. Goodlad, "Studying the Education of Educators: Values-Driven Inquiry," *Phi Delta Kappan*, 1988, *70* (2), 104-111; K. A. Sirotnik, "Studying the Education of Educators: Methodology," *Phi Delta Kappan*, 1988 *70* (3), 241-247; and R. Soder, "Studying the Education of Educators: What We Can Learn from Other Professions," *Phi Delta Kappan* 1988, *70* (4), 299-305.

5. By "rational," I do not mean to suggest a mode of thought restricted to pure reason of the type used in mathematical inquiry. I am referring to all modes of reason (for example, inductive, deductive, and dialectical) and all modes of inquiry (for example, historical, philosophical, empirical, hermeneutical, and critical).

6. H. Arendt, *The Human Condition* (Chicago: University of Chicago Press, 1958), p. 5.

7. M. Horkheimer, *The Eclipse of Reason* (New York: Seabury Press, 1974).

8. Arendt, *The Human Condition*, p. 325. The quotation is from *Cato the Elder* as reported by Cicero; see, for example, *Cicero: Selected Works* (Michael Grant, trans.) (Baltimore: Penguin Books, 1960), p. 159.

9. N. Postman, *Amusing Ourselves to Death* (New York: Penguin Books, 1985).

10. J. Dewey, *Reconstruction in Philosophy* (Boston: Beacon Press, 1967), pp. 212–213.

11. A critical discussion of education and knowledge using the banking metaphor can be found in P. Freire, *Pedagogy of the Oppressed* (New York: Continuum, 1982), pp. 57–74.

12. E. D. Hirsch, Jr., *Cultural Literacy: What Every American Needs to Know* (Boston: Houghton Mifflin, 1987).

13. See W. J. Goode, "The Protection of the Inept," *American Sociological Review*, 1967, *32* (1), 5–19.

14. Arendt, *The Human Condition*, p. 22.

15. N. Noddings, *Caring: A Feminine Approach to Ethics and Moral Education* (Berkeley: University of California Press, 1984), p. 7.

16. Noddings, *Caring*, p. 16.

17. Noddings, *Caring*, p. 80.

18. R. N. Bellah and others, *Habits of the Heart: Individualism and Commitment in American Life* (New York: Harper & Row, 1985); Etzioni, *The Moral Dimension*.

19. Arendt, *The Human Condition*, p. 324.

20. Arendt, *The Human Condition*, p. 4.

21. J. Madison, "The Federalist No. 51 (February 6, 1788)," in A. Hamilton, J. Madison, and J. Jay, *The Federalist Papers* (G. Wills, ed.) (New York: Bantam Books, 1982), p. 262.

22. By *dangerous*, I am referring not only to issues of personal safety but to issues of human cruelties of all types—physical, emotional, social, psychological, economic, and political. *Well-being* will refer to safety from all these dangers.

23. R. Dworkin, "Liberalism," in S. Hampshire (ed.), *Public and Private Morality* (Cambridge, England: Cambridge University

Press, 1978). See also R. Dworkin, *Taking Rights Seriously* (Cambridge, Mass.: Harvard University Press, 1977).

24. J. Rawls, *A Theory of Justice* (Cambridge, Mass.: Harvard University Press, 1971); A. Gewirth, *Reason and Morality* (Chicago: University of Chicago Press, 1978). See also Rawls's revised thesis in "Justice as Fairness: Political Not Metaphysical," *Philosophy and Public Affairs*, 1985, *14* (3), 223–251.

25. Gewirth, *Reason and Morality*, p. 47.

26. Gewirth, *Reason and Morality*, p. 135.

27. Gewirth, *Reason and Morality*, p. 147.

28. A. MacIntyre, *After Virtue: A Study in Moral Theory* (Notre Dame, Ind.: Notre Dame University Press, 1984); M. J. Sandel, *Liberalism and the Limits of Justice* (Cambridge, England: Cambridge University Press, 1982); W. Sullivan, *Restructuring Public Philosophy* (Berkeley: University of California Press, 1982); M. Walzer, *Spheres of Justice: A Defense of Pluralism and Equality* (New York: Basic Books, 1983).

29. D. L. Phillips, *Toward a Just Social Order* (Princeton, N.J.: Princeton University Press, 1986), pp. 106–115.

30. Phillips, *Toward a Just Social Order*, p. 113.

31. Phillips, *Toward a Just Social Order*, p. 113.

32. See, for example, Feinberg's comments on "first principles" (Chapter Five) and Sockett's concern for local control of content for ethical codes of practice (Chapter Seven).

33. L. Kohlberg, "From Is to Ought: How to Commit the Naturalistic Fallacy and Get Away with It in the Study of Moral Development," in T. Mischel (ed.), *Cognitive Development and Epistemology* (New York: Academic Press, 1971), p. 222.

34. Bellah and others, *Habits of the Heart*, pp. 284, 335.

35. A. Etzioni, "Toward an I & We Paradigm," *Contemporary Sociology*, 1989, *18* (2), 171–176.

36. S. B. Sarason, "And What Is the Public Interest?" *American Psychologist*, 1986, *41* (8), 899–905 (p. 904).

37. M. Oakeshott, *Rationalism in Politics* (London: Methuen, 1962), pp. 197–247.

38. Phillips, *Toward a Just Social Order*, p. 115.

39. In our study of schooling, we found that the strongest factor defining the classroom learning environment as perceived by

students was "teacher concern" (that is, teachers as friendly, attentive, honest, fair, respectful, and so on). Interviews with students during the pilot study confirmed these findings. See J. I. Goodlad, *A Place Called School: Prospects for the Future* (New York: McGraw-Hill, 1984).

40.   See K. A. Sirotnik, "Equal Access to Quality in Public Schooling: Issues in the Assessment of Equity and Excellence," in J. I. Goodlad and P. J. Keating (eds.), *Access to Knowledge: An Agenda for Our Nation's Schools* (New York: College Entrance Examination Board, 1989).

41.   D. H. Kerr, "Authority and Responsibility in Public Schooling," in J. I. Goodlad (ed.), *The Ecology of School Renewal*, Eighty-Sixth Yearbook (Part I) of the National Society for the Study of Education (Chicago: University of Chicago Press, 1987), p. 25.

42.   K. A. Sirotnik, "The School as the Center of Change," in T. J. Sergiovanni and J. H. Moore (eds.), *Schooling for Tomorrow: Directing Reform to Issues That Count* (Boston: Allyn & Bacon, 1989).

43.   J. Oakes, *Keeping Track: How Schools Structure Inequality* (New Haven, Conn.: Yale University Press, 1985).

44.   See, for example, S. J. Gould, *The Mismeasure of Man* (New York: Norton, 1981).

45.   See the collection of writings in Sergiovanni and Moore, *Schooling for Tomorrow*.

46.   Educational Policies Commission, *The Structure and Administration of Education in American Democracy* (Washington, D.C.: National Education Association and American Association of School Administrators, 1938), pp. 67–68.

47.   Sirotnik, "The School as the Center of Change."

48.   J. Habermas, *Communication and the Evolution of Society* (Boston: Beacon Press, 1979). See also T. McCarthy, *The Critical Theory of Jurgen Habermas* (Cambridge, Mass.: MIT Press, 1978).

49.   A number of technical reports on the Study of the Education of Educators are currently being prepared and are the supporting documents for the findings being previewed here.

50. G. S. Counts, "Break the Teacher Training Lockstep," *Social Frontier*, June 1935, *1*, 6–7 (p. 6).
51. Strike has made an important suggestion in Chapter Six that a substantial curriculum strand based on the analysis of educational *cases* (as in law school) be integrated into teacher education curriculum. Cases would consist of fundamental educational issues and moral and ethical dilemmas. See, for example, K. A. Strike and J. F. Soltis, *The Ethics of Teaching* (New York: Teachers College Press, 1985); K. A. Strike, E. J. Haller, and J. F. Soltis, *The Ethics of School Administration* (New York: Teachers College Press, 1988). In one of the more insightful and ignored reform reports on teacher education, B. Othanel Smith also recommends the use of case studies; see B. O. Smith, *A Design for a School of Pedagogy* (Washington, D.C.: U.S. Department of Education, 1980). Harry Broudy and his colleagues at the University of Illinois are currently at work developing a curriculum based on the use of cases; see H. S. Broudy, "Toward a Case Study Method in Teacher Education," *Teachers College Record*, in press.
52. G. J. Clifford and J. W. Guthrie, *Ed School: A Brief for Professional Education* (Chicago: University of Chicago Press, 1988); H. Judge, *American Graduate Schools of Education: A View from Abroad* (New York: Ford Foundation, 1982).
53. R. Peters, *Authority, Responsibility and Education* (London: Allen & Unwin, 1973), p. 44.
54. R. J. Bernstein, *Beyond Objectivism and Relativism: Science, Hermeneutics, and Praxis* (Philadelphia: University of Philadelphia Press, 1985), p. 231.
55. G. Bateson, *Steps to an Ecology of Mind* (New York: Ballantine Books, 1972), p. 462.

Name Index

Ackerman, B. A., 109, 128, 198–199, 200, 221
Aikin, W. M., 282–283, 286–287, 293, 294, 295
Alger, H., 57
Allen, F. L., 41, 79
Allen, J., 265
Altbach, P. G., 322–323
Andrews, R. L., 86
Apple, M. W., 323
Arendt, H., 298, 299, 302, 304, 323, 324
Atherton, J. M., 149

Bailey, S. K., 7, 31
Banta, D. H., 83
Barker, L. F., 83
Bateson, G., 71, 86, 321–322, 327
Bay, D. N., 192
Beale, H. K., 79
Becher, R., 249
Becker, H. S., 44, 79
Becker, S., 72, 86
Bellah, R. N., 231, 249, 295, 303, 324, 325
Bennett, W., 130
Berlak, A., 323
Berlak, H., 323
Berliner, D., 129
Berliner, D. C., 16, 32
Berliner, H. S., 84
Bernstein, R. J., 320, 322, 327
Berry, B., 248
Bestor, A. E., 81, 162, 163, 184
Bloom, A., 16, 32, 33, 173–175, 177, 178, 179–180, 182, 185, 231, 249
Bobbitt, F., 161, 184
Boesky, I., 221

Bok, S., 233–234, 250
Boucher, J., 45
Bourdieu, P., 171, 185
Boyer, C., 86
Boyer, E. L., 24, 33
Bredo, E., 322
Brophy, J., 129
Broudy, H. S., 327
Brown, E. R., 84
Buber, M., 303
Buley, R. C., 45–46, 80
Bull, B. L., 87, 129, 220, 304, 305, 314, 315
Bullough, R. V., Jr., 323

Callahan, R. E., 184
Carroll, S. L., 78
Carter, J. G., 158
Casanova, U., 142, 150
Cathcart, J. A., 78
Cato, 299
Chamberlin, D., 293, 294
Chamberlin, E. S., 293, 294
Chapman, C. B., 83
Chase, F., 36–37, 76
Cicero, 324
Clark, B. R., 52, 82
Clark, C. M., 251, 265, 310, 314, 316
Clifford, G. J., 11, 31, 327
Cohen, H. S., 78
Cole, M., 265
Conant, J. B., 6, 9, 30, 162
Cooper, M., 30
Cooperman, S., 32
Corwin, R. G., 250
Counts, G. S., 83, 317, 327
Coward, N., 42, 79
Cremin, L. A., 30, 186
Cronin, J. M., 129

329

Subject Index

Accountability: aspects of, for professionalism, 224–250; background on, 224–225; and code of ethics, 243–244; and code of practice, 236–244; concepts of, 227–229; conclusion on, 248; criteria for, 235–236; moral, 229–232; and pluralism of moral ends, 230; and private wants and public interest, 231; professional and moral, 226–236; and public forum, 231; reasons for, 227; school as locus of, 237; and standards of practice, 229, 230, 242, 244; and teacher education, 244–248; of teachers, 138; and trust, 232–235

American Association of Colleges for Teacher Education, 34, 85

American Association of School Administrators, 7

American Educational Research Association (AERA), 7, 8, 31, 87n

American Educational Studies Association, 185

American Federation of Teachers (AFT), 6, 9, 13, 37, 77

American Medical Association (AMA), 56, 58, 59

American Psychological Association, 236, 250

American Sociological Association, 236, 250

Anarchist left, and minimal state, 167–168, 169–171, 172

Application of Bay, and certification, 220

Assessment validity, and responsibility, 258

Association of American Medical Colleges, 150

Association for Supervision and Curriculum Development, 7

Autonomy: and admission to practice, 119–123; analysis of, 87–129; background on, 87–90; ethical issue of, 203; as freedom to protect, 108–109; implications of, 117–127; liberalism and, 90–98; professional, 98–117; and professionalization of teacher, 144–146, 148; restricted, 118; and school structure and organization, 125–127; and teacher education, 123–125

Blacks. *See* Minority students

Board of Public Instruction (Iowa), 198

Board of Regents of State Colleges v. *Roth,* and property rights, 220

Brigham Young University, school partnership with, 32

Bureaucratic model: challenge to, 165–172; of education, 160–163; and values conflict, 165–166

California: licensure in, 129; proficiency testing in, 18

California at Berkeley, University of, education school at, 11

California Supreme Court, and immoral conduct, 193–194

Caring: commitment to, 301–304, 308, 310, 311–312, 315, 319, 320; and justice, 217–218; and teacher education, 246–247; for teachers, 214–219; and trust, 234
Carnegie Forum on Education and the Economy, 12, 19, 31, 37, 76
Carnegie Foundation for the Advancement of Teaching, 284
Carnegie Task Force on Teaching as a Profession, 127, 128, 129, 141–142, 150
Central Intelligence Agency (CIA), 43
Certification: denial of, 192; withdrawal of, 193. *See also* Licensure
Chicago, University of: criticism of, 174; and school responsibilities, 161
Children: disruptive, in moral learning community, 267–270; protection of, 108–109, 259; rights of, 74. *See also* Students
Coalitions, professional, unraveling of, 6–12
Code of conduct, and autonomy, 97, 116
Code of ethics: and accountability, 243–244; insufficiency of, 207
Code of practice: accessibility of, 238–240; and accountability, 236–244; content of, 240–241; form of, 237–240; sanctions in, 238–239; and status, 241–243; and teacher education, 244–248
Collective bargaining: and coalition of interests, 9; and policy trust agreements, 145
Commission on the Relation of School and College, 275, 277, 278, 279, 284
Community: moral, 307–308; moral learning, 266–295
Competence: commitment to, 300–301, 308, 310, 311–312, 315, 319, 320; elements of, 113; implications of, 118–119, 123; and licensing, 112–115; and risk-laden freedoms, 95–96
Compulsory education: development

of, 156–157; and minimal state, 166–172; moral dimensions of, 22–24; and moral learning community, 266–267; and moral praiseworthiness of teaching, 73–74; political function of, 170–171; problem of moral foundation of, 155–156
Conduct, code of, 97, 116
Cornell University, criticism of, 174, 175
Culture: and limited moral vision, 178–179; and literacy, 175–178; and overinterpretation, 179–180; unity destroyed for, 173–175

Danforth Foundation, 13, 32
Decision making: decentralized, 126–127; ethical, 209; moral, 252; by students, 279–280; by teachers, 5–6, 12–13, 24, 26, 27–28, 209
Desert View Elementary School, restructuring of, 142
Donohue v. *Copaique Union Free School District,* and educational malpractice, 128

Education: in age of uncertainty, 179–183; bureaucratic model of, 160–163; compulsory, 22–24, 73–74, 155–157, 166–172, 266–267; to create a public, 181–182; enculturation function of, 309; ethical aims of, 205–206; and ethical outcomes, 204–205; fairness model of, 163; liberal society's goals for, 90; moral and philosophical continuities in, 158–163; moral mission of, 153–327; professional model of, 158–160; purposes of, 280–281, 283, 286–287, 292; rationales withering for, 163–173; renewed moral foundation for, 173–179; second wave of reform in, 224–225; taxonomy for decisions in, 27–28, 34. *See also* Schooling
Education, schools of: and access to knowledge, 22; and enculturation, 20–21; moral responsibility

Sexual abuse, in moral learning community, 270–272

Social distance, in profession, 136–137

Social justice, commitment to, 304–308, 310, 311–312, 315, 319, 320

Socialization, critical, 309–310. *See also* Enculturation

Society: aspects of moral dimensions for, 296–327; background on, 296–297; conclusion on, 320–322; and human condition, 297–308; liberal, 90, 103, 105, 205–206; and schooling, 308–311; and teacher education, 314–320; and teaching, 311–314

Standards of practice, and accountability, 229, 230, 242, 244. *See also* Ethical standards

Status: changes in, 55–63; and code of practice, 241–243; discrepancy of, 52–53, 71; of doctors and teachers, 63–66; of medicine, 56–63; and professionalization, 44–46

Students: in compulsory education, 22–24; decision making by, 279–280; and honesty, 252–256; inclusion of, 262–263; minority, 7, 20, 22; and respect, 255, 260–263; and responsibility, 256–260; teachers in moral relationship with, 251–265. *See also* Children

Subject matter, ethical values in, 204

Teacher education: and accountability, 244–248; alternative views of ethical standards in, 209–219; case method in, 327; category of, 33; character building in, 318; curriculum in, 317–318; ethical standards in, 207–219, 221; foundations in, 315–317; and licensure, 123–125; and moral transactions, 251–265; negotiating skills in, 246–247; openness and reflection in, 247; pedagogy in, 315; and professional status, 48–49, 51, 74–75; redefining, 74–75; and reform reports, 18–19;

screening and selecting in, 318–319; and society, 314–320. *See also* Education, schools of

Teachers: autonomy of, 87–129, 144–146, 148; burden of judgment for, 4, 5, 19, 27, 30, 319; career opportunities for, 144–146; commitments of, 107; constitutional rights of, 190–192, 196; decision making by, 5–6, 12–13, 24, 26, 27–28, 209; demoralization of, 290; disempowerment of, 281; due process rights of, 191–192; and ethical outcomes, 204–205; ethical standards for, 202–207; expertise of, 138–141, 148, 158; and honesty, 252–256; legal and moral responsibility of, 188–223; manner of, 134–136; as moral agents, 229–230, 290; as moral educators, 134–136, 147; in moral relationship with students, 251–265; moral role of, 159; as officeholders, 99–109; part-time status of, 26; professional development of, 284–286; and renewal process, 25–27; as resources, 284–286; and respect, 255, 260–263; responsibilities of, 14, 106–107, 118–119, 122, 183, 256–260; as role models, 195, 197, 201, 204–205; role restrictions for, 30; status discrepancy for, 52–53, 71; status of, 44–46, 63–66; and students, in compulsory education, 22–24; working conditions of, 82

Teaching: admission to practice of, 119–123; aspects of, in schools, 3–34; as calling, 15–16; categories of, 102; complexity of, 140, 143–144, 147, 229, 264; consequences of, 110–112; context layered for, 17–19; contextual factors for, 4–5; ethical concepts central to, 208; failure of, 110; functions of, 140; hierarchical differentiation in, 141–143, 146–148; implications of moral mission for, 153–327; knowledge base for, 16–17, 33–34, 50, 115, 131, 139–141, 148–149; la-